BUILDING THE
P-51 MUSTANG

The Story of Manufacturing North American's Legendary World War II Fighter in Original Photos

Michael O'Leary

specialtypress
PUBLISHERS AND WHOLESALERS

specialtypress
PUBLISHERS AND WHOLESALERS

Specialty Press
838 Lake Street South
Forest Lake, MN 55025
Phone: 651-277-1400 or 800-895-4585
Fax: 651-277-1203
www.specialtypress.com

© 2010 by Michael O'Leary
2011 Softbound Edition

Edit by Mike Machat
Layout by Monica Seiberlich

ISBN 978-1-58007-190-1
Item No. SP190

Library of Congress Cataloging-in-Publication Data

O'Leary, Michael.
  Building the P-51 Mustang : the story of manufacturing North American's legendary World War II fighter in original photos / by Michael O'Leary.
    p. cm.
  Includes bibliographical references and index.
  ISBN 978-1-58007-152-9
  1. Mustang (Fighter plane)–Design and construction–History. 2. World War, 1939-1945–Aerial operations, American. 3. Rolls Royce Ltd.–History–20th century. I. Title.
  UG1242.F5044 2010
  623.74'64–dc22
                        2010009718

Printed in China
10 9 8 7 6 5 4

On the Front Cover:
With guns blazing in the dead of night, this P-51B tests its most formidable air superiority asset at North American's Inglewood facility, highlighting the round-the-clock production schedule for America's most famous World War II fighter.

On the Front Flap:
Advertisement illustrated by North American artists shows the business end of the P-51D, as ground crewmen load ammo into the Mustang's gun bays. Partial cutaway at bottom shows special P-51 features such as a "super-speed wing." (Courtesy of Scott Bloom)

On the Title Page:
Lined up like chord wood, these P-51D Mustangs await final outfitting and pre-delivery flight testing on the East ramp at Inglewood. Both F-86 Sabres and F-100 Super Sabres occupied this same hallowed piece of real estate in the 1950s.

On the Facing Page:
The beginning of it all–North American's NA-73X prototype seen on the ramp at the company's new Inglewood, California plant during an engine run-up with main landing gear wheel firmly chocked.

On the Back Cover, left:
Final Assembly area of North American's Inglewood facility shows nearly finished P-51B models coming down the production line. Once the propellers and spinners are installed, the completed airplanes will roll out of the factory.

On the Back Cover, top:
The moment of truth! A finished P-51D–the 10,000th Mustang in this particular case–has been towed out of the final assembly building and into the California sun for the first time. Workers are shown putting the finishing touches on the airplane.

Editor's Note: While Specialty Press books usually show photo credits at the end of each caption, the photo source in this book is unique. Author Michael O'Leary culled all of the images used herein from official photographs held by the Alpha Archive. For this reason, there are no individual photo credits shown.

DISTRIBUTION BY:
Europe
PGUK
63 Hatton Garden
London EC1N 8LE, England
Phone: 020 7061 1980 • Fax: 020 7242 3725
www.pguk.co.uk

Australia
Renniks Publications Ltd.

3/37-39 Green Street
Banksmeadow, NSW 2109, Australia
Phone: 2 9695 7055 • Fax: 2 9695 7355
www.renniks.com

Canada
Login Canada
300 Saulteaux Crescent
Winnipeg, MB, R3J 3T2 Canada
Phone: 800 665 1148 • Fax: 800 665 0103
www.lb.ca

TABLE OF CONTENTS

DEDICATION

To the men and women who designed, built, tested, and flew
the North American P-51 Mustang

ACKNOWLEDGMENTS

As most readers realize, a book of this scope is the result of the contributions of dozens, if not hundreds, of individuals. Since this volume is being published during the seventieth anniversary of the North American Mustang, I would like to devote a few lines to people that have helped preserve and further the history of the P-51. The following individuals are not presented in any order, except the first, and if I have left anyone out it is not intentional.

A long time ago, aircraft companies were comprised of people who loved what they did. Today, unfortunately, the few companies left are governed by a mean-eyed capitalism that places the accountant at the head of the line. Gene Boswell certainly fit into the first category. Gene had worked for North American almost from the beginning and had become NAA's unofficial historian and keeper of fabulous files that defined the heartbeat of NAA over the decades. Gene's dedication was such that he would not only spend hours with historians researching North American products, but would also take time to answer each and every child writing in for photographs or plans. Without Gene's enthusiasm and realization that NAA's history had to be preserved for future generations, this book would have been much less comprehensive. Also, thanks must be given to Dave Arnold, Mike Machat, and the staff of Specialty Press for setting such a high standard in aviation publishing.

I had the good fortune to meet a number of people involved with creating the Mustang, including designer Edgar Schmued and test pilot Bob Chilton.

Although of completely different backgrounds, both of these men shared a common decency and were generous of time and memory. Other principals included Ed Horkey and Lee Atwood. There is an informal network of aviation historians and photographers including William T. Larkins, Harry Gann, Emil Strasser, Robert O'Dell, and Gerald Liang who also contributed to the book.

Other contributors include Brian Baird, Dave Zeuschel, Ralph Payne, Pete Regina, Steve and John Hinton, Bruce Lockwood, the staff of the San Diego Aerospace Museum, David Price, Ed Maloney and the staff of the Planes of Fame Air Museum, Jack Roush, Bill Klaers and the staff of WestPac, Stallion 51, Tony Ritzman, Carl Scholl and the staff of Aero Trader, everyone involved with Aero Sport at Chino Airport, Scott Bloom, Simon Brown and the staff of Square One, King Monty, John Lane, Connie and Ed Bowlin, the staff of the National Museum of the USAF, Paul Mantz, Jimmy Leeward, Chuck Greenhill, Jim Larsen, John Muzsala and the staff of Pacific Fighters, and a host of restorers and pilots who keep the surviving Mustangs up and flying. These companies and individuals are ensuring that the legend of the Mustang will continue for decades to come.

Michael O'Leary
Los Angeles, California
July 2010

INTRODUCTION

What, another book on the Mustang? Well, yes! Ever since its inception, there have been many, many books written about the North American Aviation P-51 Mustangs and the role those legendary aircraft played in winning the Second World War. Then there are books on Mustangs in foreign service, Mustangs in the Korean War, and Mustangs in racing configuration. So, the world of aviation literature is not exactly lacking when it comes to this particular single-engine fighter aircraft.

In this book, I have attempted to chart a relatively new path—an examination on how the Mustang was designed and built. In many ways, it was almost an accident that this great aircraft achieved production. The prototype was wrecked, its initial customer, Great Britain, was not entirely sure they wanted more P-40s or this dazzling but untried aircraft, while in America the Mustang had many detractors in the military… and the list goes on. However, from the very start it became clearly evident that the North American team had the winner for which the free world was waiting.

There is the old axiom of KISS—"Keep It Simple, Stupid"—and Edgar Schmued and the Mustang design team did just that. The P-51, compared to other fighting machines such as the Lightning, Spitfire, and Thunderbolt, was a superbly simple airplane that combined a number of different technologies to create a high-performance fighter.

The design of a fabulous aircraft is one thing—building it is another. The simplicity of the Mustang lent itself to good old-fashioned American mass production—something that no country during World War II, or even now, could hope to emulate. Very little credit has been given to NAA president Dutch Kindelberger's genius when it came to establishing an extremely efficient production line that was capable of growing and keeping up with the increasing flood of orders. In these pages, I hope to give Dutch his due—he was more than just the president of a great aviation concern.

This book goes deeply into the production line and the construction of the Mustang—how all those tens of thousands of pieces came together to create the sleek fighter that rolled out the factory doors. Men and women—the majority of whom had never even been in an airplane—traveled to southern California from all corners of the United States to join the expanding aviation industry and escape the lingering effects of the Great Depression. Even before Pearl Harbor, foreign orders as well as orders from an American government that had suddenly realized how woefully its military was equipped, led to a modern industrial revolution. Across the country, aviation companies were hiring and expanding at an unprecedented rate.

The skilled work force was small and was quickly snapped up, but there was an almost insatiable demand for workers. Companies such as North American set up their own training programs to teach boys fresh off the farm along with housewives straight from the kitchen how to work in the aviation industry. After Pearl Harbor, huge numbers of women became soldiers on the production front—women that had never been employed were now learning and mastering new technical skills that would have an impact long after the war was over. Along with North American, sleepy postwar southern California was transformed almost overnight as factories such as Douglas, Northrop, and Lockheed expanded to meet the demands of a difficult war.

As the Mustang evolved, so did the American workforce. New workers had to be housed, fed and cared for so new housing tracts and businesses went up almost overnight. The Mustang not only changed the course of the war, but it also helped change America.

Hopefully, this book will give you a glimpse of that hectic, short time period during which the Mustang was built, and how a factory capable of building just a few planes a month, soon was constructing hundreds of warplanes in the same time period. Even though the Mustang's production life was short, its global reach wasn't. The Mustang was the fighter plane that changed history.

CHAPTER ONE

CREATING A PROTOTYPE

It took a gathering of very select individuals to create an aircraft that would change the course of World War II.

NA-73X having its Allison F3R engine run-up prior to a test flight.

By mid-October 1940, North American Aviation (NAA) had become firmly established at Mines Field in southern California—part of the massive airport that is now Los Angeles International. Building its rugged series of NA-16 training aircraft, NAA had decided to move from Maryland to join the many other aviation companies that were now calling southern California home. Mines Field was picked as NAA's new location since it offered an established airfield that was not only close to supply sources, but was also cheap (NAA's original 20-acre site was leased to the company for some $600 per year!).

The new NAA complex was opened in 1936 and covered 159,000 sq ft, while 150 employees were on the payroll and engaged in the production of the NA-16 trainer and the portly O-47 observation aircraft. The many problems that beset a small and new company were met and conquered by NAA president James H. "Dutch" Kindelberger and his small hard-working staff. In many ways, Kindelberger's contributions to the advancement of aviation have been overlooked. Learning to fly with the Air Service, Dutch

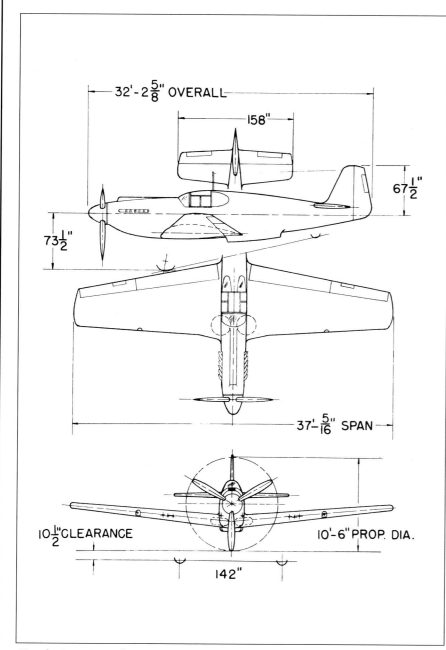

32'-2⅝" OVERALL

158"

67½"

73½"

37'-5/16" SPAN

10½" CLEARANCE

10'-6" PROP. DIA.

142"

North American factory artist's three-view technical illustration of the prototype.

would work his way up the aviation ladder. Kindelberger had been vice president of design at Douglas and had a lot of input into the DC-1, which would, of course, turn into the DC-3. During 1938, Kindelberger, much like Charles Lindbergh, had been invited to Germany for a tour of that nation's advancing aviation industry. Kindelberger was able to meet with key people and designers and also study German methods of mass production. Afterward, he was able to visit British aviation plants, but he came away most impressed by the Germans' superior production techniques based on simple tooling. Lindbergh returned to the United States and proclaimed through America First that this country's aviation industry was so far behind that of the Nazis that there was no way we could ever catch up. Kindelberger had other ideas.

Britain had become interested in the NA-16, which had turned into the AT-6 Texan, and in 1938 began ordering the sturdy advanced trainer for the Royal Air Force (RAF) and other Commonwealth air forces as the Harvard. Because of the rapidly escalating tensions with Hitler's Germany, the European nations were operating at an unprecedented pace and attempting to buy as much military equipment as possible.

During this time, a young man by the name of Ed Horkey was a California Institute of Technology (Caltech) graduate student working on his Master's degree in aeronautical engineering and spending as much time as humanly possible in the Caltech wind tunnel. Since the tunnel was in such demand by California's growing aviation industry, Horkey soon knew all the designers by first name. During one evening in 1938, Ed was running the Caltech wind tunnel (a student job that was bringing him all of 25 cents an hour) and he had a one-third-scale model of the super secret Lockheed XP-38 Lightning in the tunnel. However, a safety system malfunctioned, the expensive model came adrift, and before the tunnel could be shut down, the tunnel's propellers had made short work of the model. However, chief designer Kelly Johnson came over and patted the young man on the shoulder and said accidents just happen. That attitude, combined with the willingness of other engineers, aerodynamicists, and designers to share their knowledge and take young students into their confidence, answer their questions, and give them advice did the most to determine Ed Horkey's future in aviation.

With school completed, he found that aviation companies were hiring and Ed had an aerodynamicist's knowledge of wind tunnels that was second to none. Kindelberger hired the young man for $150 per month and this would include workweeks of 60 to 80 hours—with no overtime! Dutch put him to work on the NA-16 and Ed was off and running.

Britain had also ordered the Curtiss P-40 Tomahawk, and because of the large numbers purchased, was interested in perhaps having NAA build the type under license. The small, but creative, NAA management team decided that it

Although appearing a bit crude by today's standards, this airframe is being thoroughly studied as more and more lead weights are added to test ultimate structural integrity. A temporary wooden partition encloses the aircraft from the rest of the factory as such testing could be hazardous since there was always a chance of catastrophic structural failure that could send bits of metal flying about at high velocity. This incomplete airframe (often referred to in testing documents as XX-73) was tested to destruction to provide accurate data on the airframe's strength and then scrapped after trials had been completed. Testing progressed in a very logical manner, finally culminating with crucial wing strength trials—the flying surface failed at 105 percent of its design load. This very detailed photo was taken on 16 January 1941.

ESTIMATED NA-73 PERFORMANCE

NORTH AMERICAN AVIATION, INC.
Report No. 1620
Page 7
24 April 1940

D. GENERAL REQUIREMENTS

D-1. The Pursuit type airplane, North American Aviation Model No. NA-73, as covered by this specification, shall be designed and constructed in accordance with the requirements set forth in the publications referred to in Paragraph "A," and are hereinafter set forth in this specification.

D-2. Military Characteristics: It is estimated that this airplane will meet the following military characteristics.

D-2a. Performance (with Design Useful Load)

High Speed 384 mph @ 19,000 feet** (Future Military Rating)	Climb to 20,000 feet 9.64 minutes (Normal Rating)
High Speed 375.5 mph @ 16,500 feet** (Present Military Rating)	Cruise 311 mph (75% Normal Power)
High Speed 354 mph @ 14,000 feet** (Normal Rating)	Cruise 294.5 mph (65% Normal Power)
High Speed 316 mph @ Sea Level (Present Military Rating)	Endurance (65% HP) Normal Fuel 2.17 hours Overload Fuel 3.51 hours
High Speed 298 mph @ Sea Level (Normal Rating)	Range (65% HP) Normal Fuel 640 miles Overload Fuel 1,022 miles
Max Rate of Climb 2,720 fpm (Military Rating)	
Max Rate of Climb 2,330 fpm (Normal Rating)	Takeoff Speed 93 mph
	Landing Speed 82.5 mph
Climb to 20,000 feet 8.80 minutes (Military Rating)	Stalling Speed 78.5 mph
	** Altitudes include ram.

would be much more beneficial to the company to create their own fighter design to present to the RAF. What NAA wanted to do was take the Allison V-1710 (the most powerful production V-12 engine in the United States) and wrap it around a new airframe that would outstrip the P-40 in performance.

During 1936, NAA hired a new employee—German-born Austrian Edgar Schmued. For a bit of confusing company history we must go back to the late 1920s when General Motors (GM) created a holding company with the name North American Aviation. This company existed solely to acquire stock in other aviation concerns—giving GM a possible shot at controlling the rapidly emerging aviation market. In 1929, NAA took over the Fokker Aircraft Corporation and Schmued, who worked for GM as a field service manager in Brazil, moved to the United States to work with aircraft—something he had always wanted to do, with his training as a mechanical engineer.

Fokker soon became General Aviation, but the Airmail Act of 1934 forced airmail carriers to rid themselves of holdings that controlled aircraft construction. This meant that GM had to get rid of NAA, which, in turn, took over General Aircraft. Kindelberger had come from Douglas Aircraft a year earlier, and was now president of the "new" NAA. Dutch moved the company west and asked Schmued to join him, but Schmued's wife did not want to move to California so the designer joined the firm of Bellanca—a decision he soon regretted.

However, Dutch kept the job offer open, and Schmued and his family finally moved west. However, just 100 miles from Los Angeles, the family was

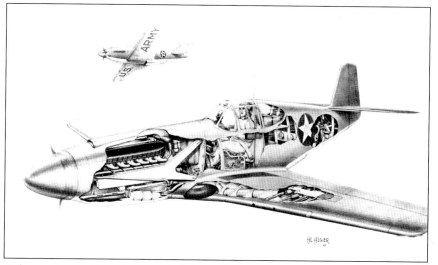

Schmued considered several fighter design concepts before settling on the NA-73X.

involved in a serious car accident that killed Schmued's wife and left the designer seriously injured—it took him until February 1936 to recover.

Once British interest in what NAA was proposing became more solidified, the problem of creating a new airframe around the V-1710 was just the type of challenge enjoyed by Schmued. The inline V-12 required a large radiator for cooling, and its placement would greatly influence performance. At the time, Leland Atwood was Dutch's right-hand man and chief engineer for the company. Atwood, a component designer and mathematical analyst at Douglas Aircraft, was hired away by Dutch and was responsible for the NA-16. In the early 1990s, Atwood would claim he came up with the idea of placing the radiator for the new fighter "behind" the pilot. However, several other surviving NAA employees from the time period, who stated that the location was the obvious choice, rebuffed Atwood's claim.

By placing the radiator to the rear, a modest increase in thrust could be achieved by taking in cold air, which would rapidly expand and reduce in velocity before traveling through the radiator. This led to an efficient heat exchange that created energy, which moved through a narrow duct, exiting through a movable duct. Thus, it was estimated that around 90 percent of the cooling system drag would be eliminated by the efficient thrust of the exiting air.

In his new position at NAA, Schmued worked on various projects including the B-25 Mitchell bomber and the NA-35 primary trainer, but he also kept working on his own personal concept of an "ideal" fighter. As interest from the British Purchasing Commission increased in having NAA license-build P-40s, a proposal was presented to the Brits on the new fighter. To give an indication of how events progressed during this trying time period, the British liked what they saw in their April 1940 meeting with Atwood and issued an order for 320 examples of the new aircraft. Ed Horkey had met Edgar Schmued and, despite the age difference, the two men hit it off and became strong working colleagues.

Dutch placed Schmued in charge of the project (Dutch also let Edgar pick whatever employee he found useful), but the British also put in a requirement that NAA purchase wind tunnel data from Curtiss on their new XP-46 (an

Natural aluminum finish gleaming in the early morning mist at Mines Field, the NA-73X was being prepared for its first flight. The adjustable front radiator scoop can be seen in the down position.

"improved" version of the P-40 design and one of world's less attractive aircraft). Curtiss made a quick $56,000 profit from the sale and Atwood went to Buffalo, New York, to collect the papers and data. In correspondence with Sir Henry Self, Atwood would write on 1 May 1940, "We have reached an extremely satisfactory agreement with the Curtiss Aeroplane Company of Buffalo whereby they are furnishing us data covering a comprehensive series of wind tunnel, cooling, and performance tests of a similar airplane, which data will assist us in the design and manufacture of these airplanes."

Schmued now had Horkey on his team as chief aerodynamicist and Ed examined the data and found it virtually useless. Ed's most difficult assignment was persuading old time engineers to accept the data the new science was revealing. Some, like Edgar, did. Schmued would later state that he never even saw the Curtiss data.

Schmued started with about eight design engineers and scheduled this number to increase to 37 in two or three weeks. A careful time study was made

Stenciling on the spinner indicates that the last propeller inspection had taken place on 3 January 1941, so this is the rebuilt NA-73X (which can also be identified by the addition of the anti-glare panel). Tight cowling was the handiwork of race pilot Art Chester.

Opening the canopy to get some air, Vance Breese returns in the NA-73X after the successful five-minute first test flight.

COSTING THE MUSTANG

Compared to today's multi-billion-dollar defense contracts, it is interesting to examine the costs for the first Mustangs and to discover what the British and NAA expected from each other along with how the contract was awarded. The following is a letter from North American's Lee Atwood to Sir Henry Self of the Anglo-French Purchasing Commission. Dated 1 May 1940, the letter appears, by today's litigious societal standards, to be almost a gentlemen's agreement:

"In accordance with our understanding, we are proceeding with the design of single-seat fighter airplane, our Model NA-73, incorporating an Allison engine and fitted with provisions for equipment and armament as detailed more completely hereunder.

"We have reached an extremely satisfactory agreement with the Curtiss Aeroplane Company of Buffalo wherein they are furnishing to us data covering a comprehensive series of wind tunnel, cooling, and performance tests of a similar airplane, which data will assist us in the design and manufacture of these airplanes. We have also received release from the United States Army for the manufacture and export of these airplanes and wish to assure you that all arrangements are entirely satisfactory.

"We are prepared to construct and deliver to you 320 of these airplanes before 30 September 1941, and guarantee to effect [these] deliveries in accordance with the following delivery schedule:

NAA was forced to buy technical data on the Curtiss XP-46A. This aircraft was supposed to be an improved follow-on to the P-40, but proved to be a dismal failure. Aircraft featured the same Allison as the NA-73X.

	JAN	FEB	MAR	APR	MAY	JUN	JUL	AUG	SEP
Airplanes	1	5	20	40	50	50	53	51	50
Spares*	1	3	5	5	5	5	10	15	15

*(Equivalent Aircraft)

"We further offer to continue the manufacture of these planes at the rate of 50 airplanes per month until at least the end of the year 1941, should you desire to incorporate and exercise an option for these additional airplanes prior to 30 April 1941.

"We have constructed a mockup and have completed the initial phase of the detail design and are submitting to you herewith certain data and information regarding the characteristics of the airplane. You will note that we have provided for armor protection for the pilot and a sealing arrangement for the fuel tanks. Provisions are being made for the installation of four .50-cal. machine guns, two of which are in the fuselage and the other two in the wing. As a normal load we are specifying 200 rounds of ammunition per .50-cal. gun, but are making additional provisions for more ammunition as a special load. Provisions are being made for four British Type 330 machine guns with ammunition boxes to accommodate 500 rounds of ammunition per gun as normal load.

"Strictly for comparative purposes, we are including the results of a study showing the difference in size and performance between the airplane offered and one which might be offered with a minimum armament and without protective armor, but is otherwise the same. It will be noted that the high speed in this condition is 400 mph with a wing area of 190 sq. ft. With a full complement of armament and armor plate protection front and rear, the weight is increased from 6,450 to 7,765 pounds and the wing area is increased from 190 sq ft to 230 sq ft in order to maintain the same landing speed. The resulting performance is materially reduced and high speed is 384 mph under the same conditions.

"The speeds quoted above are based on a power of 1,030 hp at 16,000 feet altitude, using 90-octane fuel. Since we do not have precise and final information on the power rating of the engines to be furnished for these airplanes, this rating is still somewhat of an estimate. We believe the Anglo-French Commission has, or will shortly have, accurate information on this matter. When we receive the exact figures, the performance guarantees will be arithmetically adjusted accordingly.

"The general provisions for armament have been discussed with Air Commodore Baker and Mr. Thomas and it is believed that the arrangement offered is the most practical possible at this time, consistent with the general instructions we have received. It is possible to increase the firepower through the installation of additional guns if absolutely necessary, but the performance will suffer a proportionate loss. We feel there will be no difficulty in making any changes or modifications that you may feel are essential or desirable, and are prepared to co-operate with your technical staff to the fullest extent. We do feel, however, that the design as presented is close to an optimum condition, all things considered. Details of equipment and installation are yet to be covered, but our previous experience with Harvard aircraft, which incorporate much British equipment, leads us to believe that we will have no difficulty whatever in arriving at satisfactory agreements in all these matters.

"We have made a careful estimate of the price, including sufficient structural tests to guarantee the structural integrity of all parts, wind tunnel testing, and flight-testing. We have included a price breakdown, separating and pricing all items of equipment to be installed and supposedly furnished by us. We have not considered the price of the engine, propeller, radio, oxygen, machine guns, or other items of armament or military equipment, and it is assumed that these items will be furnished to us free of charge for installation in the airplanes. The price summary for airplanes, exclusive of crating or transportation, but covering all other charges is as follows:

A) Powerplants, engine accessories	$983.95
B) Instruments	1,787.35
C) Electrical Equipment	890.75
D) Miscellaneous Equipment	528.40
E) Radio Equipment	Customer furnished
F) Armament	Customer furnished
Total contractor furnished equipment	4,190.45
Base airplane	33,400.00
Total per Airplane	37,590.45
Total for 320 Airplanes	12,028,944.00
Spare parts (20%)	2,405,788.80
Crate per airplane at $675 total	216,000.00
Crating for spare parts (4%)	96,231.35
Total Contract Amount	$14,746,964.35

"Within 60 days after the contract has been executed we will furnish a complete percentage breakdown and a recommended list of spare parts to approximate 20 percent of the contract prices of the airplanes. Spares will be delivered in accordance with the delivery schedule attached hereto, provided a spare parts list is approved and agreed upon within 60 days after submission of such a proposed list by us.

"We are prepared to proceed immediately upon receipt of a letter from you accepting this proposal and receipt of down payment. We desire a down payment of 10 percent of the contract amount upon approval of this proposal and a subsequent monthly payment of 2.5 percent of the contract amount each month until 5 percent of the contract has been paid. Details of final payments and acceptance will be as mutually agreed upon and in general accordance with our previous contracts with the British Government. We feel there will be no difficulty in the preparation of the final contract at our convenience inasmuch as we have reached agreements with your staff concerning all principal points involved in a contract of this type.

"The prices quoted above are intended to include all normal and reasonable modifications and changes which you may require, provided that such changes are agreed upon within three months of the date of the agreement and provided there is no considerable additional expense to us as might be involved in the purchase of additional material or equipment. Changes initiated after this time may involve a delay in delivery or a cost increase.

"May we request that you give this matter your early attention as we are prepared to proceed on receipt of a letter of approval from you and receipt of down payment as requested above. We will consider the date of receipt of this payment as the date of the contract.

"If there are any matters not properly covered in this letter or the enclosed data and it is necessary to withhold the letter until such matters are clarified, we will greatly appreciate it if you will notify us of these matters by telegram or telephone at our expense in order that there will be no delay."

When the accident with the NA-73X took place, much of the area surrounding Mines Field was rural so Paul Balfour was able to put the powerless craft down in a field.

Damage to the NA-73X can be seen in this view of the crumpled wing and horizontal tail which also offers a view of the sprayed-on civilian registration NX19998 and the painted gun ports.

As soon as Schmued and his team surveyed the damage to the NA-73X in the bean field, plans were being put together to rebuild the machine, so it was carefully raised from the field. Note the adjustable radiator scoop.

British optimism for the NA-73X was not dimmed by the accident that befell the prototype. Engineering test pilot Louis Wait is seen examining the tail section.

and each group leader led a particular assignment—landing gear, fuselage, wing, etc. Edgar recalled that, "We had planned to use an NACA-23 series airfoil and then heard NACA had developed a laminar-flow airfoil. That airfoil was specifically adapted by Ed Horkey, our first and only aerodynamicist, and his assistants, who developed the ordinates of the laminar-flow airfoil."

Edgar had an aeronautical vision: "At the outset, an airplane has to be designed in such a manner that the air can flow evenly around the body. There is one simple way of really designing smooth curves. That is to use conic sections to produce the surfaces that are used on all parts except the wing and tail. This means primarily the fuselage; so all curves on that fuselage were designed by conic sections. Conic sections are very simple. If you take a cone and section crosswise, you get a circle. You make a section that is under an angle and you get a parabola. All these curves are smooth, which can be calculated and then precisely shaped, and the air likes that. This is the kind of shape the air likes to touch. The drag is at a minimum and it was the first time that a complete airplane [referring to the NA-73X], with the exception of the lifting surfaces, was designed with second-degree curves. I laid out the lines myself and it was a first."

Kindelberger was concerned that this new wing might not work, but Edgar assured him that he would design and build another wing in just one month. Regarding the wing, Ed Horkey later wrote, "Our concern was that we didn't get all of the great laminar flow projected, since 20 percent would be too thick an airfoil, even in those days. It was decided to lay out new airfoils, which were around 16 percent thick at the root and 11 percent thick at the tip… In other words, what we did is pick the pressure distribution we wanted. Then we drew an airfoil shape, and… we could check our pressure distributions. If it didn't match, we could make a change to the airfoil contour, then go back and recalculate the pressure distribution." This spirit of gaining knowledge and working together were key elements in creating the NA-73X.

Constant innovation could have been the term that defined the project. Problems were met and quickly solved while new ideas were born and incorporated into the design. Schmued wrote, "We discovered that when the wing was very thin, the aileron control system had to be extremely well designed to fit into the small space that was available. We used some rather unorthodox systems for the aileron control by using a wobble plate. That is a term for a special form of mechanism which we used that was very successful."

On 10 April 1940, the British signed the go-ahead letter for the NA-73X project (73 for the NAA model number, X for experimental), while the formal contract was signed on 23 May. The small NAA engineering department issued drawings to the fabrication shops in a never-ending stream that included 16-hr working days, seven days a week. Dutch and his team were aiming for a delivery date of a complete airframe in January 1941. However, the NA-73X was rolled out of the hangar in 117 days—although incomplete

THE BACKYARD DESIGNER

The 1939 National Air Races held during September in Cleveland, Ohio, were attended by tens of thousands of spectators eager to see the fastest aircraft compete around the pylons for the Thompson Trophy or fly cross-country to gain the Bendix Trophy. However, few attendees could anticipate what was happening when the loud speakers announced that Germany had invaded Poland and that England and its allies had declared war. One of those taken by surprise was race pilot Art Chester. The self-taught pilot, engineer, and race plane builder was ready to compete in the event with his sleek Menasco-powered *The Goon* racer, but he also realized the world would soon be encompassed in war and air racing would be over for the duration.

Knowing he had to find another means of employment, Chester, who was based in Los Angeles, applied for a job at North American Aviation. He desired a position as an engineering test pilot, but was turned down since, at the time, the company was hiring only Air Corps–trained pilots. This stung Art, but he was informed that there were plenty of open positions in the engineering department. Filling out the required forms, he was told that he would be contacted by NAA.

Returning home, Chester decided to get his clubs and go play a few rounds of golf, but as he was walking out his wife Trudy picked up the ringing telephone. It was Edgar Schmued and he wanted to know if Art could report to work… immediately! It is not known if Chester and Schmued knew each other, but the NAA designer would certainly have known of Art's speed achievements.

Reporting to Schmued a few hours later, Art was immediately assigned to designing the Menasco engine installation for the new NA-35 primary trainer that Schmued had designed. The front end of the little trainer would look not unlike Art's speed ships. Schmued was impressed, but some of the other engineering higher-ups, including Raymond Rice, scoffed at Art's extensive experience and lack of a college education—calling him a "backyard designer."

Schmued had faith in Art and liked the powerplant installation so much that he assigned Art to be in charge of the NA-73X powerplant design group, which would be responsible for everything from the firewall forward. It should come as no surprise that the front end of the NA-73X was as sleek as the most contemporary of racing planes.

As production for the Mustang built up, the ever enterprising Chester soon saw that subcomponents coming from other suppliers were not only late, but often overly expensive. For example, the nearest spinner manufacturer was in far-away Kansas City so Art made the bold proposal to Schmued and Kindelberger that he could build spinners not only faster, but also cheaper.

He and Trudy used their life savings to buy a lot in Inglewood and set up a small factory under the firm name Air Craftsmen. A contract was obtained and the first Chester spinners were delivered in May 1941. The chief accountant at NAA complained that Art was working for NAA full-time while also running a side business supplying components to the company and stated this was against NAA policy. Art quit, but the engineering department—including Raymond Rice—insisted they needed Art. An arrangement was made and Art continued working on the Mustang program for another year while Trudy managed Air Craftsmen. The company supplied NAA with Mustang spinners, employed 135 people, and supplied sheetmetal components to other aeronautical companies. Not bad for a "backyard designer."

Art Chester with his Menasco-powered The Goon racer. Chester's innovative ideas for tight cowling design were applied to the NA-73X.

Form ASB 453

UNITED STATES OF AMERICA
CIVIL AERONAUTICS AUTHORITY
AIR SAFETY BOARD
WASHINGTON
- - -

(Certificate number and symbol)

(Aircraft—trade name and model)

REPORT OF AN ACCIDENT INVOLVING AIRCRAFT
(Other Than Scheduled Air Carrier)

*Complete at once and deliver to an Air Safety Board Investigator or Civil Aeronautics Authority
Inspector or mail to the nearest office of the Air Safety Board as indicated below*

NEW YORK CITY, N. Y.   KANSAS CITY, MO.   SANTA MONICA, CALIF.   ATLANTA, GA.
CHICAGO, ILL.   SEATTLE, WASH.   FORT WORTH, TEX.

I. LOCATION OF ACCIDENT: City Los Angeles   State Calif.   Date 11-20-40 Hour 7:23 am
   Name airport, or if not on airport, describe location
                150 yards west of L.A.M.A.

II. PILOT, INSTRUCTOR, OR SOLO STUDENT:
   1. Name and address P. B. Balfour, North American Aviation, Inc.
   2. Age 32   3. Injuries Cuts and bruises
   4. CAA certificate class and number Comm. #12596   Ratings 2S and 3S Land.
                                         (If temporary, date issued)
   5. Total solo flying time 2298:40   6. Time last 90 days 26 hours
   7. Time in type involved ---   8. Night flying time ---
   9. Instrument flying time None   10. List types of aircraft flown 1; 2S; 3S; and
                4M, land and water.

III. CREW, OTHER THAN PILOT (copilot, dual student, other):
   1. Names, addresses, CAA certificate class and number, and ratings if any
                None
   2. Injuries ----

IV. PASSENGERS (revenue or nonrevenue—please denote which):
   1. Names, addresses, injuries None

V. INJURIES TO PERSONS ON THE GROUND (spectators, ground crew, or others):
   1. Names, addresses, injuries None

VI. IF ACCIDENT RESULTED IN INJURY TO ANY PERSON GIVE NAME OF ATTENDING PHYSICIAN OR HOSPITAL:
                Dr. Smitgen, 325 East Hillcrest, Inglewood, Calif.

(1)   16—4821

Civil Aeronautics Authority's accident report for the NA-73X.

in some details and sitting on tires and wheels from the Harvard production line. NAA would later record that the company had expended 78,000 man-hours engineering on the NA-73X.

Also, Allison had not delivered the engine on time and it would be another 20 days before the V-12 arrived to be mated to the airframe. The sleek firewall forward design was courtesy of race pilot Art Chester ("Since Art was about the right size, I designed the cockpit around him," said Schmued). Ray Rice was very skeptical about Art because of his lack of formal education, but he was also the only NAA employee who designed, built, and flew his own high-performance aircraft. Art designed an engine mount that utilized a riveted-aluminum box beam structure instead of the usual welded-steel tube structure of the time. Schmued praised the mount for its rigidity, lightness, and accessibility. Allison engineers had rated the F3R (civilian designation for the V-1710-39) at 1,100 hp, but had fixed the critical altitude at 11,000 feet, and here lays the inherent weakness of the engine. This critical altitude figure meant that the performance of the fighter would start to fall off at any altitude over 11,000 feet, thus giving a critical advantage to enemy fighters with powerplants that had a higher altitude rating.

NAA hired freelance test pilot Vance Breese—a colorful and often outspoken personality—to do the first test flight. At the time, several freelance pilots vied for such test work (and there was a lot of it), and the pay was often very lucrative and much more than a pilot on the company payroll would make. NAA had previously used Breese to test fly Schmued's NA-35 trainer.

The morning of 26 October 1940 found the NA-73X parked on the ramp with Breese—wearing his usual double-breasted suit—in the cockpit, going over a mental checklist. Hitting the starter, the Curtiss-built propeller jerked a few times and the Allison burst into full staccato life, with just a hint of smoke dissipating from the exhaust stacks. The powerplant had been warmed up by the mechanics earlier that morning.

Breese began to taxi the prototype—the long nose obscured forward vision, which made S-turning mandatory. Pointing the nose into the wind and standing on the brakes, Breese gave the Allison a thorough run-up. Once satisfied, the pilot took the active runway and moved the throttle smartly forward. After rolling 100 feet, he brought the engine up to full power and pointed the nose down the centerline of the runway, shoving in right rudder to counteract the rapidly increasing torque.

The lightly loaded NA-73X was quickly airborne, but the first flight was a rather sedate affair, Breese keeping within gliding distance of Mines Field. After flying for about five minutes, he came back to land. He went over initial handling data with Schmued and others, and then Breese went off for his second flight, which was about 10 minutes in length. He found that the gleaming craft exceeded initial performance estimates. Throttling back, he brought the NA-73X in for a smooth landing.

ATWOOD AND THE MEREDITH EFFECT

*L*ate in 1992, Lee Atwood summarized his contributions to the NA-73—particularly regarding the Meredith effect:

"As Chief Engineer at NAA, I had regularly reviewed the National Advisory Committee for Aeronautics (NACA) reports on aerodynamics and related subjects and, in 1939, one came to my attention that was a review of some British experimental radiator work at RAE Farnborough, England. An investigator named Meredith had experimented with energy recovery from aircraft radiators. This, of course, was not anything new conceptually, since energy recovery in steam and heat engines was common, as in triple-expansion cylinder engines and in turbine applications, but these all started at relatively high temperatures. In reciprocating internal combustion engines, the coolant out temperature cannot be allowed to exceed something like 250 degrees F, which is at about the temperature of the end of a heat recovery cycle in a steam engine. However, Meredith experimented with fully ducted radiators and showed that substantial recovery was possible.

"Aircraft radiators had been generally treated like those in automobiles, using the speed of the airplane to force air through the radiators [ram air] and dissipating the heated air at random, but aircraft cooling has to be effective for various speeds and power settings, so the conventional radiator had to be able to cool an engine at full power in a climb at perhaps half its possible speed in level flight with the same power and cooling requirement. It also had to cool on the ground, but at only an idle or taxi speed power output. So, an airplane climbing at full power at 150 mph would require about four times the radiator exposure as the same plane at full power in level flight at twice the speed, 300 mph. This fixed radiator exposure, of course, led to an unnecessarily high drag at high speed and absorbed a great deal of the engine's power.

"Radiators constructed of tubing and metal fins considerably restrict airflow and so Meredith experimented with ducting the air in to the radiator face and ducting it out to the airstream. By making the outlet variable, he could restrict the air passing through the radiator to just that amount needed for cooling. By closing the outlet partially, the pressure behind the radiator could be maintained to the level that permits just enough air to pass through for cooling purposes. It is also apparent that the intake opening can be much smaller than the radiator size and, therefore, the drag is much less.

"In passing through the radiator, the air is heated and expands in volume. A 200 degree F temperature rise expands the air considerably, so it can be seen that the discharged air—although having the same mass as the incoming air—has a larger volume and for a given pressure requires a larger discharge opening, providing some forward thrust.

"With this insight from the Meredith report, I began to gradually think about some way it might be applied to the P-40. However, with a little more consideration, I began to believe that, for the best effect, the radiator should be in the fuselage, with only the duct openings exposed. The P-40 had the cooling system forward under the rear of the engine, and to balance the plane properly for stability the pilot was rather far back, somewhat compromising his view and limiting fuselage space.

James "Dutch" Kindelberger and vice president Leland Atwood (right) pose for a company portrait.

"The idea of a redesign, and even possibly a new design, looked attractive, but the thought of such a possibility seemed somewhat fanciful since I had never seen any government buy a production plane without a set of requirements in detail, some kind of competition and/or flight test approval, and a formal appropriation of money.

"In my position as NAA vice president, I had responsibility for contract administration, among other things, and so had occasion to meet with the British Purchasing Commission rather frequently to negotiate contracts, prices, spare parts, equipment, and support services. In January 1940, I told Dutch that I would like to try to get some kind of a fighter authorization and that I hoped my ideas on reduced cooling drag might be a vehicle. He was generally supportive, but skeptical, as I was myself. My best hope was perhaps a contract to modify a single P-40 or possibly to build an experimental airplane.

"H.C.B. 'Tommy' Thomas was the British Commission's senior technical man, and I used some occasions to talk to him about the subject, making the point that my confidence in the possibilities of a major improvement was based on Meredith's Farnborough papers, as well as the natural technical logic of the application.

"I made a point of visiting Tommy when I could. Coast-to-coast was just a long overnight trip in DC-3s and I could cover quite a bit of ground. I could see that my suggestion had been taken seriously after two or three visits, and I believe that Thomas established some communications with Farnborough on the subject. I used only some freehand sketches, but Tommy was very astute and technically qualified. The questions about implementation got more concrete, but no company engineering work was started—it seemed a long shot.

"I had discussed my concept with Ed Schmued, preliminary design supervisor, who, though not technically educated, had a real talent for shapes and arrangements and mechanical components [Author's Note: As time went by, it unfortunately appears that Mr. Atwood was more than ready to criticize people like Schmued—he was also an opponent of hiring Art Chester—while also perhaps inflating his overall contribution to the NA-73], but the first work authorization, designated NA-73, was not issued until April 1940.

"Finally, early in that month, I was invited into Sir Henry Self's office and was advised approximately as follows: That they had decided to accept our proposal; that I should prepare a letter contract for his signature; that it should provide for the purchase of 320 aircraft of our design; that it provide a schedule and a not-to-exceed price per airplane; that the British-supplied equipment, including engines, would be specified; and, finally, that a definitive contract would be negotiated on the basis of this letter contract.

"Furthermore, he told me that since we had never produced a fighter airplane, he considered it very desirable that we have some P-40 data as a helpful guide. He specified the P-40 wind tunnel report and the flight test report. He suggested that I attempt to obtain these data. I told him I would immediately try to do so and took the night train to Buffalo. The date was 10 April 1940, the day Hitler seized Denmark and the Norwegian ports.

"In Buffalo, Burdette Wright, general manager of the Curtiss Airplane Company, was reasonable enough, considering the competitive aspects. Ben Kelsey of the Air Corps is reported to have said that the Air Corps encouraged him to sell me the data. Later, Dutch Kindelberger quipped that we didn't even open the package, although I am sure that some of our technical staff did examine the reports [Author's Note: Wind tunnel aerodynamicist Ed Horkey]. I gave Burdy a marker for $56,000 for the copies and went back to New York, and as soon as I could, presented the letter contract [Author's Note: The passing of years have caused a bit of confusion about this data, and Schmued would remember the data as for the experimental XP-46]. After a staff review Sir Henry signed it and I went to the LaGuardia Airport. Work Order NA-73 was issued shortly after.

"It is practically impossible to quantify the Meredith Effect without extensive and elaborate flight test data and cooling information. Consequently, both pilots and writers have credited the Mustang's performance to a number of secondary or minor factors. The semi-laminar flow wing as a separate refinement which added little to the top speed [Author's Note: Another curious, and false, statement from Mr. Atwood who once again appears to be grinding what was now a quite old axe], but it materially reduced the 'tuck under' effect at high Mach diving speeds, enhancing its combat capability in pursuit and in evasion.

"In order to make a comparison in cooling drag, it is necessary to look at the benefits of the Meredith Effect. With it, as displayed in the P-51, the horsepower recovered using the same Merlin engine was over 200 hp [Mr. Atwood is comparing the Merlin-powered P-51D with the Merlin-powered Supermarine Spitfire Mk. IX], leaving some 40 hp used for actual cooling of the engine's liquid coolant. This, of course, does not take into account form drag or skin friction and certain other inefficiencies in either plane and the discharge area assumed may be somewhat overestimated, but it is an illustration of the net cooling drag reduction possibilities.

"By contrast, the two Spitfire radiators without efficient ducting to produce the Meredith Effect represent something like twice the frontal area (and drag) and there is no exit ducting to recover any significant part of the cooling energy, therefore the horsepower requirements for cooling is several times as much. The small movable flaps at the rear of the Spitfire radiator may be a partial attempt at energy recovery, but are not very effective compared to a gradually converging duct as designed into the P-51.

"This estimate correlates fairly accurately with the power/speed relationship between the Spitfire and Mustang. For equal fuel loadings and the same 1,720 hp, the Mustang is at least 20 mph faster. Some of this difference in speed can be attributed to the exposed tail wheel on the Spitfire, but the major part is the difference in cooling drag.

"To summarize, the Mustang cooling system provided just enough, but no excess, of cooling air. Ideally, the back pressure should be at a minimum, close to zero, in a low-speed high-power climb and a maximum at high speed and in long-range cruise, resulting in the lowest net drag where it is most needed."

Six more functional test flights took place (31 October and 4, 8, 11, 12, and 13 November). These were made by Breese to fulfill his contract obligations and he was then on to other testing projects after putting some 3 hours 30 minutes on the airframe. However, Breese had numerous complaints about the aircraft and it required time to correct them. Breese, an excellent self-promoter, was pretty much a very good seat-of-the-pants pilot. What the NA-73X needed, however, was an engineering test pilot.

NAA was fortunate in having access to an excellent wind tunnel facility at the California Institute of Technology where extensive tests were undertaken to prove various NAA concepts (see sidebar "Hurricane Hall" on page 30). Back at Mines Field, Paul Balfour (commercial pilot certificate number 12596) was hired by the company in 1936 and eventually assigned the post of chief test pilot for the NA-73X. Before his death in the early 1970s, Breese stated that he had bet money with NAA officials that Balfour would crash the aircraft on his first flight. Breese won.

On the morning of 20 November 1941, the ground crew prepared the NA-73X for Balfour's flight. Schmued would later recall, "Before this flight, I asked Balfour to get into the airplane and go through the routine of a takeoff and flight. He responded that one airplane is like the other and he would not need the routine checkout."

Balfour's first flight was also scheduled to be a high-speed test run for the NA-73X. The pilot took off at approximately 0710. Mechanic Olaf T. Anderson later stated that the engine had run fine on the ground and, "at about 0540, I warmed the engine up as is the usual procedure before the flight. Oil and Prestone temperatures were normal [oil, 65 degreesC; Prestone, 95 degreesC]. Oil pressure was 80 pounds and fuel, 13 pounds. The engine was run for five minutes and then shut down. When I started the engine for Mr. Balfour before takeoff, it was a little hard to start [the Allison representative said their engines have a tendency to do such]."

When the NA-73X was rebuilt, the rudder was painted with Air Corps' style red, white, and blue stripes.

PAUL B. BALFOUR

CHIEF TEST PILOT

BORN JULY 5, 1908
WITH N.A.A. SINCE MARCH 1, 1936

North American Aviation Corp. company employee file card for Paul Balfour.

As Balfour pulled the gleaming fighter up after about 12 minutes flying time, the Allison suddenly stopped running. Checking the instruments, nothing seemed amiss. However, executing a wide sweeping turn caused the NA-73X to lose altitude and Balfour quickly realized he was not going to make the runway. During the last portion of the turn, he dumped landing gear and flaps as he directed the stricken prototype toward a plowed field just west of Lincoln Boulevard. The now-glider whistled down in a correct landing attitude, but as soon as the tires touched the soft plowed soil (at approximately 0723), the NA-73X violently flipped over. The built-up structure behind the pilot saved Balfour from being crushed, and the pilot scrambled for safety from the movable side window.

Since little in the way of photography had been done with the NA-73X in its original form, NAA ordered a series of aerial photographs. However, the Air Corps must have objected about the tail stripes for in most of the photos the stripes were crudely retouched out. Note the forward radiator scoop is slightly lowered.

At the time of the accident, the prototype had accumulated just 3 hours 20 minutes of flying time (Balfour had logged 2,298.40 hours of solo time at this point). The Civil Aeronautics Authority Air Safety Board listed damage to the aircraft as "engine housing broken, both wingtips damaged, tail surfaces damaged, top of fuselage damaged, and other miscellaneous damage."

Investigation of the crash revealed that the Allison had run dry when the selected fuel tank had been allowed to be completely depleted. NAA and the British both agreed that, in spite of the crash, they had a winning aircraft and the accident was no way the fault of the design.

Some aviation historians have recorded that the prototype was scrapped after the accident, but this was not the case. Actually, the prototype was carefully raised out of the bean field by crane and transported back to NAA where it was stripped apart and rebuilt in a very short time. However, to increase the pace of flight testing, the first RAF machine was completed and joined in the flight program.

Robert C. "Bob" Chilton was hired as chief test pilot to replace the unfortunate Balfour, and a study of Bob's logbooks indicates he flew the rebuilt NA-73X on 3 April 1941 for a 1-hour familiarization flight from Mines Field. Chilton also recalled that the NA-73X had made between five and six flights with another pilot immediately after its rebuild. Chilton went on to make at least a dozen more flights with the aircraft.

Bob later remarked, "The NA-73X was a clean-flying aircraft with no bad vices. It was quite pleasant in the air and handled very similar to the later production articles."

Chilton had accrued considerable fighter experience in the Air Corps before going to NAA, flying the Boeing P-12 and P-26, the Curtiss P-36, and other fighter types. His expertise in the fighter field enabled the engineers to incorporate changes that would be beneficial to the combat pilot.

"I recall that the NA-73X was just pushed to the side after it had been retired from its last flight," stated Chilton. "It probably ended up on the company's junk pile, but I do not recall seeing it there. The NA-73X was a very attractive aircraft and its aluminum skin glowed with constant waxing by George Mountain Bear, an American Indian whose duty was to keep the airframe as clean as possible to pick up those few vital miles per hour."

With the first RAF aircraft coming off the production line, NAA and the British decided to use these airframes for continued testing. "The 'old' NA-73X was no longer representative of the design," said Chilton. "We had orders on our hands for hundreds of new fighters and the NA-73X had served its purpose. It had established the trend for what I believe was the finest propeller-driven fighter ever built by any country."

Research indicates that the NA-73X, stripped of useable components, may have been donated to a local trade school.

NAMING THE MUSTANG

Following the arrival of this official British Purchasing Commission communiqué at NAA on 12 December 1940, the NA-73 became known as the Mustang.

EXPORT OFFICE BRITISH PURCHASING COMMISSION
9 DECEMBER 1940

IN REPLY PLEASE QUOTE BAC/C/A250 (FSC)

NORTH AMERICAN AVIATION, INC., INGLEWOOD, CALIFORNIA

CONTRACT A250
FOR THE SUPPLY OF NA-73 AIRPLANES AND SPARES
LETTER OF AMENDMENT NO. 13

GENTLEMEN:
WE ARE TO INFORM YOU THAT THE ABOVE MENTIONED AEROPLANES HAVE BEEN GIVEN THE OFFICIAL DESIGNATION "MUSTANG," AND THIS NAME SHALL BE USED IN ALL CORRESPONDENCE.
PLEASE RETURN TO US THE THREE ATTACHED COPIES OF THIS LETTER DULY SIGNED BY AN AUTHORIZED OFFICER OF YOUR COMPANY.
VERY TRULY YOURS,
HIS MAJESTY'S GOVERNMENT IN THE UNITED KINGDOM BY BRITISH PURCHASING COMMISSION
BY (SIGNED) R. F. PAYNE
FOR AND ON BEHALF OF THE DIRECTOR GENERAL

ACCEPTED: 12 DEC. 1940
SUPPLIER: NORTH AMERICAN AVIATION, INC.
BY: (SIGNED) NOBLE SHROPSHIRE
TITLE: CONTRACT ADMINISTRATOR

Even though later production variants would feature many changes, the basic profile of the Mustang remained recognizable through its production life.

The rebuilt NA-73X with the radiator scoop fully retracted. The racing-style windscreen was soon replaced with armor glass. Oddly, the eliminated rudder stripes have been touched back in for this photo.

CHAPTER TWO

THE ALLISON MUSTANGS

Because of Dutch Kindelberger's exemplary planning, production of the first Mustangs proceeded successfully.

As NAA personnel watched the camouflaged aircraft taxi in from its test flight, it seemed to be traveling toward them at a higher rate of speed than was necessary. Since none of them wanted to fall prey to the shining disk of the Curtiss Electric propeller, some nervous tension seemed to surge through the men and a few began to move away from the path of the aircraft. However, there was no reason to worry. At the last minute, Michael Crossley hit the left brake, spun the plane around so the nose was facing the wind, put the mixture control in idle cutoff at 1,200 rpm, and moved the throttle fully open. In a couple seconds, the engine ceased firing and the pilot turned the ignition switch to off along with both fuel selector valves. To ensure against accidentally starting, Crossley left the mixture control lever at idle cutoff, reached up with his left hand, and unfastened the canopy. As the men gathered around, Crossley said "Wrap it up, chaps!" and began to unfold himself from the cockpit.

Jimmy Beaton, who had worked for NAA servicing the new fighters for just a couple months, recalled decades later that, "I never could quite figure out how Mike got in and out

Lovely view of Mustang Mk. I AG345 on a test flight from Mines Field on 19 August 1941 with Bob Chilton at the controls. This angle shows important features such as the machine guns in the lower cowling and the retractable front scoop of the radiator housing. The retractable scoop proved to be less than popular and was designed out of Mustang production. AG345, the first of the Mustangs, was retained for a time at the factory to test out various modifications.

of the Mustang's cockpit. He was 6-ft 2-in tall and the Mustang's cockpit was designed for a much smaller man. Watching him get in and out was a bit like viewing a circus contortionist."

Michael "Red Knight" Crossley was mild-mannered and his quiet sense of British humor was greatly appreciated by NAA workers. However, his mild manner was a façade. Crossley had joined the Royal Air Force in 1936 at age 24 and trained as a fighter pilot. He was quite well educated, having attended Eton College and The College of Aeronautical Engineering. Rising rapidly in the RAF, Crossley became a flight commander on the eve of World War II. Flying with No. 32 Squadron, Crossley entered aerial combat during the Battle of France. By the start of June 1940, he had destroyed six Luftwaffe aircraft, including four Bf 109Es while flying Hawker Hurricanes. With the defeat of the British Expeditionary Force in France, Crossley escaped back to Britain and took command of the squadron and helped whip the unit back into fighting shape. During the Battle of Britain, he shot down a further 10 Luftwaffe aircraft between 12 and 18 August. During that same month, he was also shot down twice, but survived with minimum injury. By late August, the squadron was stood down for rest. During April 1941, Crossley was assigned as a test pilot

for the British Air Commission and sent to the United States where he flew Mustangs and a variety of other aircraft scheduled for shipment to Britain. At NAA, Crossley became one of a small and tight-knit group responsible for making sure that the Mustang was ready for combat in the skies over Europe.

The aircraft Crossley had been test flying for the final sign-off was AG346 (c/n 73-3099). Chilton had completed company tests on 1 August and the plane was handed over to Crossley. After his acceptance flights, AG346 was disassembled, carefully crated, driven to Long Beach Harbor where the crate was winched aboard a cargo ship, and began the long voyage to Britain via the Panama Canal and then the Atlantic Ocean.

When the U.S. government gave approval for the production of Mustangs for the British government, it must be remembered that America was still firmly in the grip of what became known as "isolationism." Attempting to recover from the near death spiral of the Great Depression, the majority of government officials along with most of the general population wanted to separate themselves from whatever was going on in Europe and the Far East. Heroes such as Charles Lindbergh were speaking long and passionately for *America First*—the popular movement to keep the United States out of any

As soon as it was completed, AG345 was rolled out for a series of photographs. At this point, the aircraft was unpainted except for the anti-glare panel and the rudder, which was a shade of green. For identification, the serial was painted on the rudder and repeated quite large above the left wing and below the right wing. At this point, the wing had not been filled, primed, or painted. Also note the short-lived wheel covers.

form of foreign war. Since the United States was theoretically neutral, the German embassy was bringing great pressure to bear on the government regarding supply of military equipment to the British. It also must be remembered that at the time one of the largest minority populations in America was of German extraction.

Fortunately, President Franklin D. Roosevelt had a fairly clear idea of the threat posed by Germany, Japan, and Italy and the British Purchasing Commission was very pleased when government approval was received to build Mustangs for the Royal Air Force—however, there was a codicil and that will later be explained.

Because of British interest in the NA-73, it was just as well that the fledgling NAA had established an efficient production line prior to the building of the new fighter and this fact has been mainly overlooked by the success of the NA-73. Besides cranking out a few portly O-47 observation aircraft for the Air Corps, the company's main manufacturing success had been with the BT-9/Texan/Harvard series of trainers.

"We were quite successful with the advanced trainer line and had built a couple of medium bomber and attack plane prototypes, which didn't really get anywhere until the B-25 order," recalled Lee Atwood. "In 1939, we were booked up and expanding, and a major transition in the organization was shaping up. Dutch [Kindelberger] had a lot of balls in the air with contracts, building plans, machinery orders, financial requirements, personnel expansion, government interfaces, etc.

"Dutch had put a lot of effort and talent into increasing the efficiency of airplane production. Even at high wartime rates of production, parts were made in batches, and it was most unusual to have a machine tool dedicated to making one part, or even to one operation. Many tools, especially for sheet-metal parts, were 'soft' tooling—using Masonite, plywood, or low-temperature casting materials, rather than tool steel, and were much cheaper if not as durable. However, for the purpose, they were adequate and were made much more quickly and were adaptable to the inevitable changes that came along. Dutch made many contributions to the cutting, forming, and stretch-fitting

techniques, but his greatest improvement came from rationalization of assembly and installation processes.

"It was common practice to finish the structural elements, wing, fuselage, etc., and then begin installation of equipment—electrical, hydraulic, armament, instruments, and other items—in the nearly completed structure. In large airplanes, with plenty of access room, this worked reasonably well with few bottlenecks, but in smaller planes, such as fighters and trainers, the final assembly stage was crowded, hectic, and inefficient. Starting with the T-6 series, Dutch required that fuselage and wing structures remain open in sort of half-shell condition until all wiring, tubing, and permanent equipment installations were made and that they be inspected and tested before joining into complete structures. This naturally required that the engineering design provide for this construction process—so it became part of house practice in all models."

This somewhat revolutionary view of production would go a long way toward speeding production of the first Mustangs. In comparison, the Supermarine Spitfire was a very complex fighter to build, and was not really suited for the style of mass-production techniques envisioned by Henry Ford—the creator of the concept. In some ways, the Mustang went together like a very large model airplane kit, making the type ideally suited for construction in very large numbers.

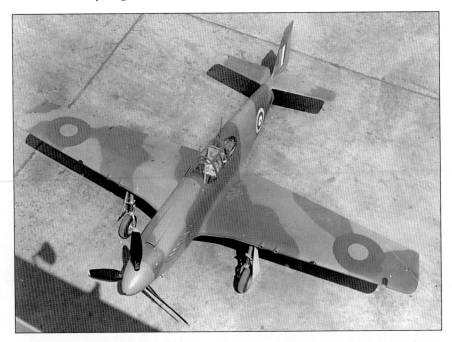

AG348 viewed from atop one of the NAA buildings. This fourth production example illustrates the very simple layout of the Mustang and also shows the angular wingtips to advantage. Most fighters produced before the Mustang had elongated curved wingtips, which were believed— incorrectly—to cut down on drag. The angular tips were much easier to build in mass quantity. The original short inlet for the Allison's carburetor was soon changed. Upper wing roundels were red and blue while those on the fuselage sides were, from outside in, yellow, blue, white, and red. Finally, the underwing roundels were blue, white, and red.

Dutch Kindelberger put the matter into more perspective when during late 1942 he wrote, "At no time prior to the late 1930s did the quantity of planes in a single contract justify even moderately high tooling costs. Even when the first orders exceeding 500 planes were placed by the British and French in 1939, and by our own government under the National Defense program in 1940, tooling costs had to be held down, simply because it proved necessary to make changes in design to meet changing needs. When NAA passed the 1,000 mark on Harvard trainers for the British and Empire air forces in March 1941, it did not mean that we had produced 1,000 identical planes. Actually, there were 2,500 change drawings made after the first Harvard was produced, and among those 1,000 trainers there were actually more than 25 different models, each varying from the others in some major or minor detail of construction. Yet, NAA shattered every then-existing production record in providing these 1,000 Harvard trainers, emphasizing the fact that we were geared to handle changes without disrupting production. The reason, of course, was flexible tooling.

"When the American aircraft industry was finally given the green light for all-out aircraft production, there was much cost for freezing designs. Then, if ever, existed an opportunity for real production tooling in the aircraft industry. Enthusiasm was high for an air war in which America could utilize its mass production techniques. Many ardent, if misinformed, prophets counted the days until the war would be won.

"Fortunately for the nation's ultimate welfare, the high commands of our Army and Navy were not stampeded by the popular cry for mass production

After being painted, AG345 was again subjected to a series of around-the-clock photographs. The position of the wing and cowling armament is evident.

HURRICANE HALL

Extensive wind tunnel testing would greatly aid the rapid development of the Mustang.

In the late 1930s, as the performance of both military and commercial aircraft started to take a quantum leap, North American Aviation was fortunate in having access to an excellent wind tunnel facility at the California Institute of Technology in nearby Pasadena. Conceived in the 1920s by Theodore von Karman (considered by many to be the father of aeronautics), the tunnel was used by NAA to prove many of its design advances. So important was the tunnel to the later war effort that armed guards were positioned around the building in which the tunnel was housed. Caltech scientists and engineers worked around-the-clock shifts. Just before the war began, Charles A. Lindbergh, who was on special assignment for the government to inspect the nation's aeronautical research capabilities, officially inspected the tunnel. The wind tunnel was built with a grant from the Daniel Guggenheim Fund, which also made possible the founding of the Guggenheim Aeronautical Laboratory (GALCIT) and an entire academic building in which to house the facility. NAA utilized the pioneering facility throughout the war.

However, the Caltech tunnels operated on a tight schedule giving a certain time to each of the many aeronautical manufacturers in southern California and at other locations. NAA officials realized the importance of having their own dedicated tunnel and, accordingly, allocated a large sum of money and critical wartime materials to construct a tunnel in a fortress-like concrete building at the Inglewood plant. While using the Caltech facility, weeks, sometimes months, of precious time were often wasted in waiting for a chance to use the tunnels. With the new tunnel, NAA engineers could run tests continuously and quickly, covering a much larger field than before.

The tunnel utilized a 3,000-hp powerplant that drove a seven-blade 190-foot propeller at up to 700 rpm, and this could get the air moving at speeds of up to 325 mph. A 200-hp auxiliary system supplied power for motors to run propellers in the models and for various other operations.

Scientific considerations governed all the details in the construction of the tunnel. The redwood test section was supported on steel I-beams, anchored at each end to the concrete portion of the tunnel. The power and propeller section was doubly strong, while the walls of the control and computing room were floating and heavily soundproofed. More than 200 years ago, Venturi discovered that, as a passageway narrowed down, the flow of liquid through it gained speed—hence, the Venturi effect—and the NAA tunnel was built on that principle. The airstream narrowed down nearly eight times, making high speeds possible through the test section.

The problem of making the air flow smoothly around the square angles of the tunnel was solved by curved metal vanes or plates set up at the corners. Since a temperature of 150 degreesC might develop in the airstream during continuous operation at high speeds, water cooling of the vanes was provided.

The building consisted of a basement, main floor, mezzanine, and top floor. The weighing system was in the basement; while the main floor housed the test section, control room, hallways on each side of the test section, the thermodynamics room, and accessories room. On the mezzanine were the computing and furnace rooms. At the top were the laboratory and model shop, consisting of woodworking and machine shops where craftsmen created the aerodynamic models.

In operation, the tunnel was quite a complex piece of equipment. Once the model was in place, engineers would make a final run-through to ensure

Engineering test pilot Louis Wait makes an adjustment to the NA-73 wind tunnel model. Note that the model did not feature a kinked leading edge and that the carburetor air scoop had been extended.

everything was functioning for the test. Powerful mercury vapor lamps were turned on while indicators were checked to make sure all doors were securely locked. If a door somehow opened during a test, the powerplant would automatically shut down. The floors were vacuum cleaned since dust had to be removed from the atmosphere, and very little air was taken in from the outside in order to keep the test section as clean as possible.

Once the test started, the clutch was set for low speed and the power was turned on. As the speed increased, there was a rising roar and slight vibration that would fill the building as engineers carefully monitored the models, graphs, and instruments to make sure that the recording graph paper was smoothly moving through the automatic recorders. When the readings for a particular setting had been obtained, the power was shut off and the engineers began rigging the model for its next test. With the second run, the graph would record the effect of the airstream on the model under new conditions.

The test section where the model was placed was a narrow tunnel throat open at both ends, its wooden walls being made of highly polished redwood and pierced by observation windows on both sides. Through the windows, NAA engineers could watch the model being tested.

Special cast-steel struts supported the model on a centerline and the struts ran down through the floor—without touching it—and were anchored to a structural steel I-beam. The weighing scales through a series of rods and levers, in turn, supported this indirectly.

There were six scales to measure the lift, drag, side force, pitching, rolling, and yawing movement (twisting force) on the Mustang model. An automatic recording system gave a complete graph of forces acting on the model. The scales measured the forces exerted against the model and transmitted the data electrically to the control room.

Using lift and drag data, engineers could take the results of wind tunnel tests and closely determine what a completed aircraft could do. Without the tunnel, if it had been necessary to change an actual Mustang and fly it to correct each fault or error, the expense and time would have been prohibitive during wartime. The tunnel was a shortcut.

NAA tested a laminated wooden Mustang model with a bubble canopy in the tunnel and found that such a modification would be perfectly acceptable. The disturbed air flowing from the bubble did not adversely affect the tail surfaces, but the removal of the upper portion of the fuselage did result in a loss of keel, and the engineers reasoned that the bubble canopy Mustang would be even more directionally unstable than earlier variants. Thus, from the earliest Mustangs through the P-82 Twin Mustang, wind tunnels played an important and essential role in defining and perfecting the abilities of the design.

As NAA and the war advanced, so did the wind tunnels. Lloyd Cook, head of the wind tunnel model shop, stands before the wind stream turning vanes at one end of the large wind tunnel. The curved metal vanes set up at the ends made the air flow smoothly around the square angles of the tunnel. They were cooled by water since a temperature of 150 degreesF might otherwise develop in the airstream during continuous operation at high speeds.

Allison Mustang wind tunnel model undergoing test with the extended carburetor air scoop and, perhaps most interesting, a dorsal fin.

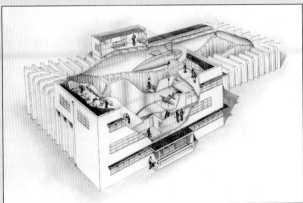

Cutaway drawing of the Dallas facility's wind tunnel during 1944.

Beautifully crafted NA-73 wind-tunnel model. Note that the three-blade propeller was made out of metal.

of frozen designs. Instead, through their respective procurement groups, the Army and Navy called upon the aircraft industry to increase production as rapidly as possible without disrupting the tooling flexibility, which is today paying dividends on the fighting fronts.

"If you have 50,000 parts to make, you can spend $45,000 (90 percent) on tooling, $4,500 (9 percent) on labor, and $500 (1 percent) on material waste and come up with a cost per part of only $1. However, reduce the quantity of parts to 500, and your cost per part becomes $100. Under this condition, it is wise to spend $100 (20 percent) on tooling, $395 (79 percent) on labor, and $5 (1 percent) on material waste. Efficiency suffers, but the cost is down to normal, and tooling and production time are reduced to only a fraction of the time required to build a $45,000 tool and knock out 500 parts.

"In wartime, this formula becomes more complicated. Among the additional factors which must be considered are: Allowable production time in the light of war needs, tooling time, production time, space required by tool, skill required with tool, and adaptability of tool to wartime allocation and flow of materials.

"Even assuming that 10,000 planes of a frozen design could be built, it would be of little wartime utility to be engaged in tooling for the duration. The war is being fought today and can be won or lost with the equipment we shipped to the fighting fronts yesterday. Ask any military leader to choose between 100 combat airplanes in the air today and 10,000 combat planes corroding on the ground when the war is over!

"Examine California's plane factories today and you will find a fair percentage of final assembly work being done under blue sky. We have expanded our facilities as fast as steel could be shipped in and men could throw it together, but we still have our production lines overflowing outdoors. Factory space required by tools is a real and vital factor in the battle of production.

"To the man in the shop, the superintendent or foreman or supervisor who is prone to grumble thoughtlessly when a small bundle of change drawings is dumped on his desk each morning, I should like to convey the thought that the lives of several brave American pilots might be depending on the speedy disposition of each of those change drawings. This is neither flag-waving nor exaggeration. In air war, second is not good enough."

The close-fitting cowl was the result of collaboration between Art Chester and Edgar Schmued and certainly would not have looked out of place on a racer. The fine metal work on the gun fairings is noteworthy along with the fact that the .50-cal. weapons were slightly offset with the left barrel protruding a bit more than the right.

Today, Kindelberger's genius in creating a production line that could accommodate constant change in order to build a great aircraft is a bit overlooked. However, throughout this volume we will attempt to show how his production line philosophy was one of the contributing factors to the greatness of the Mustang.

The year 1941 was extremely busy for NAA. Position-vacant ads in southern California newspapers brought in hordes of workers from all across the nation—men looking for steady work in an attempt to escape the Great Depression. The company was hiring by the hundreds as the initial order for the Mustang Mk. I amounted to 320 aircraft (quickly growing to 620 machines), and skilled workers were at a premium since other aircraft companies across the nation were enjoying a similar growth spurt of warplane orders. Typical of the time period, the price of the new Mustang would exclude the engine, armament, radios, etc. The RAF was getting the basic airframe, and although everything else would be added on at the Inglewood factory, the British government was responsible for supplying the remaining items. As a contract stipulation, the basic airframe price was not to exceed $40,000.

The first production Mustang Mk. I (RAF serial AG345) made its first flight from Mines Field on 23 April 1941 with Louis Wait doing the honors. The second aircraft (AG346) was disassembled and fitted in a stout wooden crate for the hazardous ocean voyage, arriving safely at Liverpool on 24 October 1941. The fighter was taken to Speke Aerodrome for assembly and initial flight-testing, which confirmed the results recorded with the NA-73X and AG345. Numerous British pilots were assigned to fly AG346, and they found the aircraft quite acceptable in its designed role.

The Mustang Mk. I (NAA Model NA-73, charge date 29 May 1940, contract A-250) was fitted with four .50-cal. and four .30-cal. machine guns. Most American fighters of the time were still well behind their European counterparts in the firepower department, and this armament fit was considered quite powerful. Power came from the Allison V-1710-39(FR), which was the first altitude-rated F series Allison, and it was also fitted with an improved supercharger. As a point of interest, the Air Corps supplied the British with the first engine and it was from a batch of five

AG348 photographed without the weapons installed. The British shipped this aircraft to the Soviet Union on 15 May 1942.

INSIDE THE ALLISON V-1710-87

*A*lthough derided by some historians, the Allison V-1710 was exactly the right engine for the Mustang's initial combat mission. We examine the -87 variant fitted in the A-36A.

The Allison V-1710-87 was a V-type 12-cylinder, liquid-cooled engine with a blower ratio of 7.48:1 and a compression ratio of 6.65:1. The engine rating at sea level takeoff was 1,325 bhp at 3,000 rpm with 47-in. Hg. manifold pressure for 5 minutes of operation only. The normal rating at 3,700 feet was 1,100 bhp at 2,600 rpm and 40.1-in. Hg. manifold pressure. The engine was to be operated with 100/130-octane gasoline. Specification AN-F-28 engine equipment included an integral oil and coolant pump, along with the following units:

UNIT	MAKE	TYPE
Carburetor	Bendix Stromberg	Model PD-12K7
Fuel Pump	Pesco	Type G 9
Vacuum Pump	Pesco	Type B-11
Hydraulic Pump	Eclipse	Type 1111-2 or -3
Starter	Eclipse	Type G-6
Generator	Delco Remy	Type G-6
Magneto	Scintilla	Type DFLN-6
Propeller Hub	Curtiss	Model C532D
Propeller Blade	Curtiss	Model 89303-27W
Governor	Curtiss	Model 100008-1
Impulse Generators (2)		Type E-8

The engine had 1,710-ci displacement, and the two cylinder blocks of six cylinders each were arranged in a "V" of 60 degrees. Each cylinder block consisted essentially of three parts: the head, the cylinder barrels, and the coolant jacket. The head was a one-piece, aluminum alloy casting. Carburized-hardened cylinder barrels were shrunk into this head. A one-piece cast-aluminum-alloy coolant jacket enclosed the cylinder barrels and was fastened to the head by a number of studs. The bottom of the coolant jacket was secured to each cylinder barrel by a nut threaded to the cylinder barrel, this completing the coolant seal for the head-cylinder-jacket unit. Each head-cylinder-jacket assembly was mounted on the upper half of the crankcase by 14 stud bolts extending through the head. These studs clamped the cylinder barrels securely between the head and the crankcase, and, in addition, transmitted all of the power stroke forces directly to the crankcase. This construction relieved the head barrel shrink-fit joint of all operating loads and provided additional rigidity to the crankcase.

Each cylinder was equipped with two intake valves, two exhaust valves, and two diametrically opposed spark plugs. The exhaust valve seats were of forged alloy steel faced with Stellite. The intake valve seats were of aluminum-bronze alloy. The valves were made of chrome-nickel-tungsten steel and were sodium-cooled.

The valve operating mechanism consisted essentially of six rocker arm assemblies operated by a single camshaft on top of each cylinder block. Each camshaft was driven through separate inclined shafts by bevel gears from the accessory housing camshaft drive gear, which, in turn, was driven through a spur gear train from the crankshaft. The valve actuating mechanism was lubricated by oil under pressure received through the camshaft locating bearing from the inclined shafts. The oil flowed through the hollow camshaft to all camshaft bearings. In addition, a small hole in the heel of each cam furnished splash lubrication to the valve stem sends, the cam follower needle bearings, and the rocker arm bearings.

The crankshaft was a conventional six-throw, seven bearing, counter-balanced type, and machined all over. The counterweights were welded directly to the steel forging, providing a compact design. At each end of the shaft was an identical nine-bolt flange. A pendulum-type dynamic balancer was bolted to the flange at the accessory housing end of the crankshaft torsional vibration damper. The driving mechanism for all accessories mounted on the rear of the engine was connected to the crankshaft through an internal spline in the dynamic balancer hub.

An internally splined coupling was bolted to the flange at the propeller end of the crankshaft to provide a drive connection for the reduction gear assembly. A front scavenger oil pump was located inside the reduction gear housing. A propeller governor drive was provided on the rear of the housing in the V between the cylinder blocks. The housing was also provided with oil passages to the governor.

The moving parts throughout the engine were supplied with oil by a single pressure pump in combination with a pressure-sensitive valve. All oil to the engine passed through a Cuno disc-type strainer incorporating a safety bypass valve. The main scavenger pump and the pressure pump were arranged as a unit on the lower right-hand side of the accessory housing. All pumps were of the conventional spur-gear type. All main bearings and connecting rod bearings were pressure lubricated. The cylinder wall and the piston pins were lubricated by oil thrown from the connecting rod bearings.

A cast magnesium-alloy accessory housing stud, mounted on the rear face of the crankcase, contained the supercharger and drives for the various engine accessories.

A centrifugal coolant pump, located on the bottom of the accessory housing, supplied coolant to each cylinder block at two inlets—one at the coolant jacket and the other at the rear of the cylinder head. The outlet scroll of the pump terminated in a tee with two flanged ends and was connected by pipes to the dual inlets of each cylinder block. The coolant was admitted to the bottom of the cylinder block through an inlet manifold, which was cast the full length of each jacket. These manifolds had an orifice at each cylinder barrel, which metered the coolant flow. The inlet at the rear of the cylinder head provided a direct rapid flow over the combustion chambers.

The Allison was equipped with a Bendix-Stromberg injection carburetor fitted with a single-diaphragm acceleration pump. This type of carburetor had a closed fuel system from fuel pump to discharge nozzle. Fuel was delivered to the carburetor by the engine fuel pump at about 16 psi pressure. It was metered according to the mass airflow rate as registered by the venturi tube and automatic mixture control unit, and was then forced to the spray nozzle, which sprayed the charge evenly across the face of the supercharger. Fuel was prevented from leaking into the engine by the spring-controlled discharge nozzle, which was closed when the nozzle fuel pressure was less than 4 psi.

The carburetor was comprised of the following five separate units, each with its own individual function:

Throttle: The throttle unit followed conventional carburetor lines incorporating a throttle, a venturi tube system for developing suction, and a group of impact tubes for collecting the average entrance pressure.

Automatic Mixture Control Unit: This unit consisted of a sealed metallic bellows, responsive to variations in temperature and pressure, which operated a contoured valve. The automatic mixture control served to maintain correct fuel-air mixture ratio in the carburetor when operating under conditions of varying air temperature and pressure such as resulted from changes in altitude.

Regulator: The regulator unit automatically adjusted the fuel pressure across the metering jets and, therefore, the fuel flow in proportion to the mass airflow through the throttle body. The unit was made up of an air diaphragm, a fuel diaphragm, and a balanced fuel valve, all mounted on one stem. Fuel entered through a strainer, passed through the balanced valve to one side of the fuel diaphragm chamber, and then to the jets in the fuel control unit. A vapor separator was provided in the strainer chamber to prevent vapor from entering the regulator.

Fuel Control: This unit, attached directly to the regulator, contained the metering jets, a fuel head enrichment valve, an idle metering valve, and a manually operated mixture selector valve. The unit was designed so that metering jets and other variables could be selected to fit the mixture ratio requirements of the engine under all operating conditions. A diaphragm that obtained its operating force from the difference between the metered and unmetered fuel pressures operated the fuel head enrichment valve. As the mass airflow to the engine increased, the pressure of the fuel delivered to the fuel control unit increased proportionately, thereby causing the enrichment valve to open. The idle valve was mechanically connected to the throttle and controlled the mixture throughout the idle range of speeds. The manual mixture control provided Full-Rich, Automatic-Rich, Automatic-Lean, and Idle-Cut positions.

Spray Nozzle and Accelerating Pump: The nozzle, which sprayed the fuel into the supercharger entrance, was mounted on the rear supercharger housing. Combined with the spray nozzle was a single diaphragm acceleration pump automatically operated by vacuum.

The carburetor air scoop consisted of an air intake duct, built integral with the top engine cowling, and an elbow duct mounted by means of a flexible joint to the carburetor intake. The air intake duct was equipped with removable baffles that could be interchanged with an air filter when the Mustang was on the ground. The carburetor air scoop elbow contained a cold- and hot-air door operated manually from the cockpit. If the cold-air intake duct became obstructed because of icing conditions, the spring-loaded hot-air door would open automatically as the result of suction existing in the carburetor intake. This duct was held rigid by cowl formers riveted to the upper section of the duct and by braces attached to the engine mount. A drain line to eliminate any water or refuse that may have accumulated in the air scoop intake duct extended from the forward part of the elbow to the lower section of the engine accessory compartment.

Engine Section/Nacelle Group

The engine mount consisted of two individual Y-shaped, aluminum-alloy box-beam structures. Each was mounted at two points of attachment to the fireproof bulkhead and extended forward on its respective side of the Allison. The upper points of attachment were the forward extremities of the upper fuselage longerons, and the lower points were at fittings on the bottom of the fuselage frame structure. The Allison was cradled between the mount beams, and attached by studs to four shock absorbing units in the mount. A lug located at the upper aft end of each beam was used for hoisting the engine of the complete airplane. Support brackets for the vacuum relief valve, exhaust manifold shroud, booster coil, and other equipment were installed on the mount. A lightening hole in each beam afforded access to the Cuno oil filter on the right side, and to the oil tank vent line at the left side.

The engine cowling consisted of a nose ring and seven readily removable panels. The nose ring was rigidly bolted to the forward end of the engine mount and contained fittings to which the cowl formers were bolted. Access to the coolant tank filler plug was gained through a hinged, Dzus-fastened door in the upper left side of the nose ring. Another door in the right side of the nose ring afforded access to the propeller brushes and propeller spinner attachment bolts. The windscreen defroster tubes passed along the exhaust stacks and were connected to two small openings in the bottom of the nose right, which supplied the inlet air for the defrosting system. The upper half of the engine cowling was a single panel with the carburetor air scoop built into the center section. All cowling panels were constructed of aluminum alloy with the exception of the stainless steel sections adjacent to the exhaust stacks.

V-1710-39s that had been built for Air Corps experimental testing. This engine had a reduction gear ratio of 2.00:1 and a supercharger gear ratio of 8.80:1 and this gave a takeoff rating of 1,150 hp with a war emergency rating of 1,490 hp at 4,300 feet and 56-in. Hg. manifold pressure.

Early testing revealed some problems that needed correction. One of the problems was with the radiator ducting. Atwood commented, "The upper edge of the intake duct had been made to be flush with the bottom surface of the wing, and we soon found that the air flowing along the surface in front of the duct became a turbulent, irregular pattern as it entered the duct and caused an audible rumble and vibration, which was unacceptable. Also, it was thought that the opening should be larger for cooling on the ground at low airspeed, so a fold-down front panel was provided to admit more air for ground operation. This leaked pressurized air and caused considerable drag.

"Both these problems required that some redesign and refinement be made. Capable aerodynamics people like Ed Horkey and Irv Ashkenas, worked very diligently on the problems, using round-the-clock wind tunnel duct models and flight test measurements to arrive at the optimum configuration of a fixed intake with rounded lip edges. Also, the intake was moved down some 2 inches to provide a gutter or scupper for the thin layer of turbulent air to bypass the intake."

The odd banging heard by Chilton and other pilots was traced to the air intake atop the cowling. The intake was too short and this caused the airflow to resonate somewhat like a pipe organ. The intake was made longer and the banging went away. Trouble with the ventral radiator opening and ducting was more difficult to eliminate. Turbulent air flowing along the bottom of the fuselage would go in at the top of the scoop and upset the internal flow. Originally, the top line of the radiator duct was in line with the bottom of the fuselage and this was generating turbulence (Schmued had originally designed the aircraft without the gutter and with a variable area entry and exit on the cooling duct). Irving Ashkenas, who later went to Northrop and helped design that company's Flying Wing, suggested that if the duct opening were dropped a few inches from the bottom line of the fuselage, the turbulent layer of air would then boil past the entrance, while the smoother flow would enter the duct. Horkey and Ashkenas tested the theory in the wind tunnel and it worked. Once this entry design was perfected, then the variable area inlet feature was eliminated and an adjustable chute at the aft end of the duct controlled the volume of air flowing through it.

Because of Kindelberger's production foresight, the RAF order rapidly began coming off the production line and, as initial problems were worked out, test flying greatly increased. One problem was the carburetor air scoop atop the cowling. It was found that when the Mustang was at different airspeeds and angles of attack, a non-uniform flow of air to the Allison's carburetor took place and this caused the engine to surge. After puzzling a bit, raising the inlet and extending the lip closer to the propeller modified the large wooden Mustang wind tunnel model. The solution worked and flying aircraft had their intakes modified while aircraft on the line received new units fabricated in the metal shop. Once again, the rapidity of a solution and its integration into production is worth noting.

In view of the Mustang's Allison-imposed altitude restrictions, Fighter Command decided to standardize on the Spitfire as their high-altitude fighter

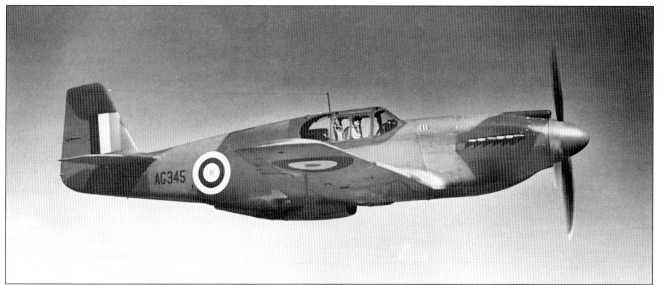

The extremely slim profile of the early Mustang is evident. The aircraft had the extended carburetor scoop. AG345 led a long life, mostly in the testing role, and it was struck off charge on 3 December 1946.

and the Mustang was assigned to the new Army Cooperation Command (ACC). The ACC was established during 1940 to co-ordinate air/ground activities with the Army—a vital task that had been neglected, with disastrous results, by the British Expeditionary Force in France. The Mustang Mk. I was ideal for the ACC since it was heavily armed, highly maneuverable, had a very good range, and could really get moving at altitudes below 10,000 feet (in fact, capable of outrunning anything flown by the RAF or Luftwaffe at or below that altitude). Until the introduction of the Mustang, ACC had been flying Westland Lysanders and Curtiss Tomahawks, neither of which was ideal for frontline operations over heavily defended enemy targets.

By the end of the year, the RAF had accepted 138 Mustangs. During January 1942, a further 84 NA-73s were accepted. On 13 February, the first production flight of AL958 took place and this was the first Mustang I of the second order (NA-83 with the date of 24 September 1940 under contract A-1493) for 300 aircraft. Even though there was a different NAA model number, the aircraft were identical and retained the Mustang Mk. I name. By July 1942, the RAF had accepted the last of 620 Mustang Is. Transit to Britain was not without its risks and a dozen Mustangs were lost when *Ocean Venture* was sunk by a U-boat in the Atlantic on 8 February 1942, and just a few days later a further eight Mustang Is were lost in another torpedoing.

AG346, still with the short scoop, was the second production Mustang.

On 5 December 1941, Mustang AG346 was previewed for the British press at Speke Aerodrome near Liverpool. It was initially planned to equip some 18 squadrons with the Mustang, but only 16 squadrons were eventually so constituted.

Enter the Air Corps

Earlier on, we mentioned that the U.S. government had given the production go-ahead for the British Mustangs, but there was a stipulation in the agreement. The fourth and tenth production Mk. Is had to be handed over to the Army Air Corps. An Authority for Purchase document (number 164265) was issued on 24 July 1940 and called for the delivery of the two aircraft with the AAC designation of XP-51. On 20 September of that same year, the Assistant Secretary of War approved an official contract. The two prototypes (assigned serials 41-038 and -039) were built in accordance with the British Model Specification, although minor modifications were undertaken to accommodate standard Air Corps equipment.

On 20 May 1941, Robert Chilton made the first XP-51 flight in s/n 41-038. Although progress with the British aircraft was relatively rapid, the same could not be said of the Air Corps Mustangs. The first XP-51 arrived at Wright Field on 24 August while the second XP-51 did not get to that location until 16 December—the two aircraft had been scheduled to arrive in Ohio during February and March (this was an Air Corps timetable and had nothing to do with NAA).

It was clear that the Mustang had highly placed enemies and that individuals more interested in products from Curtiss and Bell had purposely slowed the test schedule. In a report submitted on 15 July 1942 regarding the XP-51, Capt. W. G. Logan wrote, "Except for minor incidental changes, the project progressed at a normal rate. On 24 February 1942, an Engineering Order was issued to remove the original hydraulic gun chargers out of both airplanes and install in lieu thereof fully automatic gun charger equipment, which was being developed by the Bendix Corporation in the second airplane. This was done so that the new charging equipment could be flight tested at an early date.

Since the delivery installation, it was decided that provision only would be made for installation of this equipment.

"Preliminary flight testing was conducted on the first airplane at the contractor's plant by the contractor's personnel and government pilots in

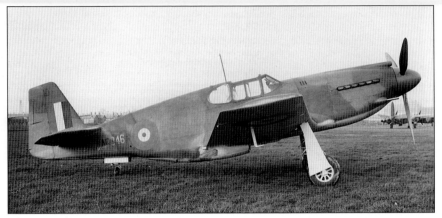

AG346 in Britain soon after arrival and assembly. All the RAF Mustangs were painted in new camouflage colors upon arrival. AG346 soon went into action and was flying with No. 168 Squadron when shot down by flak on 20 August 1944.

The Mustangs were rapidly phased into service and excelled with the Army Cooperation Command. AG654, the second aircraft in line, was serving with No. 414 Squadron when the Allison failed during takeoff from Tangmere on 3 November 1942.

Mustang I AG431 in its environment. Pilot D. W. Samson was taking a break between missions, as the crew serviced the No. 16 Squadron Mustang. Note the camera mounted behind the pilot and the cut out port in the plexiglass. The aircraft was assigned as a maintenance airframe during October 1943, probably as a result of damage.

The RAF flew their Allison Mustangs right up to V-E Day.

accordance with the terms of the contract. Considerable trouble was incurred with the Allison engine installation in the early stages of the airplane's development. At one particular throttle setting, the engine was found to be extremely rough and, in one instance, the engine completely cut out resulting in a forced landing in a plowed field. The contractor's pilot made this landing without damage to property or personal injury, although considerable damage was done to the airplane [Author's Note: This refers to the NA-73X and apparently does not take into account that the engine quit because the pilot ran a fuel tank dry].

"Under the terms of the contract, the Army was supposed to receive the fourth and tenth production articles. These airplanes were scheduled for delivery in February and March 1941. The production of the NA-73 was delayed both by the crash landing of the experimental model and by the delay of the engines for the British airplanes. To facilitate the delivery of the XP-51 models it was decided to take the fourth and tenth articles from their place in the assembly line and install the Army engines in them for delivery to Wright Field. This procedure was followed and the first airplane was accepted at the plant of the contractor and flown to Wright Field on 24 August 1941, for the purpose of conducting official performance tests.

"Upon arrival of the first airplane at Wright Field, a safety inspection was conducted. The airplane was next weighed and balanced and an actual weight-and-balance report prepared. Before flight-testing could be conducted, it was necessary to install backfire screens to prevent damage to the airplane due to engine backfire. This work took considerably longer than was anticipated due to the breaking off of studs. It was also necessary to install new aileron and flap bracket bolts to correct an unsatisfactory condition found by NAA in other airplanes. The replacement parts were furnished by the contractor and installed by Army personnel under the supervision of the contractor's representative.

"Additional flight tests were conducted on the two airplanes delivered to the Army. It was during flight-testing of the first Army airplane that it was discovered that engine difficulties previously encountered could be overcome by increasing the length of the ramming air scoop. It was only after the contractor considered the airplanes to be satisfactory that they were turned over to the Army.

"Preliminary performance tests were conducted at the contractor's plant by personnel on the contractor's first article during March 1941. Final official performance flight tests were conducted at Wright Field between 8 October and 22 December 1941. The reason for the long period of flight testing was due to the higher priority of other airplanes to be tested [Author's Note: This is where some of the delays introduced by high ranking officers came into play although one can be fairly certain that the captain knew nothing of this—higher-priority aircraft included the abysmal Curtiss XP-46],

CRATING THE MUSTANG

In order to ship the first production Mustangs to Britain, crates were built to securely house the aircraft in a minimum amount of space.

Building Mustangs for Britain was one thing. Getting them there was another. Since the nation was in dire need of aircraft, Lockheed, in nearby Burbank, had come up with a daring plan for getting their Hudson bombers across the Atlantic—they would fly them. Leaving from fields in Canada, the aircraft, fitted with long-range tanks and flown by contract civilian pilots, would land at Greenland and Iceland before making the final leap to the United Kingdom. It was a daring plan—transatlantic flight was anything but common at the time, navigation aids were minimal, weather forecasting spotty, and the Germans tried their hardest to cause havoc with the flights by supplying false radio transmissions.

For the Mustang, another solution was formulated and that was to crate and ship the airplanes by sea. At the time, woodworking businesses abounded in the United States and NAA had no problem hiring skilled carpenters while engineers devised a system to disassemble the aircraft and pack it in as small a space as possible.

Accordingly, the shipment would be broken down into the fuselage, which would include the motor, but not the spinner, propeller, air scoop, fin, or the stabilizer, and the wing, which would include the landing gear, but not the flaps, ailerons, wingtips, or gun blast tubes.

Dismantling the aircraft required two A-frames, each equipped with a 3,000-pound hoist or an overhead crane with the same lifting capability. The A-frame was approximately 9 feet wide in order to permit the crate bottom to roll between the frame.

The lifting unit was a square welded iron frame. Welded to this frame were four pieces of .5-inch boilerplate so placed that, when drilled, they would fit the four main attaching points on the wing. This frame was bolted to the wing and used as a wing lift.

The fuselage required two hoisting slings. The sling for the forward fuselage consisted of not less than seven 16-inch cables attached to an iron bar. When hoisting, these cables were fastened to two U-bolts at the point where the Allison attached to the fuselage. The rear and front slings were identical except that the front sling cables were longer. These cables attached to the lift tube, which ran through the rear fuselage. This tube was 1.75 inches in diameter and 36 inches in length.

Before disassembly, the Allison would be inhibited and prepared for its sea voyage. For the airframe, the following measures were required during general dismantling:

1. All systems carrying liquids, except the Prestone system, would be drained before disassembly.
2. Specification No. AN-C-52 would be used as a corrosion preventive.
3. All parts that were unpainted and made of materials subject to corrosion in disassembled condition were dipped in and/or sprayed with No. AN-C-52 to prevent corrosion in transit.
4. All small parts such as pins, screws, bolts and nuts, washers, clamps, spacers, etc., were bagged and tagged with reference to the section from which they were removed.
5. All open ends of tubing were closed with neoprene caps or tape.
6. All exposed threads were protected from damage by wrapping with tape.
7. All exposed bearings were coated with hard grease, such as Mobilgrease No. 5, and wrapped in oiled paper and waterproof paper.
8. All electrical wiring and control cables that had been disconnected were coiled and secured with tape to prevent chafing.
9. The nose of the aircraft would be covered with oilcloth.
10. Each exhaust port would be covered with oilcloth.
11. All detached parts such as ailerons, flaps, etc., would be wrapped in waterproof paper. Greased parts would be wrapped in waxed paper.
12. The open cowl section would be covered with black tarpaper.
13. A dry battery would be furnished and crated with the airplane.
14. Machine guns would be coated with grease when installed and plugged with rubber plugs prior to crating.
15. Only friction tape would be used for taping parts.

Dismantling the Mustang for Crating

North American employees were issued the following checklist for disassembling the Mustang airframe:

1. Remove wing-to-fuselage fairing and cowling over oil tank.
2. Support fuselage at lift tube and engine mount lift attachments. Fuselage only may be lifted by these lift attachments.
3. Support wing on movable cradle jigs.
4. Disconnect all connections between wing and fuselage:
   a. Control cables (disconnected at clevis).
   b. All lines (hydraulic, fuel, oil, etc.).
   c. All electrical connections.
5. Remove pilot's seat.
6. Remove antenna mast. Coil and tape antenna to the mast.
7. Remove control stick and gun flick.
8. Remove radiator air scoop without affecting rigging of scoop.
9. Remove connecting bolts between wing and fuselage and lift fuselage clear of wing.
10. Remove tail fairing.
11. Support empennage and disconnect all control cables, etc., from fuselage to empennage.
12. Remove rudder.
    a. Rudder trim tab cables must have tension maintained from front pedestal to monocoque turnbuckles at all times. Cables are not taped at drums, and loosening would necessitate removing the pedestal to rewind drum.
    b. Rudder control cables are not affected by removal of rudder.
13. Remove fin.
14. Remove stabilizer and elevators.
    a. Elevator trim tab cables follow the same procedure as for the rudder trim tab cables.
    b. Trim tab drums in the stabilizer are taped and the tape had to be removed after reconnecting cables.
15. Remove the ailerons, flaps, and wingtips. The electric circuits to navigation lights are disconnected in conjunction with the removal of the wingtips.
16. Grease landing gear and spray with No. AN-C-52, but do not spray tires. Wrap tires with waterproof paper prior to spraying gear. Landing gear must be retracted and locked prior to closing the packing crate.

Designers had come up with an extremely efficient method of crating the Mustang for shipment to Britain.

The Crate

North American engineers created drawings for the construction of the crate. The crates were lined on top and sides with tarpaper so lapped that any water entering the seams would drain out the side seams at the bottom of the crate. Each crate would use 1,000 sq ft of tarpaper.

All cradles and supports were padded where necessary with paper-covered kapok pads to prevent damage or chafing.

The crate floor was built with fuselage support frames for the forward section at the firewall, and for the rear section at the lifting tube.

After the fuselage was set on forward support, a steel tube was inserted through holes in the support frame and lifting tube to hold the rear of the fuselage in place.

A horizontal crossbar was bolted to the top of the forward support frame and steel straps looped over crossbar and wedges and bolted to the motor mount lift rings. Straps were made taut by tightening bolts and driving wooden wedges.

Wing cradles directly adjacent to the fuselage in its supported position held the wing in a vertical position. Cradles were located approximately at the landing gear oleo strut.

After the wing had been placed in the cradle, the second halves of the vertical supports were bolted in place, holding the wing in place.

Individually wrapped parts, stabilizer, propeller, fairings, etc., were secured to the floor and walls by means of brackets and/or webbing straps and nails.

When the crate was closed, the top was covered with heavy roofing paper to prevent leakage and any wooden knotholes were covered.

The fuselage and wing were hermetically sealed utilizing single sheet 180 P-4 transparent Pliofilm. One hundred crated Mustangs would require seven rolls of 48-inch-width Pliofilm, two rolls 36-inch, one roll 15-inch. One-inch masking tape AAF Specification No. 17000D would be utilized for the process and, again, 100 aircraft would require nine rolls of the tape. Each airframe would be filled with silica gel crystals of non-indicating type, packed in 1-pound cloth bags, Specification AN-D-6. One hundred Mustangs would require 3,500 pounds of silica and each aircraft would have 35 bags installed at various essential points.

For crating, the following procedure would have been followed:

1. The stands would be bolted through the floor and put in the A-frame, which was located at the forward lifting station. The steel straps from the A-frame would be attached to the engine mounting lugs and the slack on the straps would be taken up with wedges.
2. The inboard wing cradles would be installed.
3. Waterproof paper would be attached to the trailing edge of the wing.
4. The wing would then be placed into the crate and the outer wing cradles would be attached and secured.

5. Box No. 1 would contain all fillets, pilot seat, armor plate, cowling, etc. This box would be secured under the tail of the fuselage in the right rear corner of the crate.
6. Box No. 2 would contain loose equipment such as tool kits, slings, and heavier parts. This box would be placed in the left rear of the crate.
7. Box No. 3 held the propeller motor unit and secured to the left side of the crate between the two wing cradles.
8. Box No. 4 contained auxiliary fuel cells and mounted to the left front section of the crate.
9. Boxes Nos. 5, 6, 7, and 8 contained the machine guns. Two would be placed in the rear center of the crate and two in the left forward section.
10. At this point, the sides of the crate would be put into place. The stabilizer would be attached to the left front section of one of the sides. Then the flaps, wingtips, ailerons, fin, and the rudder would be placed in various positions along the side with the top portion being preferred. The propeller spinner would be secured to the top of box No. 1.
11. An extra stand would be added and this would be used under the propeller hub when the plane was being uncrated. The stand would prevent the fuselage from nosing over. The stand was of sufficient size to bring the top of it within 2 inches of touching the hub during the uncrating procedure.
12. The two sides would now be lagged to the bottom of the crate and then an inspector would make a tour of the entire crate. Provided everything was satisfactory and secured, the crate ends would be put in place and lagged to the sides and the center skid, which was utilized to prevent the bottom of the crate from sagging.
13. At this point, the top of the crate would be added and lagged to the sides and ends. Asphalt paper would be placed on the top and sealed at various points with roof cement. Outer siding (1 x 12) would be added as reinforcement for the sides, thus giving the completed crate double-walled sides.

Once in Britain, uncrating was basically the reverse of crating. The Grade-A wood used in the crates probably became very handy for a number of uses in that resources-strapped nation.

bad weather, and malfunctioning of the coolant scoop control and landing gear retracting mechanism during the cold weather. These difficulties and others of a minor nature were corrected by Army personnel and the contractor's representatives. The second airplane was thoroughly inspected by the Flying Branch after delivery and was then turned over to the Armament Laboratory for firing tests."

Although it is apparent that the Mustang, as with any new type, had some development problems these problems were minor in nature and it is obvious that the military either took their time solving them, or simply forged ahead on testing other types on hand. However, given the final overall contribution of the Mustang to the Allied victory, one must wonder just what they were thinking. The few supporters of the new aircraft had a long and hard fight ahead to make sure that development would continue and that the warplane would enter U.S. Army Air Force (USAAF) service.

During December 1941, NAA was building 3.5 Mustangs per day to fulfill the British order, but Kindelberger stated he could raise production to a whopping 10 fighters per day within three weeks of a substantial Army order. With the frustration of waiting for new equipment with which to battle the enemy, Col. Homer Sanders, frustrated commander of the 51st Fighter Group in India, whose pilots were finding it increasingly difficult to fight the Japanese with their Curtiss P-40s, wrote on 26 August 1942 that, "Apparently the go-ahead signal was not given [for Mustang production] or there would certainly be some available for combat duty by this time. It appeared there was a tendency by the Materiel Division to hinder the development of this airplane, which can only be accounted for by the fact that it was strictly a North American project and Materiel Division could claim no credit for it."

Back at the factory, North American was in a tremendous state of flux. Between the start of the war in Europe and the Japanese sneak attack on Pearl Harbor (a period spanning just two years and two months) the company had gone from a capability of building 70 aircraft per month to a mass-production facility that could churn out 325 aircraft in the same time period. This had also been a period of intense hiring, the company swelling from 3,400 employees to over 15,000 with buildings rapidly being erected to handle production.

Michael "Red Knight" Crossley shares a smoke with an NAA employee. At 6 feet 2 inches, the Battle of Britain Hurricane ace definitely found the Mk. I's cockpit a bit cramped. Mustang Mk. I AG347 in the background wears U.S. national markings after a government decree prohibited aircraft with foreign markings from flying in U.S. airspace. While serving with No. 4 Squadron, AG347 crashed into the sea off Scarborough, Yorkshire, on 9 December 1942.

British Purchasing Commission acceptance pilot Chris Clarkson (center) and Michael Crossley pose with L. A. Costello, the resident technical officer with the British Air Commission.

Well before the two XP-51s had been tested, NAA received a contract for 150 P-51s (NAA Model NA-91 with charge date of 7 July 1941). NAA documents state that Contract DA-140 was a USAAF order on the part of Britain and fell within Defense Aid spending. This order fell under the new Roosevelt Lend-Lease program and was viewed as a replenishment order for the RAF, but with the provisions of Lend-Lease all the Mustangs were considered the property of the American government and were given USAAF designations and serials in conjunction with RAF serials. This contract would extend production of the fighter into September 1942, but Dutch knew that direct USAAF orders were needed to guarantee production of the fighter.

During October 1941, Bob Chilton flew to Wright Field where he would be given instruction in the Supermarine Spitfire Mk. V and Hawker Hurricane Mk. II in order to gain familiarity with aircraft the British Allies were building. Chilton was very surprised to find the XP-51 tied down on the ramp. When inquiring, he found that the aircraft was under the control of junior 2nd Lt. Winthrop Towner. Asking to see the aircraft's logs, Chilton was puzzled to

Chris Clarkson prepares to fly another Mk. I on an acceptance flight before delivery to the RAF.

Sir Hugh Dowding and Dutch Kindelberger at the NAA plant on 10 February 1941. Dowding, on an inspection tour of U.S. factories building equipment for Britain, holds a Mk. I presentation model.

find that the plane had flown only one hour since arrival. However, this indifference was explained in a document titled *Future Development of Pursuit Aircraft* created by the Pursuit Board during meetings held from 11 to 30 October 1941. In the document it was stated that the purpose was to "Make a thorough study of our current program for pursuit aircraft." Some 18 experimental and eight production aircraft were listed and the Mustang was not among them. With all the advanced experimental types under consideration, the USAAF felt there was no need for the fighter. As a point of interest, the experimentals that were finally built and flown all turned out to be stunning failures in concept and performance.

While all this was going on, Kindelberger was pressing government officials to advance the P-51 program while Chilton was displaying the aircraft to almost any interested Army officer. Support for the Mustang came about in a most unusual way. During the early portion of the war in Europe, Luftwaffe Ju 87 Stuka dive-bombers had become a weapon of terror. Able to dive vertically while being controlled by efficient dive brakes, the pilot of a Stuka could place a bomb directly on target. Fleeing civilians were often the targets and, since there was little in the way of significant opposition, the Stuka seemed to be an aircraft that reigned supreme over the battlefield. In the United States, dive-bomber development was lacking and the USAAF

had obtained Douglas SBD Dauntlesses as A-24s but soon found these aircraft too slow and lacking defensive armament. In Downey, California, Vultee Aircraft was developing the rather clunky Vengeance two-seat dive bomber for the RAF, but this aircraft was also found wanting. With few other choices, the USAAF was setting up to buy large quantities of Vengeance dive-bombers, but on 4 February 1942, Col. K.B. Wolfe, Chief of the Production Engineering Section, wrote a report stating, "We will not have a useful dive-bomber before March 1943." Within the report was a recommendation to cancel the Vultee aircraft and obtain, "a suitable dive-bomber, low-altitude attack fighter in its place."

NAA was approached on the dive-bomber concept and the company reasoned that the Mustang could easily be converted into such a weapon. NAA's George Gehrkens drove the short distance to Vultee Field and spent a day examining the Vengeance. Returning to NAA, he suggested the Mustang be modified with a system of horizontal wing spoilers. The company assigned this modification Model NA-97 and work on the project started on 16 April 1942. The Army specified that the aircraft be able to carry a 500-pound bomb under each wing. Mustang AM118 was modified as a dive-bomber and Bob Chilton began testing the aircraft on 30 May, and by 18 July he was performing actual dive-bombing missions.

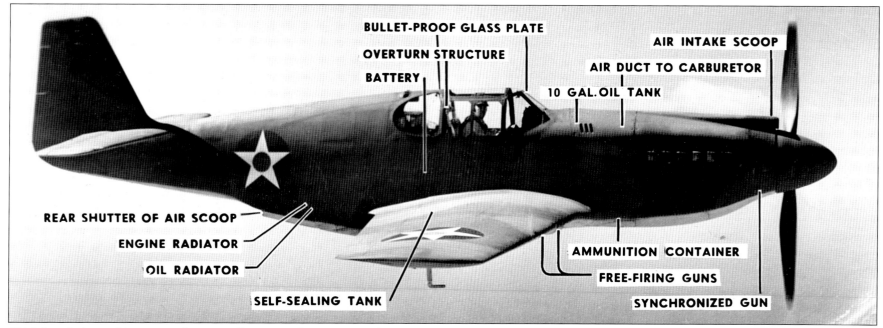

NAA handed out this press release to illustrate salient points of the Mustang Mk. I.

PAINTING THE KING'S MUSTANGS

When North American painted the Mk. I, IA, II, and III Mustangs purchased by Britain, the company complied with DTD360, USAAF Spec. 98-241123/3A and instructions included in the relevant erection and maintenance manual for each variant. In order to reduce costs and production time, camouflage paints and materials of near specification to the DTD equivalents were recommended by the authorities to be used. Army-Navy Aeronautical (ANA) specification numbers are quoted together with those from Federal Standards FS595, which gives the equivalent match for the original ANA color codes that it replaced.

British	USA	ANA Spec	Du Pont Spec	FS595
Dark Green	(Dark) Olive Drab 42	613	71-003	34087
Dark Earth	Dark Earth	617	71-009	30118
Sky	Sky	610	71-021	34424
Ocean Gray	Sea Gray	603		36118
Sea Gray (Med)	Light Gray	602		36440
Roundel Red	Dull Red	618	71-007	30109
Roundel Blue	Insignia Blue	605	71-002	35004
White	Insignia White	601	71-001	37875
Yellow	ID Yellow	614	71-000	33538

Note that color designation or name is not of equivalent RAF/Ministry of Aircraft Production (MAP) colors nor was it mandatory that the U.S. designations match that of the DTD360 titles:

All RAF Mustangs had wheel wells in aluminum or aluminized lacquer or dopes. The rear face of the wheel well was also the main spar of the Mustang and was finished in Zinc Chromate Yellow protective anti-corrosive paint FS595/33481. Insides of the main gear doors were left natural metal. Anti-glare panel (if applied) was Dark Olive Drab 41. Pilot's seat/seat covers: Medium Green 42, Dull Dark Green FS595/34092, and ANA612.

Floor of cockpit: Dull metal or wooden covered slats, latter ANA612. Sides and bulkheads of cockpit, up to and including Mk. IIIs: Yellow Green.

NOTE:

Yellow Green: 1-gallon Zinc Chromate (Yellow) Primer, 1-gallon Toloune Substitute, 1-gallon Black Enamel or Paste. Originally, the specification for Yellow Green included 4 ounces of aluminum powder, but this was eventually deleted. The "mixed color" resulting from the above was coded with ANA611, FS595/34151.

Fast, able to deliver bombs directly on target, and able to defend itself, the USAAF issued contract AC-27396 on 21 August for the construction of 500 dive-bombers with the designation A-36A. This was a huge boost for NAA.

While all this was going on, interest in the Mustang began to pick up. Work was progressing on the Lend-Lease P-51s. The Brits wanted the plane fitted with four 20mm cannon in place of eight machine guns on their original Mustangs. This took some rework, but the cannons were fitted and each weapon had 125 rounds that were belt fed. Five cannon rounds with linkage weighed 3 pounds and this compared to 1 pound for three .50-cal. rounds with links, and 1 pound for five .30-cal. rounds with links. Bob Chilton started flying the first drag tests on AG347, which had been fitted with dummy cannon. By 8 June 1942, the actual cannon had been installed on AM190 and testing was underway.

By this time, the first P-51 was ready (USAAF s/n 41-37320) and Chilton took the machine aloft on 30 May 1942. With the global battlefield situation changing on a daily basis, the USAAF decided to reclaim the first 20 (increasing to 57—and two of these machines would be assigned to a very special project) of the new P-51s coming off the production line to utilize for armed tactical reconnaissance. At the factory, P-51-1-NA 41-37324 was fitted to carry two Fairchild K-24 cameras—one on the bottom of the rear fuselage aimed downward, the second behind the pilot's armor plate and pointing to the left. After flight-testing, the modification proved quite successful and the remaining conversions were carried out at the depot level with designation changed to P-51-2-NA, but these would be redesignated F-6A in recognition of the mission. During this time, the names Apache and Invader were kicked around for the P-51 and A-36A, but in the end the USAAF stayed with the name Mustang.

With all these various programs proceeding at a fast pace, the momentous decision was made to order a USAAF fighter variant of the Mustang. Fitted with the new Allison V-1710-81, a stunning 1,200 aircraft with the designation

P-51A were ordered on 23 June 1942 under contract AC-30479 with the NAA model designation NA-97. As production forged ahead, reports were coming back from the combat fronts calling for modification or improvements to the basic design and one of these was a sand filtering system for the Allison carburetor since North African sand was reducing the powerplant's overall life. The P-51A would be fitted with four .50-cal. Brownings (two in each wing panel) supplied with 1,260 rounds of ammunition. As with virtually any other combat aircraft, weight began to grow and the combat weight of the P-51A was 8,600 pounds, growing to 9,600/10,300 pounds when 75/150-gallon drop tanks were fitted. Bob Chilton took the first P-51A (43-6003) aloft on 3 February 1943 and found the new aircraft satisfactory in all aspects.

With the awarding of the P-51A contract, Kindelberger's genius for mass production kicked in and assembly lines capable of churning out some 20 air-craft per day were set in place. By this point, the USAAF need for sufficient fighter aircraft was so great that a further contract for an additional 1,050 was soon negotiated. However, the P-51A was soon to become a fairly limited production item as orders were soon slashed to just 310 of the Allison-powered aircraft. The reason? Those two airframes that had been pulled from the P-51 production line were slated for very special modifications—modifications that would change the course of World War II.

RAF ALLISON MUSTANG DELIVERIES

Serials	Dates	Numbers	Marks
AG345-AG664	11/1941-4/1942	299	Mk. I
AL958-AM257	4/1942-8/1942	200	Mk. I
AP164-AP262	7/1942-8/1942	100	Mk. I
FD438-FD449	9/1942-1/1943	92	Mk. IA
FD470-FD509	2/1943-5/1943	40	Mk. II
FR890-FR939	6/1943-7/1943	50	Mk. II

The production line was always a good location to show the customer his product. Dutch Kindelberger in the cockpit of a Mk. I (minus the comfort of a seat) explains the Mustang's virtues to a visiting British official. As can be seen, the fuselage was on a wooden mobile platform and various bits and pieces were affixed to the airframe (like the box containing the Parker engine primer on the firewall) along with a list of NA-73 shortages for the

As production began to ramp up, non-flying static airframes were tested to destruction to prove that the aircraft could take (and hopefully exceed) the design loads. An NA-99 airframe is lowered into position for loading sacks of lead shot. As can be seen, none of the hydraulic or electrical systems had been, nor would be, installed. Various portions of the airframe were daubed in paint with "do not use," meaning that these over-stressed components were not to be utilized on any flying airframe.

CHAPTER THREE

BUILDING THE ALLISON MUSTANGS

One reason many aircraft builders picked southern California to construct their new factories was the weather. Benign weather conditions meant that test flying could take place virtually year around. As orders outpaced factory space, many aircraft were completed in the open and North American was no exception. This view shows P-51As undergoing completion outside the building facilities while new factory space was undergoing construction. Note how the Mustangs are on jacks, and that the NA-99 model designation has been rather crudely applied to the rear fuselage of each aircraft, along with the last two digits of the manufacturer's construction number (also featured on many other components including the fuselage inspection panel).

With time being absolutely critical, the Mustang was designed for ease of production. This section describes the components that made up the P-51A.

Fuselage

The fuselage was semi-monocoque in design and, with the exception of the armor plate firewall and the armor plate aft of the pilot's seat, was fabricated entirely of aluminum alloy. The fuselage was divided into three sections: engine mount, main section, and tail section. All sections were bolted together.

The main fuselage section was constructed around four longerons. The upper longerons, which were extruded H-sections, extended aft from the firewall and terminated in a tapered form slightly forward of the aft end of the main section. The lower longerons, which were formed by an H-section and a rolled U-channel bolted together, extended the full length of the section. The fuselage was covered with aluminum-alloy sheet stock. An aluminum-alloy tube was installed in the aft lower end of the section for lifting or tying down the aircraft.

The firewall, which was a combination armor plate and firewall, was bolted to the forward end of the main section of the fuselage. The outer portion of the firewall was .019-inch stainless-steel sheet. The stainless-steel sheet was formed to provide room for the installation of the oil tank. The oil tank, engine, electric junction boxes, fuel booster pump, and fuel strainer were installed on the forward side of the firewall, and the hydraulic system reservoir and generator control panel were installed on the aft side of the firewall. Stainless-steel angles were attached to the forward edge of the firewall for the attachment of the engine cowling. Dzus fasteners and aluminum-alloy angles at the aft edge of the firewall served to attach the windshield cowling and the fuselage covering to the main section of the fuselage.

The side panels of the windscreen were made of laminated glass, and the upper panel was of a plastic sheet material. The forward flat section of the windshield was made of armor plate glass. The armor plate glass was a crystalline high-test multi-plate consisting of five plies of the following thickness: one inner ply .75-inch thick, two inner plies .25-inch thick, and two outer plies .125-inch thick. The windshield panels were held in place by screw-fastened restraining strips; consequently, the panels could be easily replaced in service. The windscreen cowling extended from the lower forward end of the armor plate glass to the firewall and down the sides to the upper longerons. A shroud, integral with the windshield assembly, extended aft from the windscreen. The aft edge of the shroud was covered with a circular rubber extrusion. The shroud contained the windscreen defrosting unit, optical gun sight, and two handholds, and also provided stowage for the optical gun sight plug and the ring-and-bead sight.

The cockpit enclosure consisted of three panels: an upper and two side panels. The sections of the panels were made of plastic sheet material. Both side panels had two sections, the forward section being utilized as a sliding window. The sliding windows were guided by an upper and lower stainless-steel track and controlled by a window-locking handle. The windows were controllable from within the cockpit only. The upper and right panels were hinged together, the upper panel hinging upward. A linkage attached to both panels was used as a stop for the upper panel when opened. The left panel hinged downward against the side of the fuselage. The upper and left panels were provided with locking facilities, controllable from inside and outside the cockpit. The inner control handle was situated forward and the outer control handle aft and flush with the upper-left panel frame.

The hood was attached to the fuselage by means of four hinges secured to brackets on the upper fuselage longerons. Each hinge fitted into a U-shaped spring-loaded release cam that was held in the normal position by a rod over each pair of release cams. The rods were interconnected to the emergency control handle by a cable extending forward of the instrument panel to each rod. The rods were grooved at the proximity of the release cams so that when the control handle was operated and the rods moved, the grooves were placed in direct alignment with both ends of the U-shaped release cam. With rods in the above-mentioned position, the release cam was free to operate upward, thus releasing the complete hood.

Two indicator pins were provided in the right-hand sliding window track to indicate the position of the release cams. If the emergency enclosure release handle had been pulled, the pins would release upward into the sliding window tract and would prevent the sliding window from closing.

The two windows aft of the cockpit were easily removable for access to the radio equipment. The transparent panels were of plastic sheet material molded to fit the contour of the fuselage. A spring at the aft end and two latches at the forward end held the windows in place. These latches could be released from the inside only.

The air inlet and outlet scoop sections of the radiator air scoop were of Alclad aluminum alloy and were mounted fore and aft of the oil-coolant radiator, respectively. The rear scoop section was hinged to the fuselage by Oilite bearings and operated by means of the hydraulic system. Dzus-fastened covers in the forward section permitted access to the fuel tank drain cocks, and a Dzus-fastened dome above the aft section permitted access to the oil coolant lines and the radiator.

Two wooden bulkheads in the fuselage prevented any objects dropped within the cockpit from rolling aft and fouling any of the surface control cables or sectors, and also prevented a draft from entering the cockpit. One of the bulkheads was attached by screws to the cross-members at the bottom of

Production of the first Mustang Is was a fairly straightforward process as fuselages were assembled directly alongside Harvard trainers also destined for the Royal Air Force, which already have had their exterior portions painted in trainer yellow.

the nose-over structure and to an angle attached to the trailing edge of the wing. The bulkhead was provided with openings for the warm and cold air ducts, and a cutaway at the center provided clearance for the forward elevator cable bell-crank. The second bulkhead, constructed in two sections, was attached by screws at the aft end of the radio shelf and extended upward to the roof of the fuselage.

The extreme trailing edge of the left fuselage-to-wing fairing was fitted with a reinforced rib, thus providing a footstep. At the left side of the fuselage below the trailing edge of the rearview window, a flush-type spring-loaded door, which opened inward, was provided as a handhold.

Early Mk. I fuselages roll down a relatively crude production line, the fuselages being mounted on rough, green-painted wooden dollies. The dollies were fitted with castor wheels for ease of work. The 10-gallon oil tank had been secured to the firewall through the use of strong straps. As time progressed and orders poured in, the Mustang production line changed almost every time as new items were being added and lessons were coming in from flight test and early operational units.

While the fuselage of this Mustang Mk. I was still on its jig, the photographer took advantage to get this unusual and extremely detailed view of the instrument panel and cockpit topped off by the ST-1A gun sight on 17 September 1941.

Tail Group

The tail section of the fuselage was bolted to the main section just aft of the fuselage lift tube. The tail section consisted essentially of two longerons, a flat shelf, formers, and a solid bulkhead covered with aluminum sheet stock. The two longerons and the flat shelf produced effective longeron characteristics, as well as resistance to side and torsional shear. The solid bulkhead was located at the fuselage rear section to main section attachment station. Provisions were incorporated in the tail section structure for the installation of the tail gear and the empennage.

The empennage consisted essentially of a stabilizer, a fin, a rudder, and two elevators. The rudder and the elevators were conventionally controlled by means of the pilot's control stick. Fuselage-to-empennage fairing streamlined the empennage installation.

The stabilizer was constructed as one unit with detachable tip. The construction consisted of a forward and aft spar, flanged ribs, and extruded stringers covered with Alclad sheet stock. Dual stringers were utilized for the lower covering to resist compression. Four bolts secured the stabilizer to the aft end of the fuselage.

The tips of the stabilizer were constructed of aluminum-alloy sheet stock formed about two supporting ribs. The forward part of the tip contour was butt-welded. The tip was connected to the main panel of the stabilizer with screws.

Fabric-covered elevators were attached to the trailing edge of the stabilizer. The right- and left-handed elevators, complete with trim tabs installed, were interchangeable. The elevators were connected at the center with a horn assembly to which the elevator control cables attached. The elevators were

View of the left side of a completed Mk. I cockpit details the trim controls for the ailerons, rudder, and elevator. The landing gear handle is at the bottom of the side console, where the compact throttle and propeller controls are conveniently placed for the pilot's left hand. The large switch directly to the left of the stick is for gun heat while the large placard by the switch indicates position of the flaps. Another placard located directly in the middle of the British-style spade grip stick reminds the pilot that maximum diving speed is 505 mph, while also reminding him not to lower the flaps above 165 mph. Fuel measurements were marked in Imperial gallons.

Right side of the Mustang Mk. I cockpit is dominated by the map and data case and the switch panel directly above that controlled generator main line, landing lights, navigation lights, flood lights, and pitot heat. The round device directly above the panel is the Morse key unit. The long bar between the two is the tail wheel lock. Looking directly down to his right, the pilot could easily see the Mk. VIIIA oxygen regulator. For additional lighting, a lamp is directly above the regulator while the spare bulbs for the instrument panel, cockpit, gun sight, and landing gear indicator are located in a small compartment immediately to the left of the switch panel.

hinged to the stabilizer with five sealed-type hinge bearings: one at the outboard end and at the center of each elevator, and one at the horn assembly. Each elevator was statically and dynamically balanced by means of a cast lead weight attached to the outboard end of its leading edge.

The elevator structure consisted of 18 flanged aluminum ribs, one main front spar, a V-section trailing edge, and a short intercostal beam. The intercostal beam was installed forward of the V-section trailing edge so that a cutout section was formed in the trailing edge of the elevator for the trim tab. A formed aluminum sheet covered the entire leading edge of the elevator back to the main spar with the exception of the cutouts provided for the attachment of the elevator hinge fittings.

The entire elevator structure was covered with Grade A mercerized cotton. The fabric cover was hand-stitched to the metal leading edge at each of the three cutouts in the leading edge. Canvas patches reinforced the fabric cover around the two holes, which were cut through each side of the leading edge of the elevator for the two outboard attachment bolts. The fabric covering was cut back to the intercostal beams from the trailing edge of the elevator at the trim tab cut-out and folded under the trailing edge of the beam where it was held by a cap strip riveted to the beam. The fabric cover was sewn to pinked

This complex piece of machinery is a master wing jig that allowed the Mk. I/P-51 wings to be built with watch-like precision. The wing was firmly held in place while finishing work took place (note the pulley peeling back a portion of wing skin that would be riveted in place once internal equipment was installed). At this point, the main gear leg had not been added, but the forward 40 percent of the wing had been filled, sanded, and primered. Note that the interior is bare metal and devoid of zinc chromate. The completed wing would house two 90-gallon fuel cells that weighed 1,080 pounds when filled. The right wing was built on the other side of the jig and the two panels would be finished in conjunction for mating to the fuselage. The clipboard on the right leg of the jig holds work orders for this particular unit, which was assigned to Ship No. 590. To the extreme left and in shadow is a nearly completed Ship No. 217. Each aircraft would have its assigned number liberally splashed in paint on virtually all components.

The Mustang design team was inspired to make the airframe as simple as possible. This goal is illustrated in an entire Allison engine unit being moved along the production line by a nattily dressed pre-Pearl Harbor employee. The Allison engine and all accessories were firmly fixed to the Mustang's motor mount and ready for installation on the firewall. The nose ring cowl has been installed (another sits on the floor to the right of the employee) while various cowl components are stacked to the right of the Allison. The ability to attach a ready-to-go Allison to the Mustang greatly reduced the number of man-hours required to complete the fighter. Note the serial NA 73-46081 on the kidney-shaped piece of armor plating.

tape at the trailing edge of the elevator. The fabric was fastened along each rib with Parker-Kalon screws that were screwed through dimpled washers into holes in the flanges of each rib. Cotton drain washers were cemented along both sides of the trailing edge of each elevator. Drain holes were cut through the center of the drain washers on the lower side of the elevators only.

The construction of the fin consisted of a forward and aft spar and flanged ribs covered with Alclad sheet stock. The tip, which was formed about two supporting ribs, was not detachable.

The fabric-covered rudder was attached to the trailing edge of the fin. The rudder was hinged to the fin with three sealed-type hinge bearings: one at the top, one at the center, and one at the bottom of the rudder. The rudder actuating rod attachment fitting was an integral part of the lower hinge fitting. A formed aluminum cap was placed over the lower end of the rudder after it had been completely installed. The electric wire for the light on the trailing edge of the rudder extended through a slot in the leading edge of the rudder and into the tail of the fuselage. The rudder was dynamically balanced by means of a cast lead weight attached to the upper end of its leading edge.

The rudder structure consisted of 20 flanged aluminum ribs, one main spar, a V-section trailing edge, and a short intercostal beam. The intercostal beam was installed forward of the V-section trailing edge so that a cutout section for the trim tab was formed in the trailing edge of the rudder. A formed aluminum sheet covered the entire leading edge of the rudder back to the main spar with the exception of the cutouts provided for the attachment of the rudder hinge fittings.

The entire rudder structure was covered with Grade A mercerized cotton. The fabric cover was hand-stitched to the metal leading edge at each of the three cutouts. Canvas patches reinforced the fabric cover around the two holes cut through each side of the leading edge of the rudder for the center and upper

These Mk. I fuselages had received a light spray of primer and were individually marked with #31 in the foreground followed by the other fuselages in ascending order. Early production was a bit haphazard, but the line was an almost organic thing—constantly changing and growing as production efficiency increased. At this time, welded steel units had replaced many of the wooden dollies. Clipboards with work orders are attached to each fuselage. The aircraft nearest the photographer have had their windscreens attached before moving on to the next stage of completion.

The two main panels of the wing consisted essentially of a main spar, an aft spar, pressed ribs, and extruded stringers covered with aluminum sheet stock. A tank bay at the inboard end of each wing panel provided space for four free-firing Browning M2 machine guns; and a wheel bay in the inboard leading edge of each wing panel provided space for the retraction of the main landing gear into the wing. When the main landing gear was retracted, fairing doors enclosed the gear completely within the wing so as to present a smooth contour to the airflow in flight and thus preserve the laminar flow. Provisions were made for installation of a bomb rack on the lower surface of each wing panel just outboard of the main landing gear. A landing light was built into the leading edge of the left-hand wing panel just outboard of the dive brake installation. Each panel was finished from the leading edge aft to the 40 percent chord point with fast-drying red putty and gray primer so that the leading edge of the wing caused a minimum of turbulence in flight. The wing panels were bolted together so that the inboard rib of the left-hand panel became the center rib of the wing.

The wingtips, consisting essentially of spar and pressed flanged ribs, covered with a formed-aluminum sheet stock, were attached to the wing panels by means of screws. Navigation lights were installed on the upper and lower surface of each wingtip.

Metal-covered sealed-type ailerons were installed on the trailing edge of the main wing just inboard of each wingtip. The ailerons were statically and dynamically balanced by means of two lead weights attached to the forward edge of each aileron. The main structure of each aileron consisted of two spars and 12 flanged ribs covered with .020-inch aluminum sheet stock, and the trailing edge was formed from a single sheet of aluminum reinforced with nine-sheet aluminum supports in the form of tapered hat sections. The forward spar consisted of two aluminum sheets formed into U-channels and then riveted together to make an I-beam. The aft spar consisted of a single aluminum sheet that was formed into a U-channel. Three aileron hinge brackets bolted to the forward spar provided hinge bearing attachment points. The ailerons hinged on three sealed-type bearings.

Production lines move in different directions as A-36As receive tail surfaces, Allisons, and wings. The fuselage on the extreme left is marked 155, while the fuselage to the right that has just received its Allison QEC is liberally marked on every component (including individual cowl pieces) with 135. Even though on a production line, each airframe required individual attention for missing components or for corrections. For example, orders have been taped on the fuselages while note boards carry further instructions. Missing rivets or other anomalies have been marked directly on the aluminum skin with soft pencil or china marker.

With parts bins strategically placed, Mustang fuselages make a U-turn as they have components added at each station. It is interesting the aircraft on the extreme left is P-51A 99-7 (which has a large "Hold" scrawled in pencil on the rear fuselage) followed immediately by A-36A 97-485 (note dive brakes). In the background, B-25 Mitchell forward fuselages are built on a series of jigs, illustrating NAA's massive wartime production effort and "Get 'em Built To Keep 'em Flying" spirit.

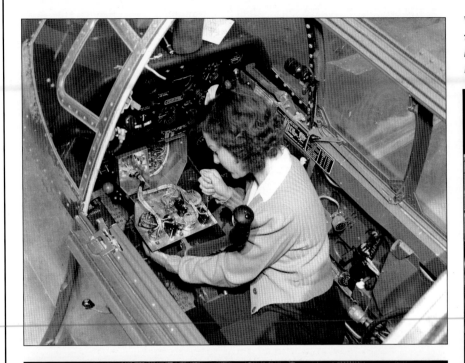

With the wooden pilot's seat removed, a female worker has easier access to cockpit instrument panel wiring although the control stick remains a barrier (aircraft's radio call sign is 36-044). During the early portion of Mustang production, workers usually just wore their normal day clothes.

At each step of the production line, components were added to the Mustang in an orderly fashion. In this case, a worker installs the SCR-274 command radio behind the P-51A pilot's position. This radio was the main communication between the pilot, ground bases, and other aircraft. The substantial rollover structure immediately forward of the radio compartment would save many pilots during takeoff and landing accidents.

Snaking lines of A-36As head toward completion. To the far left, incomplete fuselages head toward the camera before making a U-turn and being fitted with engines, cowlings, etc. On the right, rapidly completing A-36As move to the camera. Closest aircraft is 97-297.

Plywood trim tabs were installed on the ailerons. A metal bracket on each trim tab provided an attachment point for the trim tab actuating rod. The two holes in the tab for the bracket attachment screws were spot-faced on the side opposite the bracket so that the head of the screw was below the surface of the tab. After the bracket was installed, the holes above the heads of the screws were filled with wood filler. Each tab was hinged to the respective movable surface by three hinge bearings attached at the cutouts provided in the leading edge of the tabs.

Metal-covered sealed aileron-type wing flaps were installed on the trailing edge of each wing between the fuselage and the ailerons. The main structure of each flap consisted of two spars, 12 nose ribs, 11 main ribs, and a series of rolled section stringers. The main ribs and stringers were covered with .032-inch-thick sheet aluminum. The trailing edge of the flap was formed from a single .020-inch-thick aluminum sheet reinforced with 27-sheet aluminum supports in the form of tapered hat sections. The forward spar was a single

The nearly completed fuselage of P-51A 99-132 is lowered onto its wing. Exact alignment markings on the factory floor allowed precision fitting of the two components.

.040-inch-thick aluminum sheet with both edges braked at right angles to the surface of the spar. Flanged lightening holes in the spar surface permitted access to the inner structure of the flap after the skin was on the flap. The aft spar consisted of a single .032-inch-thick aluminum sheet formed into a U-channel. A stainless steel rubbing strip curved forward and down on the nose ribs from the top of the forward spar. Three flap hinge brackets bolted to the forward spar provided hinge bearing attachment points. The flaps hinged on three sealed-type bearings.

Landing Gear

The landing gear consisted of two retractable main gear assemblies with disc-type brakes and 27-inch smooth-contour wheels, installed in the main wings, and a retractable auxiliary tail gear assembly with a 12.5-inch, smooth-contour wheel, installed in the tail of the fuselage. When the alighting gear was retracted, the main gear was completely enclosed in the wings, and the auxiliary tail gear was completely enclosed in the fuselage by the landing gear fairings. The mechanical and hydraulic operation of the landing gear was controlled by means of the landing gear control handle on the lower left side of the cockpit. The tail wheel was steerable and full swiveling. The air-oil system of shock absorption was used in all of the landing gear struts. Baffles and a metering pin in the shock strut cushioned the shock of a landing. A mineral-base hydraulic fluid was used in all of the shock struts.

The landing gear locks were all actuated by means of mechanical linkage from the landing gear control handle bell-crank, with one exception; the main gear down-lock pin was actuated hydraulically.

Cables extending aft from the upper and lower ends of the landing gear control handle bell-crank actuated the tail gear up-latch and down-lock pin.

A push-pull rod system, which extended forward from the lower end of the control handle bell-crank, actuated the lock system torque tube in the main wheel bay. Lock rods connected to the inboard bell-crank on each end of the torque tube actuated the main gear up-latches.

The fairing door locks were actuated by a push-pull rod system connected to the outboard bell-crank on each end of the torque tube and was transmitted through bell-cranks, which were installed on the forward spar of the wing, to the upper arm of the fairing door lock assembly in such a manner that the lock assembly rotated vertically. The upper arm of the lock assembly was slotted so that the spring-loaded lock assembly could be pushed open against the spring pressure to engage the fairing door locking lug. A rod extended outboard from each lock assembly to bell-cranks just above and outboard of the main gear retracting cylinder. A bracket on the main gear retracting strut piston contacted the inboard arm of the bell-crank when the landing gear was in the down position.

MUSTANG I TACTICAL DEPLOYMENT

The Royal Air Force Mustangs were so effective in their missions that consideration was given to putting Allison-powered aircraft back into production. This document gives proof as to the value of the Mustang I.

HEADQUARTERS
NORTHWEST AFRICAN STRATEGIC AIR FORCE
APO 520
26 AUGUST 1943

SUBJECT:
   BRITISH ARMY COOPERATION TACTICAL EMPLOYMENT
OF THE MUSTANG I (P-51)

   TO:
   COMMANDING GENERAL, NORTHWEST AFRICAN AIR
FORCES, APO 650 (ATTENTION: TACTICS OFFICER)

1. The following report on the Cooperation Tactical Employment of the Mustang I (P-51) has been submitted by Colonel C. W. Bunch, Operational Engineering Officer, Northwest African Strategic Air Force:

Introduction

1. Wing Commander Peter Dudjeon, a former squadron commander of one of the Army Cooperation Units, was contacted on 31 May 1943, for the purpose of obtaining information on their daylight intrusion raids (Rhubarbs) using the North American Mustang I and IA aircraft. Wing Commander Dudjeon was most helpful and cooperative in spite of the fact that the Army Cooperation Activities were being, that day, taken over by RAF Fighter Command and all personnel were engaged in moving to the new post. Additional time was spent with him after he had moved to the new headquarters.

General

2. This phase of the Army Cooperation effort started as a photo reconnaissance operation using the Mustang I fitted with two cameras; a vertical camera in a quick detachable mount and an oblique camera mounted aft of the pilot's head and shooting out of the left side of the canopy through a small hole cut in the plexiglass. The cameras were automatic in their operation and controlled by the pilot.

3. These aircraft were equipped with four .50-cal. and four .30-cal. machine guns with a total of 1,000 rounds for the .50-cal. guns and a total of 3,492 rounds for the .30-cal. guns.

4. The long range (fuel capacity 180 U.S. gallons) of this aircraft made it an excellent tactical reconnaissance aircraft and its armament made it effective against most ground targets. As their operation progressed, they swung more and more to offensive reconnaissance and began to take advantage of targets of opportunity until the operation finally developed into a strategic effort against ground objectives such as railway locomotives, canal barges, heavy motor transport vehicles, and aircraft on the ground.

5. These daylight intrusion raids (Rhubarbs) were very successful largely due to the care and effort that went into the planning and operation of their missions. The theme was the destruction of those targets designated with the minimum of casualties. That this was achieved is attested by the record of this squadron that in 18 months of operation destroyed, or damaged severely, 200 locomotives, over 200 barges, and an undetermined number of enemy aircraft on the ground. This was accomplished with only one ship being shot down by enemy fighters, five ships lost by enemy flak, and two ships vanished without any record or information as to what happened to them. During this period of operation, they were never once intercepted over enemy territory. This included raids over Holland, occupied France, Belgium, and Germany: The longest one having been a flight of more than 1,000 miles. Their furthest victory was a locomotive shot up just outside Wilhelmshaven, a distance of approximately 350 miles from their base.

6. The results of a typical raid are as follows: Two ships were gone from the base 3:40 (90 miles flown over Germany), each ship used approximately 118 U.S. gallons of fuel. The two Mustangs destroyed or damaged five locomotives, five loaded goods barges, and one "R" boat. The Mustangs were unharmed.

7. It is felt that with the present load on the enemy ships, and the possible shortage of the high quality steel necessary for the boiler tubes, that a locomotive that has been holed by .50-cal. fire will be out of service from three weeks to six months, depending on the location with reference to repair facilities. In some cases, the locomotive explodes; if it does not explode, often the escaping steam blows the fire out of the firebox into the cab. The repetition of these attacks has definitely made the profession of locomotive engineer unpopular in that part of Europe within range of the Mustangs.

8. In general, their tactics consist of sending into a given target area a sufficient number of ships to saturate the enemy air defense warning system and to cause the maximum confusion through a multiplicity of plots and through pre-determined zigzag courses laid out in short legs (6 minutes each) arranged so as to carry them parallel to their objectives (canals and railways). The most unusual formation employed is a pair line abreast, although four line abreast, or two and sometimes three flights of four abreast, have been used. It was found that the smallest unit of two abreast worked out better in most cases. The formation proceeds to a given point off the enemy coast at which time it breaks up into the smaller units who then fly their respective predetermined course so as to cover the particular section to be attacked. All crossings of the enemy coast are at as nearly the same time as possible.

9. The flight from the home base to within 40 miles of the point of crossing the enemy coast is made at 200 IAS, 1,100 rpm, and 30-in. Hg. at between 25 and 50 feet altitude. Upon reaching the above-mentioned point, the power is increased to maximum cruising (250 to 275 mph, 2,600 rpm, 34.5-in. Hg.) and left there during the entire time over enemy territory and until 40 miles away from enemy coast on the return trip. If a landfall is not made within 5 miles of the predetermined point at which the enemy coast was to be crossed, then the flight should return home immediately because the entire flight plan will be thrown off too much and, also, since the entry point is chosen with careful regard for the flak map, there is apt to be serious trouble from this cause.

10. Just at the point of crossing the coast, an attempt should be made to flash in as quickly as possible—pulling up slightly and then diving with a burst of gun fire in the direction of any gun locations that may be firing—once across the coast, going back to tree-top height, taking advantage of all natural cover possible. Attacks on locomotives should never be made near stations or other locations where flak defenses are apt to be concentrated, but should be made between the stations out in the country where there is usually only single track; in which case the damaged locomotive holds up traffic until a wrecker or another engine can be brought in to tow the disabled engine to a siding. It often happens that the locomotive explodes, which usually causes damage to the track and roadbed, further disrupting traffic. Attacks should be alternated between the two members of the flight; one covering while the other makes the attack. Each pilot of the pair should be constantly searching for enemy aircraft so as to avoid a surprise attack by enemy pursuit. Attacks should be made from one side of the railway, canal, or roadway to the other—never along. An attack should never be repeated even though the objective has been missed, because the protecting element of surprise is no longer present. At a speed of 270 mph and at zero altitude, the search area is comparatively limited and targets appear quickly. Experience and alertness are required to pick out these targets in time to make an attack. It has been found necessary for inexperienced pilots to fly at not over 250 mph until they acquire the necessary skill and experience. It has also been found that depressing the flaps 5 degrees will have little effect on the speed, but it will change the attitude of the aircraft so that targets can be more easily seen over the nose.

11. The route in enemy territory usually involves about 90 miles, following the predetermined zigzag course, which has been laid out with reference to the latest flak map and with maximum target possibilities in mind. The 6-minute legs of the courses just about give the enemy time to pick out a plot, determine the speed and course, and dispatch interception. The course is then changed and the interception is always about 6 minutes behind time or out of phase. Strict adherence to the original flight plan must be maintained for many reasons, one of which is so that the rendezvous after the enemy coast is left will not be prevented and thereby deprive the entire flight of the protection offered by supporting numbers during the trip home when interception is more likely.

12. At the point of leaving the coast, flash out as fast as possible, weaving and changing place in the flight. Make use of cloud cover if possible. After 40 miles from the coast, throttle back to 200 mph (1,100 rpm, 30-in. Hg.), and proceed to the home base.

13. It has been found that speed is not protection or at least not sufficient protection from ground fire and weaving must be employed for the maximum protection.

14. The use of cloud cover is an important feature of these operations. Ten-tenth clouds at 500 feet would represent an almost ideal condition. For operation deep into Germany, 10/10 clouds at not over 1,500 feet is required while 6/10 to 7/10 clouds at 1,500 feet is allowable for operations into Holland, Belgium, and France. Since the only interception has been at sea, every effort is made to take advantage of such cloud cover during the over-water portions of the return trip. On the outgoing trip, low flying and proper selection of the approach course gives comparative security from detection by radar until a landfall is made. Absolute radio silence must be observed on the outgoing trip and if for any reason this silence is broken, the flight must return to the home base immediately since the enemy will have been alerted. Once the coast is crossed, there is no longer any great necessity for radio silence, since security and complete concealment are no longer possible, however, even then it is desirable to use the utmost discretion in the use of the radio, preserving silence unless an emergency warrants the use of the radio.

Training

15. Specialized pilot training is a very important phase in this operation. New pilots coming with the unit are not allowed to go on an operation flight for several months. They must have become familiar with every phase of the operation before going out on their own. They are thoroughly instructed in radio procedure and discipline. They must know their airplane completely and have responsibility for keeping their own ground crew on their toes. They are allowed to make changes in their own aircraft for their personal comfort and are encouraged to keep the wings polished and free from scratches. In fact, no one is allowed to climb up on the wings without a pad in place. The pilots enter from the front, stepping on the wing at only two designated spots. They must run slow-speed fuel consumption tests so that they are convinced that it is possible to operate at 200 mph and approximately 20 gallons per hour if they keep the RPM down to 1,100. They must supervise the swinging and checking of their own compass in order to increase their confidence in their equipment. Blind flying practice is carried out at all times. Each pilot is so trained that he can lay on a complete mission in all details.

16. Each day there is range estimation and gunnery practice. Pilots are encouraged to go out in pairs and practice shadow shooting over the water in addition to the carefully scored aerial gunnery practice. Competition is introduced in all phases of the training with the possibilities of becoming a flight leader as a reward.

17. Formation flying is practiced continually by twos and fours until the pilots are automatic in their ability to handle themselves in a formation of either type. After they have been paired off, they are usually not separated, but continue to fly with the same partner—developing their own system of signals for target designation, etc. The four-plane line abreast formation is very maneuverable, but it is difficult to fly. Proficiency is acquired only through constant practice. The two-plane line abreast formation is most usually used, as it is the more flexible.

18. Pilots are briefed constantly on enemy tactics and the capabilities of their own aircraft compared to the enemy opposition.

19. It has been found that the Mustang is faster than the Bf 109 and the Fw 190, and that 4,000 to 8,000 feet is a good altitude at which to catch the enemy. At sea level, the Mustang can run away from any enemy aircraft they have encountered to date. The pilots are schooled to run rather than fight because their main objective is the destruction of ground targets, not to fight enemy aircraft. They are instructed in the use of flaps in combat to reduce their turning radius (which with flaps is shorter than the Bf 109 or Fw 190.) At least one Fw 190 has been made to spin in through the use of a small amount of flap by the Mustang when engaged in a turning contest at low altitude; the Fw 190 tried to tighten his turn to keep the Mustang in his sights after the pilot had dropped his flaps slightly, but spun out of the turn. Pilots practice combat, evasion, flak evasion, and low-altitude flying continually.

20. Pilots are taught the importance of proper flying equipment. Goggles must be worn at all times while over enemy territory to protect their eyes from windscreen and hood splinters. They must wear escape boots, flying suits (so as to provide two or more layers of clothing), helmets, and gloves at all times for the protection those give in case of a fire in the air. In short, they are taught to know their aircraft and equipment and how to use both to the maximum.

21. A considerable amount of time is spent in training for emergency situations. Pilots practice forced landings under all conditions—particularly the conditions following an engine failure at low altitude over land. It has been found that if the Mustang must be ditched it will go under like a shot and that ditching must be avoided. If the engine fails at 200 mph and 25 feet altitude, the aircraft can be pulled straight up to about 500 feet at which point the pilot jumps, but this must be

practiced in order to convince the pilots that it is possible if everything is done without delay. In case of such a failure over water, the IFF [in-flight formation] should immediately be shifted to switch position No. 3, which is an emergency position giving a wide emergency plot on any radar screen that happens to be following the aircraft at the time. All stations will drop all operational plots and follow an emergency plot giving the location immediately to the nearest Air Sea Rescue Unit. If the aircraft must be ditched, pilots are told to use coarse pitch, no flaps, radiator shutters closed, slow up as much as possible, and stall onto the water along the swell regardless of wind. The hood should be off, parachute harness off, safety belt and Sutton harness taut, one hand on the instrument panel, and the head slightly forward and rigid. Pilots are cautioned that as long as the engine will run enough to fly, they should keep the aircraft headed for home and endeavor to reach home even if the engine is ruined. Pilots are taught how to handle their engines in such emergencies; if the oil temperature goes up—reduce RPM and increase boost; if the glycol temperature goes up, increase RPM and reduce boost. During their period of operation, the squadron did not have any complete engine failures, nor did they have any internal glycol leaks.

22. Pilots are continually lectured by intelligence officers concerning the general situation in the countries or territories over which they are flying. Particular emphasis is placed on the problems of escape and the changes in the escape situation from time to time. The customs and dress of people are studied—stories of escapes are discussed and wherever possible people who have escaped discuss their experiences with the pilots. Everything is done to make pilots more escape conscious. They are encouraged to have personal weapons with them in the aircraft (knife or blackjack rather than a gun) and to exercise their own ingenuity in concealing compasses, small saws, etc., in their clothes. They have many types of such compasses; a few are made more or less obvious so that they will be taken—leaving the concealed ones for later use. Battle dress should consist of clothing that will not look out of place or strange in the locality where a pilot is apt to be forced down.

23. If pilots are down in enemy territory, they are taught never to do anything without a plan. Each stage of the escape must be planned. First, their aircraft must be destroyed—then clothes must be arranged so as not to attract attention. Pilots must know thoroughly the contents of their escape kit and how to use everything. They

should avoid doing anything that would attract undue attention, such as over tipping—lack of knowledge of money, etc. It has been found that the poor people of a country are always more ready than any other class to help in escaping. Pilots should remember the names and addresses of people who help them and should always avoid all people of their own nationality.

24. At the operations room, there is a canvas bag for each pilot with his name on the bag. In this bag are his escape kit; his pass, which has a civilian photograph and his name, rank, and serial number; two photographs (to be used on forged passports if necessary) in which he duplicates as close as possible the appearance of a native of the locality where he is apt to land (manner of dress, moustache or not, etc.); and official money of this locality. Also in this bag are personal weapons, sheath knife, wooden flashlight, whistle, small razor, mirror, goggles, and gloves. He removes this equipment from the bag and into the bag puts the contents of his pockets (the items mentioned above are all that he can carry with him on a mission), papers, notebooks, his necktie, etc. His escape boots should be kept with the bag and not worn until he leaves the operations room; otherwise they will be partially worn and may not last when he needs them most. His shirt collar is opened and tie removed because of the danger of shrinkage in case he gets in the water and is then unable to loosen his clothes.

25. As the pilots leave the operations room, their flying equipment is inspected and the last thing he fastens on is a sheath knife placed outside everything and in easy reach so that if a chance hit should cause his Mae West to inflate in the air, he can puncture it.

26. During their training period, the pilots are first sent on shipping reconnaissance missions to allow them to get familiar with the airplane, navigation, and to check fuel consumption, while doing something they feel is operationally important. They are next required to simulate three practice Rhubarbs over friendly country—then they are sent out to sea, out of sight of land, and required to fly a predetermined three-leg course and simulate an approach to the coast and an attack on a land objective. When they are proficient at the above, they are then ready for their first operational Rhubarb.

Objective Planning

27. If the desired target destruction and damage is to be secured with minimum casualties, then very careful training alone is not enough—it

must be supplemented with the most careful planning. Requests for hurry-up or flash missions will have to be ignored and only those missions attempted in which there is time available for planning all details or complete laying on of the mission in which no details are slighted.

28. An experienced unit with all facilities available can lay on a mission in 1.5 hours, including the briefing. They have more or less control over their target selection since their effort is unsupported and requires no coordination other than in a general way. Their targets are chosen by information contained in photographs, by information obtained from previous missions, and by a general knowledge of the transportation system of a given locality.

29. Once a target is decided upon—for instance, a certain area where there are several important rail lines and perhaps a canal—all the latest intelligence is made available. This includes flak maps, radar locations, locations of airfields, fighter strength and disposition, knowledge of other friendly simultaneous action, etc. The number of aircraft is set and those pilots alerted. Pilots do not leave the post after being alerted, nor are they allowed to drink. They are sent to bed early.

30. The points of entry into enemy territory by the various flights are carefully chosen with regard to the flak map, the air defense warning system, enemy fighters and target proximity, and coverage. Separate zigzag courses of approximately 6-minute length at 275 mph are planned so as to give the maximum coverage in the target area without the separate fights interfering with each other or crossing the path already covered by another fighter (in this case, a flight is assumed to be the smallest unit—two abreast). Every element that will contribute to the surprise of each flight is taken into consideration. The distance to be covered by each flight in enemy territory is usually in the neighborhood of 90 miles for each flight. The point of exit is chosen with regard to the exit points and the route home plotted on the overlay.

31. The course for the mission for any one flight consists of a number of legs of varying distances and directions. At the early morning briefing, pilots are allowed to do most of the work in obtaining data for his particular flight. One pilot will measure all the distances with another checking. Another pilot will obtain all the true tracks with proper checking. All the data is entered on a Form 433-A and from the last minute meteorological report and the compass card of each airplane, the pilots work out their magnetic courses, true airspeeds, and times. All times, airspeeds, and directions will be the same from the base to the dispersal point (50 to 60 miles from the coast), but different for the individual flights over enemy territory and then the same again (usually) for the trip home from the rendezvous point. Gun cameras in the left landing light location take pictures of all action and verify claims.

Performance of the Mustang I and IA

32. The record of the Mustang I is excellent. The pilots like to fly it and its success has been due to its reliability, simplicity, and the fact that it is faster than any contemporary aircraft at low to medium altitudes.

33. The aircraft is powered with the Allison V-1710-39 having a rated power of 1,150 hp at 3,000 rpm and 44-in. Hg. at 12,000 feet. The engine was originally equipped with an automatic boost control limiting the manifold pressure at the lower altitudes to 44-in. Hg. The British remove this so as to get the vastly increased performance at lower altitudes through the judicious use of over-boost. As has been mentioned, they have had exceptionally good service out of these engines and due to its smoothness at low RPM, they are able to operate it so as to obtain a remarkably low fuel consumption giving an operational range greater than any single-engine fighter they possess (the fact the Merlin engine will not run well below 1,600 rpm prevents them from obtaining an equivalent low fuel consumption and, therefore, limits its usefulness for similar operations).

34. Actual combat has proven the aircraft can run away from anything the Germans have. Its only inferior points are that it can't climb as well as the Bf 109 and Fw 190 and that at the slower speeds of close combat, it loses effectiveness of aileron control and therefore has a poor rate of roll—but its turning radius with a slight amount of flap is shorter than either of the German aircraft.

35. In view of British experience, it is felt that we have a plane excellently fitted and suited for long-range, low-altitude daylight intrusion and for a medium altitude escort fighter to accompany our medium bombers. It must be realized that an aircraft that will fulfill the conditions for a medium bombardment escort fighter might not be completely suitable for a long range intruder due to the inability on the part of the engine to run at the exceptionally low RPM necessary for such long range operation. This is also assuming the operation will allow a major portion of such missions to be made over water where interception would be unlikely, such as from North Africa or the Mediterranean islands to the mainland.

36. In view of the British operation and the fact that we have an approved war emergency rating on the V-1710-39 engine of 56-in. Hg., it is suggested that immediate steps be taken to remove the automatic boost controls from our P-51 airplanes in this theatre and that the instrument dials be marked with the proper lights. The British have operated at full throttle at sea level (72-in. Hg.) for as much as 20 minutes at a time without hurting the engines. According to them, the Allison is averaging 1,500 hours between bearing failures compared to 500 to 600 hours for the Merlin. The Allison, they have found, will drag them home even with the bearing ruined.

37. It is suggested that the Allison-powered P-51A may lend itself better to a combination low-altitude fighter-intruder and a medium bomber escort than will the Merlin-powered P-51B due to the inherent difficulty of operating the Merlin at the low RPMs necessary for low fuel consumption. It is felt that definite engineering and flight information should be secured for these two aircraft immediately.

Charles F. Born,
Brigadier General, CSC,
Asst. Chief of Staff, A-3

When the landing gear control handle was moved to the up position, the cable attached to the lower end of the control handle bell-crank was pulled forward so that the tail gear down-lock pin was retracted, and the cable attached to the upper end of the bell-crank was slacked off to allow the spring-loaded tail gear up-latch to move to the locked position. When the control handle was moved to the down position, the action was reversed.

Obviously set up photograph of a Mk. I near a hasty piled wall of sandbags with two soldiers watching the proceedings.

When the landing gear control handle was moved to the up position, the torque tube turned so that the up-latch linkage was pulled aft, and the latch was moved to the locked position. When the control handle was moved to the down position, the action was reversed.

When the landing gear control handle was moved to the up position, the fairing door lock linkage moved outboard so that the spring-loaded locking lug was free to move into the locked position. While the main gear was still in the down position, the bracket on the main gear retracting cylinder held the outboard bell-crank and, consequently, the fairing door lock assembly, inboard against spring pressure. As the main gear was retracted, the bracket on the actuating strut moved outboard, and the lock assembly moved toward the locked position. In the meantime, the fairing door had opened. When the landing gear reached the up position, the fairing door closed and the locking lug on the door forced the lock assembly open against spring pressure until the lock engaged the locking lug.

The safety lock for the landing gear control system consisted of a flexible control cable, with one end attached to the upper torque link of the left main shock strut, and the other end attached to a bell-crank located in the wheel bay just forward of the main spar of the wing. The flexible cable moved the bell-crank up and down as the shock strut was extended or compressed. One arm of the bell crank was held in direct alignment with a rod that extended outboard from the fairing door lock bell-crank when the shock strut was compressed; consequently, when the weight of the airplane was on the alighting gear, the bell-crank prevented the rod from moving, and the entire landing gear control system was blocked. When the shock strut was extended, the bell-crank was held above the rod, and the landing gear control system could be operated.

The main landing gear electrical position indicator on the lower left corner of the instrument panel indicated the down and locked, or up and unlocked, condition of either gear. Switches operated by the main gear down-lock pins and by the main gear actuating rods controlled the indicators. If either gear was not down and locked, the indicator for that gear would indicate that the main gear was in the up position, and the green lights indicated that the main gear was in the down position and locked. The switch actuating rods for the down-lock pins extended aft to the forward switch box on the first rib inboard of each main landing gear support casting. Switch actuating buttons screwed into the main gear actuating rods operated the switches in the switch box, located just above the actuating rods.

A tail gear position indicator on the lower left corner of the instrument panel indicated the down and locked, or up and unlocked, condition of the tail gear. Switches operated by the tail gear down-lock pin and the tail gear shock strut controlled the indicators. A red light indicated that the gear was in the up position, and a green light indicated that the gear was in the down position and locked. The switch actuating rods extended forward from the tail gear shock strut and the down-lock pin to a central switch box.

The main landing gear assembles were supported by the landing gear support castings, which were installed on the forward side of the front spar in each wing at the outboard end of the wheel well. The support castings were bolted to the front spar of the wing and to the lower and upper skin of the wing in order to dissipate the landing gear thrust into the entire wing structure. Each gear retracted inboard and into the wing by means of a hydraulically actuated retracting strut mounted on the front spar of each wing inboard of the landing gear support casting.

Each main landing gear was a full-cantilever shock strut with a half fork and axle bolted to the shock strut piston, and a pivot shaft bolted to the upper end of the shock strut cylinder. A scissor-type torque link attached at the top of the half fork and at the lower end of the shock strut cylinder transmitted the torque load applied on the axle and fork to the shock strut cylinder. The landing gear assemblies were secured to the landing gear support castings by the shock strut pivot shafts, which permitted the gear to pivot laterally.

A spring-loaded lock pin controlled by a hydraulically actuated down-lock valve locked the main gear in the down position. The lock pin assembly was located in the landing gear support casting just inboard of the main gear pivot shaft. A threaded cap held the lock pin

assembly to the support casting; and the lock pin lever pivot casting, which was bolted to the main gear support casting after the lock pin was installed, secured the lock pin cap. A link rod between the down lock valve and the lock pin assembly provided a means for adjusting the lock pin travel. The lock pin engaged the main gear torque arm when the gear was in the down position.

The main gear up-latch was located in the center of the wheel bay and was operated by a link rod connected to the landing gear control system torque tube. The latch engaged the strut-locking roller at the lower end of the main gear shock strut when the gear was in the retracted position. The latch was

Utilizing the belly photographic position in one of the company's O-47 observation aircraft, this interesting plan view of a Mk. I was recorded. USAAF markings replaced RAF roundels while undergoing flight-testing in the United States.

AL958 was the first of the NA-83 Mustang Is. After flight-testing, the aircraft would survive service with four RAF combat squadrons before being struck off charge on 28 November 1944.

Not everything went smoothly at NAA. When union workers demanded a 10-cent-an-hour raise, in June 1941, the Army moved in and NAA was taken over by the military in a direct order signed by President Roosevelt, who was not about to let the strikers cause production delays. Fortunately, the matter was settled in fairly short order.

spring-loaded so that it would snap into place after the strut-locking roller pushed it forward in passing.

Mechanical position indicators were provided for the right and left main landing gear. The indicators were located on top of the control pedestal in the cockpit. A cable attached to the top of each main gear pulled the luminous buttons of the indicator to the Up position as the gear was extended. The indicators showed only the relative position of the main gear shock struts, and not a true up-latched or down-locked position.

Aluminum shock strut fairings for the main landing gear were hinged to the wing just outboard of the shock struts, and were connected to the center of the shock struts by adjustable link rods. When the main gear was in the retracted position, the shock strut fairings were pulled up flush with the skin of the wing.

Hydraulically operated main gear fairing doors were hinged to the castings installed on the center rib of the wing. The doors were controlled by hydraulically actuated struts, which were mounted on the top skin of the wing. Fairing door locks incorporated in the landing gear lock rod system engaged the locking lugs on the aft sides of the fairing doors when the main gear was retracted. The fairing doors closed flush with the lower skin of the wing when the main landing gear was fully extended and when the gear was in the retracted position. The hydraulic system was timed so that the fairing doors opened to permit the landing gear to pass as they went up or down.

Tail Gear Assembly

The auxiliary tail gear located in the aft end of the fuselage was fully retractable, free swiveling, and steerable. The gear was installed in a trunnion-like manner to a single support casting, which was bolted to the two lower longerons. The tail wheel moved forward and up as the tail gear retracted; and in the retracted position, the tail gear fairing doors enclosed it completely within the fuselage. The tail gear was retracted by means of a hydraulically actuated strut, controlled by the landing gear control handle in the cockpit.

The tail gear shock strut assembly consisted of a shock strut cylinder and piston, a torque tube, a post assembly housing, and a post assembly, which supported the rudder and the tail wheel when the declutching mechanism was engaged was five to one; that 30-degree turn of the rudder resulted in a 6-degree turn of the tail wheel. Springs installed aft of the tail gear assembly pulled the steering cables clear of the shock strut when the tail gear was retracted.

The tail gear declutching mechanism installed on top of the tail wheel post assembly was operated by means of the tail wheel lock control on the inboard side of the control pedestal in the cockpit. A control cable attached to the lever on top of the declutching mechanism extended aft through a bracket at the top of the shock strut housing, aft of the tail gear assembly, and down to the bottom of the fuselage where it reversed direction on a set of two pulleys and then forward to the control handle in the cockpit. A Shakespeare casing protected the declutching cable where it extended across the tail gear assembly. The declutching mechanism consisted of a pin that was an integral part of the tail wheel post assembly. The pin engaged the tail wheel steering arms when the control handle was in the locked position, so that the tail wheel had to move with the steering arms. The steering arm was released when the control handle was in the unlocked position, so that the wheel could swivel 360 degrees without the steering arms.

A spring-loaded lock pin down-lock support casting, which was bolted to the upper structure of the fuselage just above the tail gear assembly, locked the tail gear in the down position. The lock pin was controlled by means of cables from the landing gear control handle in the cockpit. A bell crank just outboard of the lock pin was connected to the lock control cable in such a manner that one arm of the bell-crank retracted the lock pin when the cable was pulled. The spring inside the lock pin returned the lock pin to the engaged position when the cable was released. The lock pin was beveled so that the locking lug on top of the tail gear shock strut could force the lock open as the gear closed.

The tail gear up-latch was located aft of the tail gear assembly between the two lower longerons. A control cable from the landing gear control handle in the cockpit controlled the up-latch. When the control handle was in the down position, the cable held the up-latch in the open position. The up-latch was spring-loaded so that it automatically snapped to the closed position when the landing gear control handle was placed in the up position. The up-latch engaged the strut locking roller at the top of the tail gear assembly.

The tail gear fairing doors were hinged to the lower skin of the fuselage at each side of the tail gear assembly. The fairing doors were actuated by turnbuckles attached to a bracket that was hinged to the tail gear support casting. A short link connected to the tail gear assembly pulled up the fairing doors as

the gear moved toward the retracted position. When the tail gear was fully retracted, the fairing doors were closed flush with the skin of the fuselage.

Brake System

The brake system consisted of two master cylinders, one connected to each brake by means of brake lines. The brake hydraulic system was entirely separate from the general hydraulic system, except that the brake system received its supply of hydraulic oil from the general hydraulic system reservoir. A stand-by arrangement with this reservoir provided a reserve of oil for brake operation, even though the supply of oil for normal operation of the general hydraulic system had been lost.

The brakes were selectively controlled by means of toe pedals incorporated in the rudder control pedal assembly. These pedals were connected by means of a mechanical linkage through the brake master cylinders. The left pedal operated the left brake, and the right pedal operated the right brake. When a toe pedal was depressed, braking pressure was generated in the respective brake cylinder; and when the pedal was released, the braking pressure was released by means of a spring arrangement in the brake cylinder.

Stripped of paint and its aluminum skin polished, XP-51 s/n 41-039 gave the appearance of being much more sleek than its camouflaged RAF brethren. On 4 May 1940, NAA signed a Foreign Release Agreement with the AAF for the foreign sale of the Model NA-73 airplane that entitled the AAF to two airplanes of the type contemplated for sale. The release specifically set forth that the AAF would receive the fourth and tenth articles from the production line.

A parking brake, controlled by means of the parking brake control handle just below the center of the instrument panel, was incorporated in the brake system. The parking brake was designed to hold the wheels in a locked condition over long periods of time without pressure being maintained on the foot pedals.

Goodyear hydraulic multiple-disc brakes were installed on each main gear leg. The brakes were essentially metal-to-metal clutches especially designed and built to function as aircraft brakes. Bronze discs keyed to the wheel were alternated in the brake assembly with steel discs that were keyed to the brake anchor bracket. The discs were held in position on the brake anchor bracket by a steel anchor nut, which could be tightened or loosened to obtain the proper clearance between the brake discs. The anchor nut was locked in position by a lock screw threaded into the nut.

When the brake pedal was depressed, the brake discs were pressed together by means of an annular ring piston located in the brake cylinder; and cantilever-type release springs forced the piston back into the brake cylinder and released the pressure on the discs when the brake pedal was released. The fluid of the brake system located in the brake cylinder activated the piston.

The brake cylinder was sealed by means of a synthetic rubber gasket held in position against the cylinder walls by a circular leaf-type spring. An insulator disc, between the brake piston and the first steel disc, kept the excessive heat of the brake discs from the brake piston and prevented vaporization of the brake fluid. Cutouts in the insulator discs permitted the return springs to bear directly against the piston. There was a bleeder connection on the top centerline of the anchor bracket casting, and an inlet boss was installed on each side of this centerline for connecting the fluid line from the master cylinder of the system to the brake cylinder. The brakes were interchangeable for the right- and left-hand landing gear.

The brake master cylinders were installed forward of and in line with their respective actuating bell-cranks, which were incorporated in the rudder pedal assembly. When the brake piston was in the normal position (no pressure applied to the brake pedal) and the poppet valve held open by the cylinder wall, the brake fluid could flow freely to or from the brake. The brake fluid flowed by gravity from the hydraulic system tank into the cylinder so that the master cylinder constantly maintained the correct volume of fluid under either extremely hot or cold conditions. When the linkage connecting it with the brake pedal pulled the piston rod back, the spring forced the poppet closed. With the poppet closed, the brake pressure obtained was directly proportional to the force applied on the brake pedals. The brake pressure flowed through the outlets in the piston sleeve, around past the parking brake stem assembly, and out to the brakes.

A parking brake valve was incorporated in each brake master cylinder. After the brake pedals had generated braking pressure, the parking brake was applied in order to lock the pressure in the brake lines and hold it after pedals were released. When the parking brake was applied, the arm was pulled up, which in turn pushed the stem assembly down until it was firmly seated on the cylinder body; when the brake pedals were slowly released, the pressure below the stem assembly was released. The pressure in the brake lines held the stem assembly seated until

After rollout, both XP-51s would have a long fight to earn acceptance with some Air Corps higher-ups. For the XP-51s, engines, propellers, and other normal items of regular government-furnished equipment specified for AAF airplanes were specified as GFE for the two airplanes.

enough pressure was generated in the brake cylinder by the brake pedals to overcome the pressure in the lines and unseat the stem assembly. The stem assembly was spring-loaded so that it remained in the open position during normal operation of the brakes.

When the parking brake was on, a vent around the stem assembly permitted the brake fluid to enter an expansion chamber containing a spring-loaded piston, which compensated for the expansion and contraction in volume of the brake fluid as the result of changes in temperature when the Mustang was parked.

Aluminum-alloy tubing 52SO was used throughout the brake system for all the rigid lines. All the tubing, with the exception of the brake supply lines connecting the hydraulic reservoir to the brake master cylinders, had a 5/16-inch outside diameter and a .042-inch wall thickness. The brake supply lines had a 3/8-inch outside diameter with a .042-inch wall thickness. So that the brake lines would not interfere with normal operation of the gear, flexible hose was used from the top of the main gear shock struts to the nose section of the wing, and from the shock strut cylinder to the strut fork.

Goodyear 27-inch drop-center wheels with 27-inch regular smooth-contour tires and tubes were mounted on the main landing gear axles. The wheels were mounted on Timken bearings at each end of the axle openings in the wheel hub. The inboard bearing was held in place by a felt grease retainer and a metal washer secured in place by a wire locking; the outboard

Following RAF practice, the XP-51s received national insignias above and below both wing panels. Following completion of negotiations between NAA and the Anglo-French Purchasing Commission, Authority for Purchase No. 165265 for two XP-51 airplanes was initiated on 24 July 1940 and followed by a contract, which was approved by the Assistant Secretary of War on 20 September 1940. The airplanes were built in accordance with the British Model Specification except that certain modifications were made to accommodate standard AAF equipment. In its polished metal finish, the two small vents directly behind the cockpit are more evident.

At this early point in Mustang construction, some T-6 parts were still being used in the XP-51s.

Even though Robert Chilton flew the first XP-51, 41-038, on 20 May 1941, the craft was not delivered to Wright Field until 24 August 1941. The head-on view of 41-039 shows the slim lines to advantage. Oddly, 41-038 survived to be restored back to flying condition and is now on display at the EAA Museum in Oshkosh, Wisconsin. 41-039 did not fare so well. The aircraft was transferred to NACA at Langley Field for high-speed testing, but after newer aircraft became available the prototype was apparently scrapped.

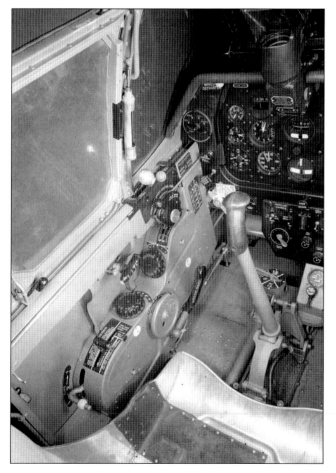

bearing was held in place by the wheel retaining nut and washer on the axle. Steel tubes pressed into the inboard side of the wheel protruded partially inside the brake drum and engaged the rotating discs of the multiple-disc brake when the wheel was installed. A retaining disc, secured by screws to the wheel hub, covered the inboard end of the steel tubes. An aluminum-alloy tab was provided between two of the steel tubes on each wheel to prevent the steel tubes from being inserted between the tube slots in the brake discs. The wheel rims were integral parts of the wheel casting and could not be removed to mount the tires.

A Goodyear 12.50-inch smooth-contour wheel, having a detachable flange and a 12.50-inch channel-tread-type casing and tube, was installed on

The left and right sides of the XP-51's cockpit illustrate small differences compared to the British aircraft. For example, the large British compass had been removed while the control spade had been replaced with the more standard American stick.

the auxiliary tail gear axle. This conducting type of tire formed the static ground for the entire airplane. The wheel was mounted on Timken bearings at each end of the axle openings in the wheel hub. The inboard bearing was covered by a seal ring for retaining grease and protecting the bearing from dust. The outboard bearing was provided with a coverplate to keep dirt out, and a dust cover protected the entire outboard axle opening. The detachable flange was held on the outboard rim of the wheel hub by a lock ring, which caught in a groove in the wheel hub and a ridge in the flange. When the tire was deflated, the flange could be pushed toward center of the wheel hub and the lock ring installed or removed. When the tire was inflated, the wheel flange was pushed to the outboard edge of the wheel hub so that it covered the lock ring and locked it in place.

Surface Controls

The ailerons, elevators, and rudder were conventionally controlled by a control stick and foot pedals in the cockpit. Tinned-steel control cables guided by fiber pulleys and fairleads connected the control stick to the respective control surfaces. All of the pulleys were equipped with sealed-type bearings. Turnbuckles were incorporated in the control system for rigging purposes. The wing flaps (and, on the A-36, dive bakes) were hydraulically actuated surfaces regulated by control handles in the cockpit.

The control cables were fabricated of pre-formed tinned-steel cable. The main control cable terminals were of the die-swaged friction type. The remaining cables were either sweat-soldered into tinned terminals or woven-spliced.

The control stick was a swaged tube of aluminum alloy. The lower portion of the tube was fitted into a socket, the lower end of which was attached to the elevator control tube. The point of attachment of the socket had a seal-type bearing. The above unit was mounted in a trunnion-like manner to a fitting, integral with the aileron torque tube, having stops that controlled the angular movement of the ailerons. The lower portion of the control stick and the fitting integral with the aileron tube was covered with a detachable cloth shroud. The upper portion of the control stick was equipped with a piston-type grip.

The locking gear for the primary surface controls, which was mounted forward and at the base of the control column, locked the ailerons and rudder in the neutral position and elevator in the down position. The portion of the surface control that engaged into the control stick was an inverted V-shaped bracket. The top of the bracket was slotted and had a spring-loaded plunger. A lip integral with the control stick socket engaged into the slot in the bracket, and a spring-loaded plunger engaged into the hole in the center of the lip. A rod attached to the bracket extended forward to interconnect with a locking lever pivoted on a bracket immediately aft of the firewall. When the surface

control lock was engaged in the lock position, the locking lever engaged between the stops on the rudder balance cable.

A safety lock, consisting of a lever attached to the surface control lock and interconnected to the locking lever actuating rod, prevented the surface control lock from accidentally engaging with the control stick during flight. To engage the surface control lock, it was first necessary to depress the lever to allow the control lock to be sprung aft and engage with the control stock.

Conventional rudder pedals were provided in the cockpit. These were adjustable for length by means of a release on the inboard side of each pedal. When the release was pushed inboard, the pedal was free to move forward or aft without moving the control cables. The pedal release was spring-loaded so that it automatically locked the pedal when the pilot's foot was removed.

The ailerons, controlled by lateral movement of the control stick, were not differentially controlled; that is, the angular movement of each aileron was from 10 degrees up to 10 degrees down. Motion was imparted simultaneously to each aileron from the aileron torque tube. The control stick was attached to the forward end of the torque tube, and a V-shaped bell-crank was linked to each of the inboard aileron cable drums, which were attached to the aft side of

Dutch Kindelberger was justifiably proud of the reputation NAA rapidly earned for particularly fine metal work—illustrated in this view of an XP-51 spinner and cowling.

the rear spar of the wing. The aileron cables extended along the rear spar of the wing to the outboard aileron cable drums on the spar at the inboard end of each aileron. A fork and block assembly connected each outboard cable drum to the aileron. The outboard cable drums imparted an eccentric motion to the fork and block assembly so that the ailerons moved up and down as the cable drum rotated.

A booster tab was provided on the right-hand aileron and a combination booster and trim tab on the aft left-hand aileron. A control knob on the pilot's control pedestal operated the trim tab on the left-hand aileron. The control knob was geared to a link rod inside the pedestal. A series of link rods extending aft from the control knob shaft actuated the inboard aileron trim tab cable drum, installed just above the rear spar of the wing. The trim tab control cables extended outboard along the rear spar of the left wing to the cable drum; the drum was attached to a bracket bolted to the rear spar of the wing in line with the outboard end of the aileron trim tab. The trim tab actuating rod was attached to the screw assembly in the cable drum. The angular travel of the aileron trim tab was 10 degrees up and 10 degrees down, and was limited by means of stops fastened to the cables just outboard of the inboard aileron hinge fitting.

Alfred P. Sloan was General Motors' chairman of the board and GM was, of course, parent company of Allison.

The fore-and-aft movement of the control stick controlled the elevators. A push-pull rod extended aft from the base of the control stick to the elevator bell-crank on the flap torque tube. A duplicate set of cables extended aft through the fuselage from the bell crank to the two elevator horn assemblies, between the elevators, which formed an integral part of the elevator torque tube. When the control stick was moved forward or aft, the resulting movement of the control cables and elevator horns rotated the torque tube so that the elevators moved down or up. The angular movement of the elevators was 30 degrees up and 20 degrees down from the neutral position.

The elevator trim tabs were operated by a control wheel on the inboard side of the control pedestal in the cockpit. The wheel revolved a cable drum inside the pedestal, which, in turn, moved the trim tab control cables fore and aft. The trim tab control cables extended aft through the fuselage to the center of the horizontal stabilizer, and then outboard to the cable drum in each side of the horizontal stabilizer just forward of the elevator trim tabs. The trim tab actuating rods were attached to the screw assembly in each cable drum. The angular travel of the elevator trim tabs was 10 degrees up and 25 degrees down, and was limited by stops fastened to the cables just forward of the horizontal stabilizer.

The rudder pedals in the cockpit controlled the rudder. The rudder control cables extended aft from each pedal to a bell-crank assembly in the aft end of the fuselage. A rudder pedal balance cable, extending forward from one pedal across the fuselage and then aft to the other pedal, maintained a constant tension forward on each rudder pedal. A push-pull rod connected the rudder bell-crank assembly in the aft end of the fuselage with the rudder actuating horn; the horn was an integral part of the rudder lower hinge casting. The angular movement of the rudder was limited to 30 degrees each side of the neutral position by means of adjustment bolts on the rudder bell-crank assembly.

The control knob on top of the pilot's control pedestal operated the rudder trim tabs. The knob operated a cable drum inside the pedestal, which in turn moved the trim tab control cables. The trim tab control cables extended aft through the fuselage to the stabilizer and then up inside the fin to the trim tab actuating drum assembly. The trim tab actuating rods were attached to the screw assembly in each cable drum. The angular travel of the rudder trim tab was limited to 10 degrees each side of the neutral position by means of cable stops located aft of the wing inside the fuselage.

The wing flaps were operated by hydraulically actuated struts located in the fuselage just above the front air scoop of the radiator. The flap actuating strut was linked to a bell-crank on the flap torque tube, which, in turn, was linked to the wing flaps at each side of the fuselage. The flaps had an angular movement of 50 degrees down. The flap movement was selectively controlled by means of the flap control handle on the aft end of the control pedestal in the cockpit. The sector of the flap control was slotted in the positions, which indicated each 10 degrees of flap movement from 0 to 50 degrees. The flap control handle could be placed at any one of the slotted positions and hydraulic pressure would move the flap to the indicated angular position.

The flap position preselector linkage located just forward of the flap torque tube was connected to the flap torque tube, to the link rod, to the flap control handle, and to the flap control valve. When the flap control handle was moved down or up, rods were moved forward or aft, respectively. One rod was connected to the flap control valve actuating lever. When the flap control handle was moved down, rods moved forward, the flap control valve actuating lever depressed the upper plunger in the flap control valve, and the flaps began to go down. As the flaps moved down, the flap torque tube pulled the link and rods aft. This action continued until one rod finally pushed the flap control valve actuating lever to the neutral position and the flaps stopped moving. The action of the flap position preselector linkage was reversed when the flap control handle was moved up.

A cable attached to the flap torque tube mechanically operated a flap position indicator installed on the left side of the cockpit just aft of the instrument panel. The indicator consisted of a plate marked off in degrees from 0 to 50 and

a luminous indicator button that indicated the angular position of the flap. The indicator cable was attached to an eyebolt in the flap torque tube just outboard of the flap position preselector linkage attachment. As the flap moved down, the flap torque tube pulled the indicator cable, and the cable, in turn, pulled the indicator button down; and as the flap moved up, the flap torque tube released the tension on the indicator cable. The indicator button was spring-loaded so that it moved up toward the 0-degree mark as the torque tube released the tension on the cable.

Fuel System

The fuel system, including the main system and the auxiliary system, consisted essentially of the following units:

When Lend-Lease came into effect, the British requested certain modifications for their Mustangs and the main one was replacement of all machine guns with four 20mm cannon. NAA engineers spent a lot of time with the installation and were able to supply each weapon with 125 rounds and this made an interesting comparison with Bell's export variant of the Airacobra whose single 20mm weapon carried only 60 rounds fitted in a drum. This aircraft, the fifth P-51, illustrated the long barrels and housings for the cannon.

This interesting view of a P-51 not only shows the cannon to advantage, but also the incredibly smooth finish of the wing.

Unit	Location
Main Fuel Tanks (2)	One in Each Wing
Selective Sump Valves (2)	Between Main Tanks in Center of Wing
Selector Valves (2)	Inside Right and Left Wheel Recesses
Strainer	Right Side of Firewall, Bottom
Booster Pump	Left Side of Firewall, Bottom
Fuel Pump	Left Side of Engine Accessory Case
Drain Box	Lower Aft End of Engine Compartment
Ferrying Tanks (2)	Bottom of Wings, Outboard

The engine was supplied with fuel from the two main self-sealing tanks in the wings and from the auxiliary tanks when they were installed. The regular fuel flow was from the main tanks, through the selective sump valves to the selector valve, through the fuel strainer and booster pump, and on to the engine fuel pump and carburetor. When the ferrying tanks were used, the fuel from them passed through the auxiliary system selector valve and on to the main fuel lines. The ferrying tanks were mounted beneath each bomb rack. The main fuel lines were of the self-sealing type, and aluminum tube lining was used at critical bends. The tanks were not interconnected, and it was necessary to switch from one tank to the other and then to the reserve to provide smooth operating of the engine.

Sufficient fuel feed to the engine during steep climbs or dives was ensured by two outlet lines, one at the forward end and one at the aft end of each tank, interconnected by a selective sump ball-and-socket valve to a single line. Additional facilities for furnishing the engine with sufficient fuel when the fuel level became low were the bulkheads with flapper valves, located at the inboard end of each tank, which formed a sump chamber over the fuel outlet and the booster pump installation. The carburetor was of the fuel-injection-type containing an idle cutoff device; a vapor return line extended to the left main tank. The full capacity of the main fuel system was 180 U.S. gallons (150 Imperial gallons), Specification No. AN-F-28, 100/130 octane. All units of the fuel system were satisfactory for use with aromatic fuel.

The main fuel tanks, manufactured by the Firestone Tire and Rubber Company of California, were of pressure-molded self-sealing construction, incorporating an Aviation Flight Facilities (AFF) approved aromatic-resistant liner. Each main tank had a total fuel capacity of 90 U.S. gallons (75 Imperial gallons), but the tank in the left wing was divided into a main and a reserve supply by a standpipe. A magnetic-type fuel gauge on each tank extended into the sump compartment. Each tank was provided with a long vent line that extended into the fuselage and had its outlet at the wing fillet. The cork floats on the fuel level gauges and the filler cap gaskets were satisfactory for use with aromatic fuels.

Droppable ferrying tanks were constructed of wood and had a fuel capacity of 150 U.S. gallons (125 Imperial gallons) each. When carried, the tanks were installed on the bomb racks by means of two shackle fittings. Four sway brace fittings secured the tank. The tank fuel line was connected to the wing outlet by a rubber hose and a straight nipple, which was installed in the underside of the wing forward of the bomb rack. Access to the fuel line within the tank was gained by the removal of the access door, which also contained the filler cap. A vent line extended from the front to the rear along the top of the tank. The filler cap was at the front and top of the tank, and the drain plug was on the bottom of the tank.

Installing the top cowling on a P-51 shows the extended air scoop to advantage. Although it is difficult to see in this view, the scoop had a bulge about halfway down that gave a slight Coke bottle effect.

Final work being done on the gun bays for a P-51 prior to delivery. Note the large ejection chutes for the expended shells and the molded plexiglass cover for the landing light.

Allison Mustang Tactical Suitability

Initial USAAF testing with the Mustang viewed the basic design as having great potential.

COPY:
PROOF DEPARTMENT
TACTICAL COMBAT SECTION
ARMY AIR FORCES PROVING GROUND COMMAND
EGLIN FIELD, FLORIDA

FINAL REPORT ON TACTICAL SUITABILITY OF THE P-51
TYPE AIRPLANE
30 December 1942

1. OBJECT

To determine the relative tactical value of the P-51 type fighter aircraft for combat service.

2. INTRODUCTION

This test was authorized by letter from Headquarters Army Air Forces, Director of Air Defense, dated 13 July 1942, to Commanding General, Air Forces Proving Ground, Eglin Field, Florida, subject: "Test of P-51 Airplanes." This test was started 7 August 1942, and was finished 1 November 1942.

a. Description. The articles tested are P-51 type airplanes, Air Corps Serial Nos. 41-37323, 41-37324, and 41-37325.

3. CONCLUSIONS

It is concluded that:

a. The subject aircraft is the best low-altitude American fighter aircraft yet developed, and should be used as the criterion for comparison of subsequent types.

b. If possible, the power loadings of this fighter aircraft should be materially reduced, without increasing the wing loading.

c. To reduce the power loading of the aircraft, excess weight in the structure and accessories not vital to operational use should be eliminated, and engine performance increased.

d. Pilots become completely at home in this aircraft immediately after the first takeoff due to the remarkable sensitivity of control, simplicity of cockpit, and excellent flying characteristics.

e. The rate of roll is not as rapid as is desired for combat operations.

f. The view downward over the nose is not sufficient to allow full deflection shooting in a turn.

g. The automatic manifold pressure regulator is completely satisfactory.

h. With the exception of the radiators, the airplane is completely satisfactory.

i. The range of speeds obtainable in the throttle limits in level flight is excellent.

j. Up to 15,000 feet this is faster than all standard American fighters with the exception of the P-47C-1.

4. RECOMMENDATIONS

It is recommended that:

a. The subject aircraft be equipped with an engine that will permit satisfactory tactical combat maneuvering between 25,000 and 30,000 feet.

b. The present armament in the subject aircraft be changed from four 20mm cannon to four .50-cal. machine guns, wing mounted, and that these be high cyclic rate of fire guns when conclusive tests are accomplished with the guns and standardization is effected.

c. Provisions be provided for carrying external combat and ferrying fuel tanks.

d. The subject aircraft be equipped with the modified N-7 type gun sight to allow changing of bulb while in flight and to set dropping angle for low level bombing.

e. The subject aircraft be equipped with the Stoddard radio (Model MRT-3A) for test at this station. This radio weighs 46 pounds installed.

f. The brakes of the subject aircraft be redesignated for more satisfactory operation.

g. The throttle and propeller controls be hooked together to operate as a unit, if the pilot desires.

h. The coolant and oil radiators be redesigned for more satisfactory service, and the mountings be modified to permit much faster installation and removal.

i. Study be made of canopy structure to determine the weakness that allows the canopy to bulge at high speed, and steps be taken to correct this condition.

j. The subject aircraft be equipped with an automatic shutter control (factory has installation).

k. It be equipped with a stick locking tail wheel (factory has installation).

l. It be equipped with more effective aileron control to produce higher rate of roll at all speeds (factory has installation).

m. It be equipped with left wing landing light only.

n. It be equipped with a Demand oxygen system (now standard equipment).

o. The electrical compass indicator mangesyn remote indicating compass be installed.

p. The automatic manifold pressure regulator be incorporated on all subsequent models of this airplane.

5. RECORD OF TEST

This test was conducted according to the Test Program, Proof Department, No. 4-42-7, this headquarters, dated 3 August 1942, a copy of which is attached as Enclosure No. 1, except for the procedure called for in paragraph 3a (4). The portion of this test has not been completed.

6. DISCUSSION

a. Performance. For speed, rate-of-climb, range, and gas consumption tables, see Enclosure No. 2.

b. Maneuverability. The subject aircraft was flown in mock combat against the P-38F, P-39D, P-40F, P-47B, and the Mitsubishi "00" type aircraft.

c. The following results were obtained:
1. The subject aircraft was found to be superior in speed to the Mitsubishi "00," P-39D, P-40F at all altitudes, and the P-47B and P-38F up to 15,000 feet.
2. The subject aircraft was found to be superior in rate-of-climb to the P-39D, P-40F, and P-47B up to 15,000 feet.
3. The acceleration in dives and the maximum permissible diving speed of the subject aircraft is superior to all types tested.
4. The turning characteristics of the subject aircraft are substantially the same as the P-40F and P-39D. None of these appears to have any definite superior turning characteristics.

5. In close dog fighting the subject aircraft has the very decided advantage of being able to break off combat at will. However, if neither airplane attempts to leave the combat, the P-40F is considered to have a slight advantage.

d. Ceiling. The absolute ceiling of the subject aircraft at the date of this report was found to be approximately 31,000 feet. It is believed that the fighting ceiling of this aircraft is 20,000 feet as the engine loses power very rapidly above 18,000 feet. This limited ceiling is the most serious handicap to this aircraft, and every effort should be made to increase the power and critical altitude of the engine.

e. Range. The cruising ranges of the subject aircraft are contained in Enclosure No. 2.

f. Flying Characteristics—General.
1. The flying characteristics of the P-51 are exceptionally good and the aircraft is very pleasant and easy to fly. Its taxiing visibility is limited in view over nose as are all standard landing gear fighters having engine in front of pilot. There is no objectionable amount of torque on takeoff and the ship becomes airborne very nicely. A pilot flying

P-51 41-37324 was one of the Mustangs used for the test report.

this plane for the first time feels immediately at home when this ship leaves the ground, and he has a feeling that he has flown this ship for a large number of hours. The plane picks up speed very rapidly after leaving the ground and will climb equally well between 165 and 205 mph IAS. This ability to climb well at a high indicated speed should be a great aid in helping catch targets having altitude and attempting to escape. In level flight, trimmed up, the aircraft will fly practically hands off. There is a speed range of about 200-mph difference in which it is possible for the pilot to control the plane without aid of trim. The plane handles nicely in a dive, using a very small amount of trim, and accelerates faster than any other type of American fighter. At 500 mph IAS with small aid from the trim tabs, the plane still maintains its stability. In normal flight, the plane responds quickly to the controls, however, the aileron roll is slower than desired and tightens at very high speeds. It is very easy to put through all normal aerobatics, and it has sufficient speed to perform all these aerobatics from level flight without diving to pick up speed. At slow speeds when approaching the field for landing, there is a mushy feeling in the aileron but the control is still there. The plane lands nicely, has a tendency to skip several times if landed fast, and it rolls in a straight line without attempting to swing or break noticeably in either direction.

g. Cockpit Arrangement. The engine and flight controls of the subject airplane are conventional. A drawing for an improved instrument panel is submitted as Enclosure No. 3.

h. Armament.
    1. The present armament is considered adequate, but is functionally unsatisfactory. It is believed that four .50-cal. (high rate of fire) guns would furnish ideal firepower.
    2. The present N-3A gun sight should be replaced with the N-7 type sight in order to permit changing of the bulb while in flight.

i. Armor.
    1. The pilot is covered from behind by armor plate 1/4-inch thickness and in front by the engine and a bulletproof glass panel.
    2. All fuel tanks are self-sealing.

j. Vulnerability of Vital Installations.
    1. The engine and the oil tank are mounted in the nose of the subject aircraft and are not considered as vulnerable as those mounted to the rear of the cockpit.
    2. The coolant and oil radiators are combined into one assembled unit and are located in the belly of the aircraft just behind the cockpit.

For the reason that most hits on an airplane in combat are to the rear of the cockpit, it is believed that this radiator installation may prove to be quite vulnerable. It is recommended that the designer of the subject aircraft make a study of the possibilities of incorporating a sheet of armor plate to protect the radiator from fire from the rear.

k. Visibility.
    1. The pilot's visibility is in general very similar to that afforded him in the P-40 type aircraft. The view to the rear is somewhat restricted but not dangerously so.
    2. The visibility forward in flight attitude is good except over the nose, but on the ground is extremely poor.
    3. Every effort must be made to increase the angle of view over the nose. At present, the view over the nose is restricted to 3 to 4 degrees below the sight line. A mirror arrangement to increase angle of view should be developed.

l. Night Flying. The subject aircraft is suitable for night flying, but because of the very restricted view forward, it is a bit difficult in the run after landing.

m. Instrument Flying. The subject airplane due to its excellent stability is easily flown by the use of instruments.

n. Speed of Servicing. The subject aircraft can be completely serviced (fuel, coolant, oxygen, ammunition, and radio check) in 5 minutes by a crew consisting of the following: Four armorers, two mechanics, and one radioman.

o. Maintenance. The regular 50-hour inspection can be completed in approximately 8 hours by using the optimum crew, or a crew of two men can complete it in approximately 10 hours. The most common maintenance difficulties were found to be:
    1. Radiator leakage and the time required to remove and install the radiator unit is unsatisfactory. It is believed by the maintenance crew that most leaks in the radiator are due to poor workmanship rather than faulty design.
    2. Considerable trouble was experienced with brake action. It is recommended that both deficiencies be corrected.
    3. In order to change magnetos, retime, or change points, the carburetor air scoop must be removed. It is recommended that, if possible, the carburetor air scoop be redesigned to give more room for working on the magnetos.
    4. Cuno strainers are too difficult to remove and install.
    5. Larger inspection plates for the fuel tank sump drain are desired.

The Enclosures

As indicated in the above report, three enclosures were attached. Briefly, the first enclosure outlined how the tests on the three P-51s would be conducted under the control of Capt. George Walker, Group Project Officer.

The second enclosure is of importance since it gives a detailed outline of P-51 performance and is as follows:

Speed

The average trial true speed of the three subject aircraft are set forth in the table below (left):

Rate-of-Climb

The average of the best time of the three subject aircraft during the climb trials is set forth in the table below (right):

Long Range Cruise

Takeoff—As low a power setting as possible; climb to 15,000 feet true altitude—2,280 rpm, 30.5-in. Hg. at 200 mph IAS (shutters closed). Cruise at 15,000 feet true altitude—1,650 rpm and 22.5-in. Hg. (shutters closed and auto-lean mixture). This procedure will give a range of 1,000 miles with a 30-gallon gasoline reserve. No appreciable winds. IAS—192 mph.

Maximum Cruising

Takeoff—As low a power setting as possible. Climb to 15,000 feet true altitude at 200 mph. AS and cruise—2,280 rpm and 30.5-in. Hg. (shutters closed and auto-lean mixture). This procedure will give a range of 900 miles (55 to 60 gal/hr) with no reserve. IAS—265 mph.

Combat Range

Interception—20,000 feet   PRESSURE ALTITUDE
Climb —

TIME	RPM	MP	ALTITUDE
10 min	3,000	46 inches	20,000
		(as long as available)	

Cruise —

TIME	RPM	MP	IAS
15 min	2,600	28.5 inches	255 mph

Combat —

TIME	RPM	MP	IAS
20 min	3,000	34 inches	273 mph

Total distance covered	540 miles
Total gas at takeoff	180 gallons
Gas remaining after landing	36 gallons
Time of flight	1 hour 35 minutes

ALT (feet)	MAX CRUISE (RPM/HG)	MAX OPERATION (RPM/HG)	MAX POWER (RPM/HG)
	2280	2600	3000
5,000	284/30.5	319/37.5	343/44.6
10,000	305/30.5	343	369/44.0
15.000	330/30.5	367	385
20,000	356	373	—
25,000	334	357	—

MANI/PRESS.	RPM	ALT.	TIME	CLIMB	IAS
55 inches	3,000	5,000	2 min 10 sec	2,314 fpm	170
Dropped in		10,000	4 min 7 sec	2,427 fpm	170
Climb		15,000	6 min 34 sec	2,287 fpm	170
To 25,000 feet		20,000	9 min 54 sec	2,020 fpm	160
25 inches	3,000	25,000 feet	15 min 20 sec	1,631 fpm	135

(The rate-of-climb figures are based on the time taken from the start of the takeoff run to the indicated altitude.)

Rated Power

Takeoff—2,600 rpm at 38-in. Hg. and climb to 15,000 feet true altitude at 200 mph IAS and cruise (shutters as far closed as possible). This procedure will give a range of 480 miles (103-105 gal/hr) with no reserve. IAS—298 mph.

Range—Convoy of medium bombers at 14,000 feet. Climb to 14,000 feet:

RPM	IAS	Rate of Climb
2200	150 mph	1,000 fpm

Cruise at 14,000 feet:

RPM	in. Hg.	AUTO-LEAN	IAS	OAT
1,650	23.5	Position	193	-12 degreesC

Total distance covered on trip	610 miles
Radius of action	305 miles
20 minutes at 3,000 rpm, 41.5-in. Hg.	
Total time in air	3 hours 26 minutes
Fuel used	159 gallons U.S.
Fuel remaining	21 gallons U.S.

The electric booster pump for the fuel system was a Type G9, Model TFD-9800, manufactured by the Thompson Products Company of Cleveland, Ohio. With the ignition switch turned on, the booster pump switch located on the right side of the pilot's switch panel controlled the booster pump. The pump assembly consisted of two units—a No. A-7005 motor and a Type TFD-100 fuel pump. The relief valve, which was housed in a separate body, could be mounted in reverse position on the pump so as to permit change of rotation when this would be necessary. The booster pump could be used for either the main fuel system or the auxiliary fuel system through adjustment of the selector valve controls.

An engine-driven fuel pump, Type G9, was mounted directly on the engine at the aft end. When the Allison was being started, this pump was to be assisted by the booster pump.

Two fuel selector valves, one located in each wheel recess, provided for control of the main fuel system and the auxiliary fuel system. The control handles located side by side on the cockpit floor directly underneath the pilot's switch panel manually operated the valves.

An engine primer pump and operating handle were installed on the sub-panel at the lower right side of the instrument panel. When priming operations were completed, the handle had to be pushed in and turned clockwise to the off position.

The distributor valve was located forward of the carburetor on top of the engine. From the distributor, 1/16-inch lines ran to the forward and aft ends of the intake manifolds.

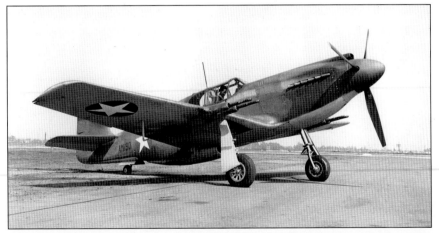

Wearing RAF camouflage and USAAF insignia, AM190 was parked on the Inglewood ramp and the heavy exhaust stain indicates the Allison had been subjected to some hard running. Once in Britain, the Mk. I would initially go to the Aeroplane and Armament Experimental Established before being assigned to No. 516 Squadron. The Mustang survived the war to be struck off strength on 31 October 1945.

Coolant System

The coolant system consisted essentially of the following units:

Unit	Location
Coolant Tank	Inside Engine Nose Ring At Top
Coolant Pump	Bottom Left Side Accessory Section
Coolant Radiator	Bottom of Fuselage, Aft of Cockpit, Between Air Scoop Inlet and Outlet
Temperature Indicator	Instrument Panel, Lower Right Side

A solution of ethylene glycol with a corrosion inhibitor, Specification No. AN-E-2, was the coolant medium, and the coolant system had a capacity of 21 U.S. gallons (17.5 Imperial gallons). The coolant was circulated by a centrifugal pump and followed from the coolant pump into the engine, through the coolant jackets around each bank of cylinders and out of the engine at the front, then aft to the coolant radiator. The coolant liquid then entered the radiator at the top, flowed through the cooling tubes in the radiator to the outlet at the bottom, and then back again to the coolant pump.

The coolant tank was interconnected with the pump to replenish the coolant supply in the system. The coolant radiator was mounted in the center of an air scoop assembly designed to concentrate a flow of air through the radiator.

The coolant tank was tubular and curved to conform to the contour of the engine nose ring cowl. The interior of the tank was entirely void of structures, baffles, etc. When heated, ethylene glycol expanded considerably; therefore, the filler flange on the tank was positioned so that when the tank was filled to overflowing, one gallon of coolant liquid was in the tank and the remaining space served

Interesting view of a P-51 showing lack of visibility over the nose when the aircraft was in the tail down position.

Wartime activity at North American in full swing and B-25s undergoing flight-testing. P-51 s/n 41-37324 was the fifth aircraft in the USAAF allocation.

In USAAF service, many of the P-51s were modified to carry cameras and were redesignated F-6A. In this view of the number five aircraft, the serial on the side of the fuselage has been censored out.

for expansion. A Parker two-way, pressure-vacuum relief valve installed on the tank and vented to the drain box, provided pressure relief at 3 +/- 3/8 psi, and suction relief at 3/4 +/- 3/16 psi.

The coolant pump was manufactured by the Allison Engine Company and was provided with the engine. It was a centrifugal-type pump and had spring-loaded packing that did not require manual tightening.

The coolant radiator, cylindrical in shape, was of the honeycomb type. The radiator consisted of an outer circular brass shell and an inner brass shell, also circular in shape except for a separation at the top. The core of the radiator consisted of a number of copper tubes grouped together somewhat in appearance like a horseshoe when viewed from either end. The opening in the center provided for the insertion of the oil cooler assembly, and the space at the top provided clearance for the oil cooler valve mounted on the oil cooler. A drain plug was provided on the bottom of the radiator. The coolant liquid seeped down between the round cooling copper tubes, the hexagonal ends of the tube being sealed with solder. A removable screen was secured to the forward end of the oil and coolant radiator. The cold weather shield assembly furnished with the Mustang consisted of two flat baffles that could be secured to the bolts that held the oil and the coolant radiators together at the aft end. The baffles served to blank off a section of the coolant radiator, and were for use only in weather of +30 degreesF (-1.1 degreesC) or below.

The forward end of the air scoop was stationary, whereas the aft end was movable and was adjusted by a hydraulic strut controlled from the cockpit by a preselector control handle. The control handle was located on the aft end of the control pedestal to the left of the pilot's seat. An indicator showing the scoop's position in degrees was located just above the forward end of the control pedestal. The opening or closing of this scoop regulated the amount of air flowing through the radiator, which in turn regulated the temperature of the oil and coolant in the radiator.

Lubricating System

The oil system consisted essentially of the following units:

Unit	Location
Oil Tank	Forward Side of Firewall at Top
Oil Pump	Lower Aft End of Engine Accessory Case
Oil Cooler Assembly	Bottom of Fuselage, Aft of Cockpit, Within Coolant Radiator
Cuno Oil Filter	Right-Hand Side of Engine Accessory Case
Temperature and Pressure Indicators	Lower Right-Hand Side of Instrument Panel

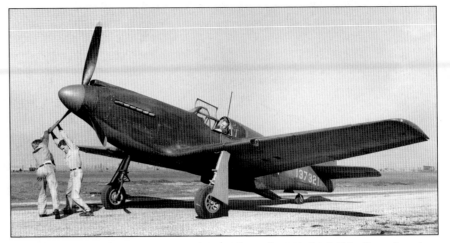

USAAF 41-37321 was the second aircraft in the NA-91 P-51 allocation, but all armament had been removed and the plane may have been retained by NAA for flight test duties.

With the buildup of production, NAA hired more production test pilots and these aviators came with a wide variety of experience—everything from flying in the Great War, to barnstorming, to serving with the early airlines.

Held by an overhead hoist, this A-36A is receiving final equipment fitting before being rolled out of the factory. To convert the basic Mustang design into the dive-bomber, NAA engineers expended some 40,000 man-hours of effort. One modification following the fitment of the dive brakes saw the pitot tube relocated to the starboard wing. This view shows the installation of the nose .50-cal. machine guns to advantage.

The oil flowed from the bottom of the tank to the oil pump and was then delivered to the Cuno filter through a spring-loaded check valve, which prevented oil flow from the tank when the engine was stopped. A pressure of only 1-psi from the oil pump side of the valve was necessary to open the check valve. From the filter outlet, oil was then distributed to the moving parts of the engine. When the airplane was in normal position, all oil drained to the oil pan and was scavenged by the scavenger pump from the accessory end of the oil pan. The scavenger pump would not pump oil when the Mustang was in an inverted position in the air. From the scavenger pump oil outlet, the oil flowed back to the oil tank either directly through the oil cooler valve, which incorporated a bypass valve, or on through the oil cooler and then back to the tank, depending on the temperature of the oil. A standard AAF oil dilution system was provided to facilitate starting. The full capacity of the oil system was 18 U.S. gallons (15 Imperial gallons).

The oil tank was a hopper type constructed of aluminum alloy. With this type tank, it was only necessary to drain the engine lubricating oil at engine change, unless a failure of an engine part necessitated an oil change before that time. The oil entered the hopper in the top of the tank and flowed down through the hopper to the reservoir in the bottom of the oil tank. Clean oil entered the reservoir from the oil tank through two flapper valves, which served to ensure an adequate supply of oil in the reservoir during maneuvers. The sump inlet was suspended on a swivel joint so that the inlet could rotate about the swivel joint and siphon oil from the greatest depth in the reservoir. A small cup directly above the swivel joint in the sump was always filled with oil; this sealed the joint and prevented the oil pump from drawing in air should the depth of the oil fall below the level of the joint. The tank was provided with two vents; one to vent the tank in normal flight, and the other to vent the tank in inverted flight. The filler cap was located below the top of the tank on the left-hand side to allow for the expansion of the oil. A drain cock installed on the right-hand side of the sump casting allowed for the removal of accumulated moisture and foreign matter.

A cylindrical, honeycomb-type oil cooler was located in the center of the coolant radiator. The complete oil cooler assembly, including the thermostatic oil cooler valve mounted on top of the cooler, could be removed from the outer coolant section as an individual unit. The cooler consisted of a series of copper cone pipes enclosed in a brass shell. The hexagonal ends of the copper tubes were soldered together, each one to its adjacent tubes; the core assembly was soldered to the shell. When the system was in operation, the oil seeped down between the round portions of the cooling copper tubes. The oil temperature control was a rotary-type oil cooler valve activated by a bimetal spring. The temperature of the oil caused expansion or contraction of the spring, which, in turn, rotated the movable ported cylinder to allow the oil

either to enter the cooler or to be bypassed back to the tank. This valve also acted as a surge valve to resist damaging surge pressures, which were encountered in cold-weather starting. An oil drain plug was located in the back of the cooler at the bottom.

The oil pump was manufactured by the Allison Engine Company and was furnished with the engine. The pressure pump and the main scavenge pump were arranged as a unit on the lower right-hand side of the accessories housing. The pump, in combination with a pressure-sensitive relief valve, maintained constant pressure. The pumps were of the conventional spur gear type.

The oil-dilution system withdrew engine fuel from a restricted fitting at the carburetor and induced it into the oil system at the oil Y-drain valve, where it mixed with the oil. This action lowered the viscosity of the oil and facilitated engine starting in cold weather. The system was set into operation by an

Because of rapid expansion and lack of facilities, some final assembly work was performed on the A-36As in the open air. This aircraft, up on jacks, was undergoing gear swings. For some reason, cowling areas around the spinner had been left unpainted, but this shows the openings for the .50-cal. weapons to advantage. The blisters around each gun, seen on the Mk. Is, had been eliminated to save production time and money. Of interest is the number of incomplete fuselages immediately behind the A-36A. These could have been spare parts being provided with the contract.

electrically operated solenoid on the forward side of the firewall at the top. The control switch for the system was mounted on the top center of the pilot's switch panel.

The Allison was equipped with an automatic Cuno oil strainer consisting of an assembly of steel discs and cleaners, and a cast aluminum mounting head with a built-in safety valve. The filter was of the self-rotating type; that is, the oil pressure turned the vane unit when the engine was operating.

The oil pressure, temperature, and fuel pressure indicators were incorporated into one instrument, which was mounted in the lower right-hand corner of the instrument panel.

Propeller

The P-51A was equipped with a Curtiss constant-speed three-blade, electrically controlled propeller, with a diameter of 10 feet 9 inches. The blades were set at a 23-degree angle for low pitch and a 58-degree angle for high pitch. The propeller pitch could be changed by either of two controls; one a manual control lever mounted on the control quadrant, the other a selector switch mounted on the pilot's switch panel. The manual control lever was used principally when the toggle switch was placed in the Auto Constant Speed position. The electric control could be used when the switch was placed in the Fixed Pitch position. Pulling the switch down to either the left or right automatically increased or decreased the RPM. When the switch was released, it snapped back to Fixed Pitch. An electric circuit breaker served to cut off the power to the propeller in case of an overload. Pressing a button located to the right of the propeller selector switch could reset the circuit breaker. When set in Auto Constant Speed, the propeller maintained a given RPM regardless of throttle setting or manifold pressure; when the propeller was set in Fixed Pitch, the RPM could be changed with the throttle lever. A streamline, dynamically balanced spinner was attached to the propeller.

Armament and Armor

The P-51A was fitted with four .50-cal. Browning M2 machine guns and two were mounted in the leading edge of each wing. All four guns fired simultaneously and were electrically controlled by the trigger switch on the control

A great deal of final paintwork was done by hand. Using masking tape to carefully mark out positioning, this painter applied the A-36A's serial number by air brushing one stencil at a time. Also note the mostly eliminated alignment markings for the national insignia.

Completed A-36A 42-83934 has been raised into flight position for bore sighting the six .50-cal. machine guns. The tight fit of the ammunition trays for the nose guns can be seen along with just how easily the flat Olive Drab paint would stain.

stick grip. The guns had to be manually charged on the ground. The four M2s were so situated in the wings that their fire passed outboard of the plane of propeller rotation. Two guns and their accessories were located in one gun compartment in each wing, and the removable ammunition boxes for both guns occupied a single ammunition compartment enclosed within the wing structure. The guns were mounted on Type A-3 front mounts and Type A-4 rear mounts. The guns were adjusted horizontally and vertically so that their fire converged with the line of sight at 300 yards.

Access to the gun compartments was by loosening the Dzus fasteners on each door handle, lifting the handle, and swinging the door forward. The coverplate was removed by sliding it forward. The ammunition coverplate was removed by loosening the six Dzus fasteners that held it to the wing. The following checklist ensured correct loading of the Brownings:

1. Remove the ammunition boxes by means of the handle on each end.
2. Prepare two belts of 280 rounds each for the outboard guns and two belts of 350 rounds each for the inboard guns. Make certain that the links are properly and securely loaded.
3. Start each belt from the inboard corner of the outboard section of the box. Load the belts in smooth and regular layers. Allow approximately 22 cartridges for the inboard gun feed chutes and 14 cartridges for the outboard gun feed chutes.
4. Place the boxes in the ammunition compartment. Push the box handles down.
5. Attach the outboard gun feed chutes first. Attach the feed chute to the gun before engaging the bolt with the grooves in the support brackets. Check the freedom of movement of the belts in the feed chutes. The belts should slide into and through the chutes easily.
6. Load each gun by inserting the double-loop end and the first cartridge into the gun feedway until the belt holding pawl holds the cartridge. Charge each gun by pulling the gun bolt back twice with a charging hook.
7. Replace the ammunition compartment and gun compartment coverplates and secure the access doors.
8. To fire the guns, turn the gun and camera safety switch, located on the armament control panel, to Guns and Camera and squeeze the trigger switch on the control stick grip. All guns fire simultaneously.

With an A-36A's V-1710 ticking over, a flight line mechanic makes some final adjustments. Note the partially completed XB-28 bomber in the right background. This was an NAA attempt to create an advanced pressurized bomber, but the type was not put into production. Fortunately, test pilot Bob Chilton managed to bail out of one of the two XB-28s when serious problems developed during a test flight.

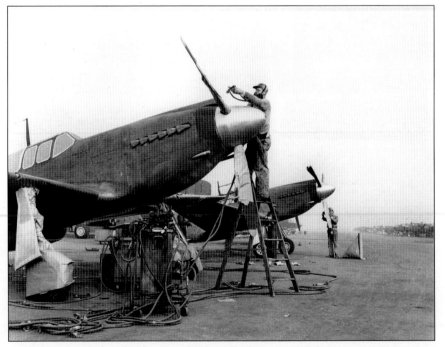

A-36As receiving a final coat of Olive Drab on a misty June morning—not the best of times for outdoor painting, but there was a war going on.

Well-weathered A-36A 42-83861 on a test flight out of Inglewood. This aircraft has had its armament removed and ports sealed which may mean that the dive-bomber had been retained by NAA for test work.

A line of A-36As is prepared for the day's test flight schedule while a B-25C Mitchell awaits its turn.

The P-51A-1s and P-51A-5s were provided with one gun heater (Type 789-V Stewart-Warner) in each gun compartment. The heaters utilized a fuel-air mixture that was piped from the engine intake manifold to a solenoid-operated valve on the forward side of the firewall; from the valve the gas passed to a tee for distribution to the gun heater in each wing. A heater switch on the armament switch panel controlled the solenoid valve and heaters. To turn on the heaters, the heater switch was lifted to On. The heater switch was turned to Off before firing the guns, and during takeoff or landing. The P-51A-2 and P-51A-10 series were provided with an electric heater for each gun. These heaters fitted over the cover of the gun and were controlled by the heater switch on the armament panel.

In the P-51A, provisions were made for the installation of a gun sight aiming-point camera (Type N-1) equipped with a 3-inch plain lens. The camera was located in the left wing inboard of the gun compartment and was adjusted to converge with the line of sight of the gun sight at 300 yards. The self-contained film magazine used with this installation was interchangeable on all 16mm gun-sight aiming-point cameras. To operate the camera simultaneously with the guns, the pilot lifted the gun and camera safety switch situated on the lower left side of the instrument panel, to the Guns and Camera position, and depressed the trigger switch on the control stick grip. To operate the camera without firing the guns, the gun and camera safety switch was placed in the Camera position and the trigger switch was depressed. When through photographing, the gun and camera safety switch was placed in the Off position.

A Type N-3A optical gun sight that functioned on the collimator principal was mounted in the center of the instrument panel shield. The gun sight assembly consisted of a reflector and sunscreen installed on the sight housing, which contained a lamp, reticule, mirror, and lens. The lamp circuit was modified for a two-wire electrical connection. A Type O-1B rheostat, on the right side of the pilot's switch panel, controlled both the lighting of the lamp and regulation of light intensity of the reticule image on the reflector.

The P-51A was also fitted with an optical sight gun assembly that consisted of an adjustable front bead sight attached to the top of the firewall forward of the cockpit, and a rear ring sight that fitted into a socket located on the windshield frame to the right of the rearview mirror. Stowage for the rear ring sight was under the right side of the instrument panel glare shield. In the event of malfunctioning of the optical gun sight, the ring sight could be installed by pulling the knurled spring-loaded plunger outward, inserting the stem of the ring sight into the socket in the windshield frame, and then releasing the plunger.

For the bombing mission, an external, removable bomb rack was installed on the lower outer wing panel of each wing. Both bomb racks were identical and each accommodated one 100-, 250-, 300-, or 500-pound bomb, one depth charge or one chemical tank. When bombs were not carried, a 75-gallon capacity

TESTING THE A-36

PROOF DEPARTMENT
ARMY AIR FORCES PROVING
    GROUND COMMAND
EGLIN FIELD, FLORIDA
FINAL REPORT ON TEST OF THE
    OPERATIONAL SUITABILITY OF
    THE A-36 TYPE AIRPLANE
15 APRIL 1943

DESCRIPTION

Three A-36 type aircraft were received at this station on 23 November 1942. One A-36 was lost as the result of the wings pulling off in a near vertical dive. Complete tests on dive-bombing were not carried out due to restrictions placed on diving speeds and pullouts by the Materiel Center, Wright Field, Dayton, Ohio.

CONCLUSIONS

It is concluded that:

a. The A-36 is an excellent minimum-altitude bombing and attack aircraft.

b. The A-36 is an inferior dive-bomber due to the fast diving speeds at angles of dive greater than 70 degrees.

c. The A-36, after jettisoning its bombs, is an excellent fighter aircraft at low altitudes.

RECOMMENDATIONS

It is recommended that:

a. The A-36 be utilized as a minimum altitude attack bomber.

An A-36A tears into a target at Eglin Field during a skip-bombing attack. Even though this document recommends that the A-36A not be used for dive-bombing, pilots in the field quickly developed the plane into a very effective dive-bomber as noted in this 1 July 1943 Tactical Bulletin No. 23: "The A-36A in North Africa: It [the A-36A] became an excellent fighter-bomber, capable of delivering its bomb load with extreme accuracy. Its high speed and good maneuverability make it an excellent aircraft for either [glide or dive] bombing, but it must be noted that the accuracy obtained by glide bombing is much less than that obtained by using the dive brakes to secure vertical dives on the target. The essential element in a successful dive-bombing attack is a vertical dive. Accuracy of the bombing varies directly with the steepness of the dive and any dive of less than 72 degrees is considered as glide bombing. The best possibilities for a successful attack [resulting from] a 12-ship formation, close line abreast, with the leader on the flank toward the target and into the sun, the leader rolling over and diving as soon as he comes directly over the target, followed as closely as possible during the dive by the other ships and then reforming in a normal fighter defensive formation. The second formation used is an echelon of flights back and away for the target. For well-defended targets, an altitude of about 12,000 feet is obtained before the bomb run. The formation loses altitude to 10,000 feet for the beginning of the dive and recovery is made between 4,000 and 5,000 feet. For lightly defended targets, the altitude at the start of the dive is from 6,000 to 8,000 feet with recovery on the deck. A higher degree of accuracy is obtained by the latter, but at the expense of greater danger to the flight from ground fire. The rollover method is much preferred to the pushover method for obtaining a vertical dive. The dive brakes are opened immediately before the rollover on signal from the flight leader. Strafing with all guns is possible with individuals of the flight during the dive."

b. All A-36 type aircraft be equipped with the A-1 variable reflector sight.
c. The dive brakes be eliminated.
d. Flame dampers be installed for night operation.

PERFORMANCE

1. Maximum speed without bombs at the critical engine altitude of 5,000 feet is approximately 324 mph at war emergency power.
2. Maximum speed with two 500-pound bombs at the critical engine altitude of 5,000 feet is approximately 298 mph at war emergency power.

DIVING CHARACTERISTICS

The A-36 has excellent diving characteristics from the standpoint of a fighter, but it dives too fast for a dive-bomber, the dive brakes slowing the airplane down approximately 83 mph. This is insufficient from the dive-bomber standpoint, as the airplane will still dive with the dive brakes open to speeds in excess of 450 mph, necessitating bomb release at approximately 4,000 feet in order to pull out of the dive. The best diving angle is approximately 70 degrees.

FLYING CHARACTERISTICS

The A-36 is pleasant to fly, being extremely stable on each axis. The controls are well balanced with little tendency to tighten up at high speeds. The airplane handles well in aerobatics and gives ample warning of a stall.

Prepared by: (signed)

M. A. McKenzie
Captain, Air Corps,
Project Officer

combat fuel tank or a 150-gallon capacity ferry fuel tank could be installed on each bomb rack. These tanks were dropped by the normal operation of the bomb control system.

The bomb racks consisted of a housing incorporating the bomb release mechanism, a solenoid assembly, and integral sway braces which were adjustable for the three different sizes of bombs that could be carried.

The bomb rack cocking arm, when positioned aft, obtained a rack lock condition by means of an internal lock within the rack. With the arm in the vertical, or selective, position, the bombs could be released electrically. When the cocking arm was moved to the forward, or Salvo, position, the internal lock was released, allowing the bombs to drop. The Lock, Sel (selective), and Salvo positions of the racks were governed by a cockpit control handle, which was connected by cables to an actuating sector above each rack.

An electrical control system was used for the selection of nose or tail arming of bombs, to release bombs, depth charges, and fuel tanks when the control handle was in the Sel position, and to ignite the chemical tanks. The control system consisted of a bomb release switch on top of the pilot's control stick, and four toggle switches on the armament control panel. A bomb safety switch connected or disconnected the bomb circuit; another switch armed the bombs on the left and right racks. The bombs were armed and released by three solenoids housed in each bomb rack and wired to respective switches in the cockpit.

Provisions were made for the installation of a streamlined chemical tank on each bomb rack. Each tank when filled weighed 588 pounds. Release of chemicals from the tanks was accomplished by pressing the bomb safety switch to On and then pressing the desired nose arming switch (right rack, left rack, or both) to the On position. Following the same procedure as used for dropping bombs dropped both tanks.

The bomb control handle, located on the forward left side of the cockpit, was provided with three positions: Aft—Lock (locked), center—Sel (selective), and forward—Salvo. The handle could not be moved from one position to another until the button on top was depressed. In order to move the handle from Sel to the Salvo position, a mechanical anti-salvo safety guard located forward of the handle had to be hinged upward. The optical gun sight could be used as a bombsight. The bombs could be released when the airplane was in any attitude of flight from a 30-degree climb to a vertical dive.

The P-51A was equipped with an M-8 pyrotechnic flare pistol mounted on a bracket attached to the fuselage at the left side of the pilot's seat. It was fired through a hole in the fuselage at the outer end of the mounting bracket. Six flares were stowed in a canvas container just behind the left side of the pilot's seat. To insert a flare in the pistol, the pilot pulled on the lower handle above the barrel and broke it in the same manner as an ordinary revolver. When the upper handle on the barrel was pulled, the pistol was released from the bracket. During flight, the pistol was kept stowed in the bracket.

The aircraft's armor plates gave forward and aft protection to the pilot against .30-cal. gunfire and against .50-cal. gunfire striking obliquely to the plates. Two plates behind the pilot's seat provided aft protection. A 5/16-inch

DESPERATE TIMES, DESPERATE MEASURES

As the United States entered World War II, final victory over the Axis was uncertain at best. America would be fighting over many battlegrounds comprising a wide variety of climatic conditions. The USAAF and North American collaborated on fitting the Mustang with skis, which would be of great advantage if the Japanese invaded mainland Alaska.

The USAAF fighter ski program began in early 1941 with the development and manufacture of a set of streamlined fixed skis for a Curtiss P-36. As a result of flight tests and service tests with these skis, design criteria began to crystallize and a Curtiss P-40 was picked in January 1942 to serve as the test bed for retractable skis.

Test results with the P-40 were mixed at best. On the ground, the P-40 handled in a satisfactory manner, but in-flight maneuverability was less than desired while speed loss was deemed excessive. The skis were then modified to fit closer to the bottom of the wing when retracted and performance improved. Further testing revealed that the concept was worth pursuing and in July 1943 the USAAF picked a Lockheed P-38 Lightning, Republic P-47 Thunderbolt, P-51 Mustang, and a Bell P-63 Kingcobra for modification and test.

All the skis would be retractable except for the P-47. That aircraft's propeller arc would not allow a retractable ski of sufficient length to be installed. The Mustang was tested between July 1943 and February 1944 at Grenier Field, New Hampshire, and Ladd Field in Alaska (at this point in time, the emergency that generated the ski modification was certainly past). First, wind tunnel tests were made at the Wright Field 5-foot wind tunnel while North American conducted static tests at Inglewood. Luscombe Engineering Company, North Wales, Pennsylvania, built the Mustang's skis, under the direction of the Mechanical Branch, Aircraft Laboratory, Engineering Division, Air Technical Service Command.

The P-51 retractable ski installation followed the same design trend as on the P-40, except that a new problem was experienced in retracting the skis inboard toward the fuselage. A universal type pedestal was required in order that the skis might retract flat against the bottom of the wing and fuselage. This type of pedestal required an off center link-down lock to keep the ski from rotating in the down position. The spring-loaded rigger cylinder was mounted between a small pedestal aft of the main pedestal and the lower torque arm fitting on the strut. The ski bottoms were covered with black iron and had two Micarta runners. A fairing along the lower engine cowling covered the nose portion of the ski, which protruded beyond the leading edge of the wing.

The tail ski was also retractable and rigged with a spring-loaded cylinder. Retraction of both the main skis and the tail ski was accomplished with the Mustang's landing gear retraction mechanism.

Once installed, the Mustang's ski installation received no further modifications, as the original design was considered satisfactory. The P-51's ground handling was not as good as the P-38, but was deemed satisfactory. While testing the P-51, deep snow was not encountered, but from past experience USAAF pilots predicted the Mustang should operate successfully in deep snow.

Slight buffeting occurred at speeds below 200 mph with skis retracted and it was believed this was due to a small amount of looseness and play of the skis in the retracted position. This buffeting was greater in climbing attitude, but was not serious in any condition. Tests were made at speeds as high as 400 mph and it was found that the effect of the skis on flight maneuverability was negligible.

USAAF fighter ski program studies began in early 1941 with the development of fixed-ski landing gear fitted to a Curtiss P-36. More advanced and streamlined retractable skis were tested on the P-51 in late 1943 and early 1944 at Grenier Field in New Hampshire and Ladd Field in Alaska. Operating from plowed runways with wheel landing gear proved to be the ultimate solution, however.

With snow of 6 inches or more in depth, both the takeoff and landing runs were exceptionally short. When landing on surfaces of hard packed snow or ice, the distances required to stop were greater than with wheels mounted with snow and ice tread tires.

The stability and trim of the Mustang were not noticeably affected with the skis either extended or retracted. There was a tendency for the skis to cause skidding of the P-51 while they were in the process of extending at low engine power, but this did not affect lateral control, even at speeds near the normal stalling speed of the airplane.

After all this testing, the USAAF determined that the P-51, and all single-engine, high-powered fighters, was not generally adaptable to ski operation. The high engine torque combined with relatively small vertical tail surface and short tail length made ground maneuverability difficult without suitable ski brakes (which had not been developed).

The final USAAF ruling was that fighter ski operations should be limited to emergency missions only. For extended operation from snow-covered bases, it was determined that runways should be rolled or kept clean of snow for operation of wheel aircraft.

Looking a bit ungainly in flight, the ski-equipped Mustang was evaluated along with the Lockheed P-38, Republic P-47, and Bell P-63. It was determined that high-performance fighters such as these were unsuited for ski operations due to several factors, one being ground handling with high torque from the engines, and lack of effective braking capability.

A-36A-1-NA 42-83767 appears to have been withdrawn from flight use and assigned to mechanics training at Inglewood. All armament had been removed and the Olive Drab paint had been given a light overspray of aluminum.

plate extended from just below the bottom of the seat to a point level with the pilot's shoulders; a 7/16-inch-thick plate was attached to the top of this plate to protect the pilot's head. The 3/8-inch-thick firewall, the engine, and the 1.5-inch-thick armor plate glass windscreen provided forward protection. An armor plate was also provided immediately forward of the coolant tank located on the forward end of the engine.

Radios and Oxygen

There were two types of radio equipment installed in the P-51A: the command set and the identification equipment. The command radio could be either of two sets: SCR-511-A or SCR-274-N. The operation of the two sets was dissimilar. Identification radio equipment could be any of three sets: SCR-535, SCR-515, or SCR-695.

Command radio set SCR-522A was a push-button type of transmitter-receiver operating on the 100 to 156 mc (megacycles) band. A control box for this equipment was located just aft of the right-hand switch panel in the cockpit. The small lever on the rear of the box controlled the momentary or permanent action of the transmit-receive toggle switch. The small lever at the forward end of the control box regulated the brightness of the indicator lamps by moving a dimmer mask over them. The microphone furnished for this equipment was of the dynamic type and was normally mounted in the facemask.

Three A-36As on the prowl over Southern California during a test flight. During flight acceptance work, formation flights were not all that common and this flight had been probably set up by NAA for specific publicity purposes.

Command radio set SCR-274-N transmitters broadcast throughout the frequency range of 4 to 5.2 mc and 7 to 9.1 mc. The range of the three receivers was from 3.0 to 9.1 mc and 190 to 550 kc (kilocycles). No spare coils were required for either transmitters or receivers.

The control box for radio set SCR-535 (radar) was located on the right side of the cockpit adjacent to the pilot's seat. Operation of the equipment was automatic, and the pilot had only to place the On-Off switch, located on the face of the control unit, in its On position to place the equipment in operation. A dual push-button switch marked Danger was located on the right side of the cockpit forward of the receiver control box. The purpose of this switch was to destroy the radar equipment should it be necessary to abandon the airplane over enemy territory. When both push buttons were pressed, a detonator inside the receiver was set off, this destroying the receiver internally without damaging the airplane.

Provisions had been made to the left and aft of the pilot's seat for the stowage of a Type AN-3089 quick signaling lamp for communication between airplanes without using the radio equipment. A sight on top of the lamp permitted accurate control of the direction of the signal beam. Four snap-on filters, usually stowed in the map case, controlled the color of the beam.

The oxygen system consisted of two Type D-2 low-pressure oxygen cylinders mounted in the fuselage aft of the radio compartment, a Type A-12 demand regulator, a cylinder pressure gauge, low-pressure warning signal, and flow indicator. Mask Types A-9, A-9A, and A-10 could be used with the system.

An A-12 demand-type regulator, mounted in the forward right-hand corner of the pilot's cockpit, normally

An odd, and obviously staged, photograph of an unarmed A-36A being serviced alongside a Boeing P-26. Built in 1933, the P-26 could have been one of the very last examples still flying or many have been assigned to the ground-training role at Inglewood. Either way, it is an interesting comparison of less than a decade in aeronautical development.

P-51A-1-NA 43-6008 was retained at the factory for various test projects. In this instance, the aircraft has been fitted with the MX-241 bazooka launchers. The P-51A series was fitted with the three-blade Curtiss Electric C.53D-F-32/50700 aluminum blade propeller. Mustang Mk. Is were fitted with steel blade props.

required no adjustment; the mixing of air and oxygen and the compensation for change in altitude was fully automatic. Should the pilot desire pure oxygen, the automatic mixture lever at the side of the case could be turned to the Off position and no air would enter the regular mixing chamber. The red emergency knob on the front of the regulator was turned on only in the event of failure of the regulator mechanism. With the emergency knob on, oxygen was then supplied at a normal fixed rate of flow. With the automatic mixture level set in the On position, the mask could be worn and connected at any altitude. Only air would flow until oxygen became necessary.

Anti-Icing System

Anti-icing systems were provided for the propeller, windscreen, and carburetor. When installed for ferry purposes, the propeller anti-icing system was comprised of a 2.9 U.S. gallon (2.41 Imperial gallon) capacity tank installed in the rear left-hand ammunition box feeding through an electric pump to the propeller feed shoes. A 1-gallon-capacity tank was installed behind the pilot's seat for propeller anti-icing during combat missions. An electric switch on the left side of the cockpit operated both systems.

A valve on the upper right side of the instrument panel controlled a spray jet that provided fluid for the windshield from the coolant system. On the P-51A-1, the pilot could shut off the rammed air to the carburetor

Detailed view of the cockpit section of P-51A-1-NA 43-6055 with the rear quarter panels removed for clarity. Original contracts called for the building of 1,200 P-51As, but this was drastically cut back to 310 aircraft when the Merlin engine was introduced to the Mustang airframe.

and allow warm air from the engine compartment to flow into the carburetor to prevent carburetor icing under some conditions. The control for this operation was on the left side of the instrument panel. On the P-51A-2 and P-51A-5, an additional control permitted the pilot to draw air heated by exhaust gases into the carburetor for ice prevention or elimination.

Miscellaneous Equipment

Pyrotechnics: A signal flare pistol was located on the left side of the cockpit within reach of the pilot. The flares for the pistol were stowed to the left and aft of the pilot's seat.

Pilot's Seat: The pilot's seat was made of plywood and would accommodate a seat-type parachute. The back cushion was kapok filled and could, therefore, be used as a life preserver. The seat was equipped with a Type B-11 safety belt and a Type 41G8725 shoulder harness attached to a spring-loaded mechanism. The control lever for the shoulder harness was on the forward left side of the seat, and the vertical adjustment lever for the seat was located on the forward right side.

Pilot's Relief Tube: The relief tube horn was stowed on a bracket at the left underside of the pilot's seat. The tubing extended along the lower inboard side of the fuselage and emerged through an aluminum scoop outlet beneath the rudder.

First-aid Kit: An AC97765 medical first-aid kit was attached to a bracket on the left fuselage side panel in the radio compartment.

Incendiary Bombs: Provision was made for two incendiary bombs, located on each side of the seat, for destruction of the airplane if forced down in hostile territory.

Rations: One kit of ordinary rations and one kit of emergency rations were stowed in the left aft end of the radio compartment.

Water Containers: A water bottle was stowed in the left aft end of the radio compartment beside the first-aid kit and a larger water container was placed in the lower right side of the fuselage, aft of the radio shelves.

Line mechanic jacks up a P-51A's left gear leg to perform work on the brake. A rare Los Angeles thunderstorm caused crews to cover portions of the Mustangs with canvas protective covers. The small hole in the wing leading edge near the fillet was for the Type N-1 gun camera. To operate the camera simultaneously with the guns, the pilot would lift the gun and camera safety switch on the lower left side of the instrument panel to the guns and camera position, and then depress the trigger switch on the control stick grip.

P-51A-1-NA 43-6004, the second of the type, went to Wright Field. Armament was removed along with pylons, and the leading edge sealed. Stripped of paint, polished, and given the name Slick Chick, the USAAF wanted to see how fast the plane would go at low levels. NAA could have told them—fast!

Even in the early 1940s, Mines Field was surrounded by a fair amount of agricultural land. The photographer positioned his camera so this shot of a P-51A returning to the field after a test flight could be captured.

Dust Excluders: Canvas dust excluders provided for the main landing gear shock struts were secured to the struts by zipper fasteners. Another canvas dust excluder was permanently installed inside of the tail wheel well. Dust excluder boots were provided for all hydraulic cylinders. A dust cover was provided for the mouth of the radiator air scoop. Each aircraft also came with an engine and cockpit cover to protect the fuselage from a point aft of the cockpit up to and including the spinner.

Engine Crank: An engine crank and extension tube was stowed on brackets at the back of the right-hand landing gear well.

Mooring Kit: A mooring kit was attached to the left side of the fuselage in the rear compartment.

Shape of things to come. An Allison-powered P-51A poses with Merlin-powered P-51B-1-NA 43-12302. In the far background are another P-51A and a P-51B that has had its spinner and the cuffed portions of the propeller blades painted white, presumably for test purposes.

THE MERLIN MUSTANGS: A MATCH THAT MADE HISTORY

By combining the Mustang airframe with the Rolls-Royce Merlin, an aviation legend was born.

With the Allison-powered Mustangs, NAA, the USAAF, and the RAF realized they had an excellent airframe mated to a not-ideal powerplant. However, this was not a criticism of the V-1710. The engine (once various problems had been eliminated) performed very well within the regime for which it had been designed. As the war progressed, it became obvious that the air war was being fought at greater altitudes—an arena for which the Allison was not suitable.

Sometimes a momentous trend starts out in a thoroughly mundane manner. During 1942, Wg. Cmdr. Ian Campbell-Orde, commanding officer of the Air Fighting Development Unit (AFDU) at Duxford, phoned his friend Ronnie Harker and told him that one of the new Mustangs was at the base, and invited him to come and fly the fighter. Harker, Rolls-Royce's service liaison pilot, quickly accepted the invitation and headed to Duxford where he flew Mustang AG422 (later abandoned in flight on 2 October 1943 when its

All the power and magnificence of the Mustang is displayed by this P-51D executing a sharp break from the camera aircraft.

engine quit while serving with No. 41 Operational Training Unit) on 30 April 1942. Harker had previously flown the Allison-powered Curtiss Tomahawk, and was very wary of American manufacturer claims regarding high-performance. However, Harker was most impressed by the Mustang, and the next day sent a report to Rolls-Royce that, in part, read, "This aircraft should prove itself a formidable low- and mid-altitude fighter. It closely resembled a Bf 109F, probably due to its being designed by one of the Messerschmitt designers, who is now with the North American Aeroplane Co. [this, of course was incorrect, as Schmued

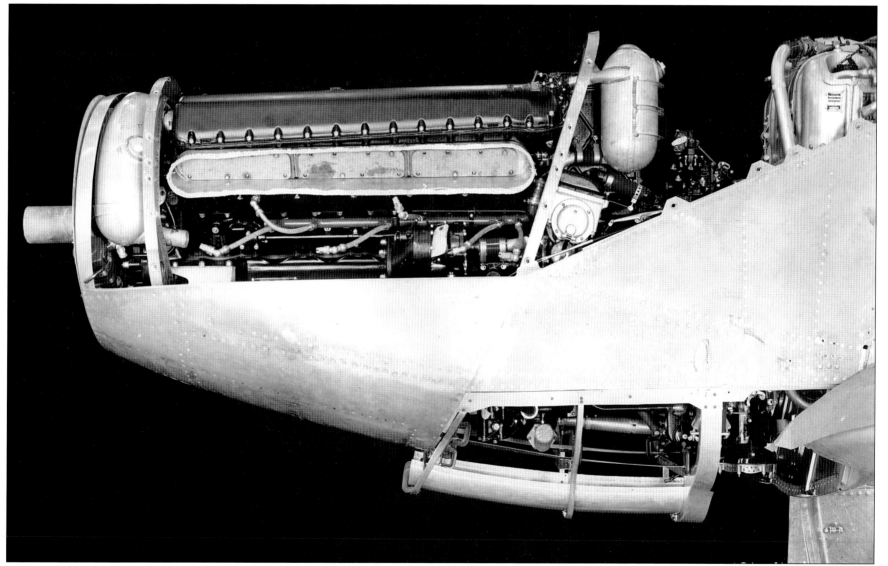

In the experimental shop, hand-formed cowling panels partially frame the Merlin engine for XP-51B 41-37352 (one of two NA-91 airframes assigned to the Merlin modification project). Note the partial ducting on the bottom of the cowl to accommodate the V-1650's carburetor.

was never employed by Messerschmitt, but this started a trail of misinformation that would bother the designer for the rest of his life]. The point which strikes me is that with a powerful and good engine like the Merlin 61, its performance should be outstanding, as it is 35 mph faster than a Spitfire V at roughly the same power." Harker's quick and accurate calculations showed that the Allison Mustang was some 30 mph faster at 5,000 feet and 35 mph faster at 15,000 feet than the frontline Mk. V.

The top personnel at Rolls-Royce took his suggestions very seriously, and moved rapidly with a secret memo dated 14 May 1942, from E. W. (later Lord) Hives, general manager for Rolls-Royce Derby, stating, "I feel

Although totally devoid of serial and data block, it is presumed that this is NA-101 41-37352 after completion. The 20mm cannon have been removed and the wing leading edge faired in smoothly. Also note that the landing gear oleos are extended to the maximum, which means they were probably overfilled.

The XP-51Bs featured an interim radiator scoop, revised ailerons, and a deepened cowling to allow for the Merlin's carburetor air scoop. They also had the new four-blade cuffed propellers and closely fitted stainless-steel exhaust stack covers.

The second XP-51B was 41-37421 and it retained its cannon armament. The aircraft is shown with the short-lived red surround to the national insignia.

MORE OCTANE, MORE POWER

During spring 1944, certain 8th AF fighter groups went through a trial testing of utilizing higher octane fuel that permitted the use of higher manifold pressures for more power. Even though this increased spark plug fouling, all 8th AF Mustang groups were ordered to change over from 100/130 to 100/150 octane fuel that summer. This was followed by an increased number of takeoff crashes and the new fuel was suspect. An extensive technical survey failed to find a correlation and the accidents were mainly blamed on incorrect operating measures to minimize the risk of plug fouling during engine operation prior to takeoff.

This increased fouling led to the addition of ethylene dibromide to the 100/150 fuel and this lessened the carbon buildup on the plugs. Known as PEP, this additive was supplied to all U.K. P-51 groups during February 1945. However, this led to another problem—valve seating now required very frequent attention due to either burning away of seating inserts or stretching of stems. During April, the problem was considered serious and a directive calling for inspection each 25 hours of operation was issued. However, engine problems became so frequent that the supply of spare V-1650 engines fell to almost zero and average engine life dropped to under 100 hours—an extremely dismal figure. Since this was affecting combat operations, a return to 100/130 fuel was ordered, but there was difficulty in obtaining and stockpiling the fuel—a true Catch-22 condition!

myself that it might pay a good dividend [the conversion to Rolls-Royce power], if it can be done quickly, to install the Merlin XX in this machine. It would be a relatively quick job, and might fill a very useful interim niche under existing conditions. I am endeavoring to obtain performance data about the aircraft so that the gain that might be anticipated can be estimated. I recall that Air Commodore R. B. Mansell and E. T. Jones, when in the USA, did suggest that the Packard [the car company now building Rolls-Royce engines under license in America—Packard had built the Liberty engine of

It is presumed that this aircraft is one of the two XP-51Bs, but it does not feature any form of identification. What is important is that the very tight cowling does not feature any form of carburetor intake—top or bottom. The only remaining theory is that the intake was inside the modified radiator housing and then run forward to the engine.

World War II fame and started Merlin production with the XX, designated V-1650-1 by the USAAF and assigned to the P-40F] should be fitted into the Mustang aircraft, but it did not get any further."

The Air Ministry voiced some concern since a strong commitment had been given to the production of the Spitfire Mk. V. The Ministry reasoned that the modification of the Mustang would draw valuable resources away from getting the Mk. IX into the frontline to combat the Luftwaffe's potent new threat—the Focke-Wulf Fw 190. This left Harker particularly perplexed, and he later wrote, "...that my proposal was unrealistic, that the Air Ministry would not approve and that there would not be any engines available anyhow as they were all required for the Spitfires—and why waste time on an untried American-built aeroplane?"

One of the XP-51Bs was taken to a NACA tunnel for further testing. The degree of boundary layer bleed for the radiator intake, as well as its shape, had to be adjusted. For, if the scoop intake were dropped too much, drag would increase. In some cases the degree of adjustment was only 1/18-inch and it was wind tunnel testing that allowed such fine tuning changes to be made.

The XP-51B's cowl shape and overall configuration can be seen in this wind tunnel model.

Simple teaching aid displays the Mustang's hydraulic system.

INSIDE THE ROLLS/PACKARD V-1650

This V-12 engine was liquid-cooled and incorporated an aftercooler in addition to the conventional cooling system. The two-speed, two-stage supercharger had a low gear ratio of 6.391:1 and a high gear ratio of 8.095:1. The compression ratio was 6:1. At sea level the engine had a takeoff speed of 3,000 rpm at 61-in. Hg. manifold pressure for 5 minutes of operation. The engine was operated with 100-octane gasoline Spec. AN-F-28. Engine equipment included an integral oil pump, coolant pump, aftercooler pump, and had the following units:

UNIT	MAKE	TYPE
Carburetor	Bendix-Stromberg	Model PD-18A1
Fuel Pump	Pesco	Type G-9
Vacuum Pump	Pesco	Type B-12
Hydraulic Pump	Pesco	Type 582
Starter	Eclipse	Type 840
Generator	Eclipse	Type O-4
Magnetos	General Electric or Delco	Type C-6
Propeller Hub	Hamilton Standard	Model 24D50
Propeller Blade	Hamilton Standard	Model J6487A
Governor	Hamilton Standard	Model 4G10-G21D
Automatic Boost Control		Packard Part No. 615333

The engine had 1,649 ci of piston displacement, and the two cylinder blocks of six cylinders each were arranged in a V of 60 degrees. The induction system consisted of a centrifugal two-speed, two-stage, gear-driven supercharger, which was supplied by a Bendix-Stromberg double-throated, injection type updraft carburetor. A plate-type heat exchanger in the supercharger section cooled the fuel-air mixture before it entered the induction

manifold. The two-piece cylinder blocks had two inlets and two exhaust valves for each cylinder, and an overhead camshaft on each bank actuated the valves. The force-feed lubrication system was of the dry-sump type having three pressure stages. Two magnetos provide ignition, each supplying one of the two spark plugs in each cylinder. On later aircraft, supercharged high-altitude magnetos replaced the Type C-6 magnetos.

The Packard-built V-1650 Merlin would revolutionize Mustang performance.

Despite official reluctance for the Merlin Mustang, E. W. Hives used his political power to have three aircraft transferred to the facility at Hucknall for conversion with Merlin powerplants. Rolls-Royce freely let NAA know what they were doing. NAA was not unaware of the benefits of the modification, and one of the champions of the re-engine program was Maj. Thomas Hitchcock, assistant air attaché at the U.S. Embassy in London. He issued the following memo, dated 8 October 1942, "The reasons for the

remarkably low drag of the Mustangs are not fully understood on this side of the ocean. The English think it is only partly due to the laminar flow wing. The Rolls people became very much interested in the possibilities of the Mustang airframe with the Merlin engine. Estimates were made as to the speeds that could be obtained with the installation of the 61 and 20 Merlin. The Air Ministry instructed the Rolls people to install five Merlin 61 engines in Mustang airplanes. Simultaneously with this development it was

V-1650-7 ENGINE PERFORMANCE DATA (STATIC)

Combat Conditions

3,000 rpm + 25 lbs/sq-in bhp @ SL = 1,940
Max power in MS gear = 1,940 bhp @ SL
Max power in FS gear = 1,810 bhp @ 12,000 feet
Supercharger change in height = 5,000 feet

3,000 rpm + 67-in. Hg. boost pressure, bhp @ SL = 1,630
Max power in MS gear = 1,700 bhp @ 5,750 feet
Max power in FS gear = 1,555 bhp @ 17,750 feet
Supercharger change height = 10,500 feet

3,000 rpm + 61-in. Hg. boost pressure, bhp @ SL = 1,490
Max power in MS gear = 1,580 bhp @ 8,500 feet
Max power in FS gear = 1,400 bhp @ 21,000 feet
Supercharger change in height = 13,400 feet

Climb and Cruise

2,700 rpm + 46-in. Hg. boost pressure, bhp @ SL = 1,050
Max power in MS gear = 1,150 bhp @ 11,250 feet
Max power in FS gear = 1,080 bhp @ 22,000 feet
Supercharger change height = 14,250 feet

Weak Mixture Cruise

2,400 rpm + 36-in. Hg. boost pressure, bhp @ SL = 730
Max power in MS gear = 820 bhp @ 13,000 feet
Max power in FS gear = 755 bhp @ 22,500 feet
Supercharger change height = 16,250 feet

arranged to have the North American Company install a Packard version of the Merlin 61 in the Mustang airframe. Requests were sent to the United States to have the Packard Company start manufacturing Merlin 61s as promptly as possible.

"The interesting qualities of the Mustang airframe were brought to the attention of General Arnold and Admiral Towers when they were in London June last, by the American ambassador [John C. Winant], Air Chief Marshal Sir Charles Portal, Chief of the Air Staff; Air Chief Marshal Sir Sholto Douglas, Commander-in-Chief Fighter Command, and Air Marshal F. J.

A P-51B left wing panel is prepared for the production line. At this stage, the gear, flaps, and ailerons are not installed. At an earlier stage, the first 40 percent of the wing chord was shot with one coat of zinc chromate primer. This was followed by enough coats of Acme Gray Surfacer No. 53N5 to cover all irregularities. Skin butt joints were then filled with Acme Red Vellunite glazing putty No. 58485. The entire area was then sanded down and sprayed with one coat of camouflage enamel. When camouflage was deleted, the forward portion of the wing (and sometimes the entire wing) was sprayed aluminum.

Linnell, Ministry of Aircraft Production Research and Development. Robert Lovett, Assistant Secretary for War for Air, was also advised by letter, dated 5 June 1942, of the importance, which English and various American representatives attach to the Mustang airframe and the desirability of energetically pursuing the Merlin development.

Dutch Kindelberger would create a very efficient P-51B production line where parts and components would smoothly flow together to create a complete aircraft.

"Mr. Phil Legarra, North American representative, reported when he came back from the United States in the early part of September that the Mustang had the lowest priority that could be granted to an airplane.

"The Mustang is one of the best, if not the best, fighter airframes that has been developed in the war up to date… its development and use in this theater has suffered for various reasons. Sired by the English out of an American mother, the Mustang has no parent in the Army Air Corps or at Wright Field to appreciate and push its good points.

"Important people on both sides of the Atlantic seem more interested in pointing with pride to the development of a 100 percent national product than they are concerned with the very difficult problem of rapidly developing a fighter plane that will be superior to anything the Germans have."

Although Hitchcock's feelings were well placed, he did not know that work was going on to make the Merlin Mustang a reality. Gen. Hap Arnold had seen the potential in the design and Brig. Gen. Oliver Echols, Arnold's Chief, Materiel Division, was instructed to get the concept into reality. From 1940 onward, Echols had been responsible for setting up the license-built Packard Merlin production line, and he quietly made sure that two new V-1650-3s were transferred to NAA for the XP-78 project (the Merlin Mustang had been given this new designation, but it was to be short-lived).

The entire right gear assembly and clamshell door had been installed as the P-51B wing panel moved down the line. Bendix made the gear under contract. Note how the leading portion of the wing had received its layer of filler and a coat of primer. At this stage, the phenolic resin external stores shackle had also been installed.

In Britain, Mustang AM121 was sent to Hucknall on 7 June 1942 to form the basis for the first conversion. The aircraft was followed by AL963, AL975, AM203, and AM208 (the last two were added to the Rolls-Royce program by the request of the USAAF). Some initial flying was done with AM121 in its stock condition to obtain performance data. At an early stage in the conversion, a decision was made to use the Merlin 65 instead of the 61, and the first aircraft made ready for flight was AL975G, which flew on 13 October 1942. The aircraft was given the designation Mustang X. The second X to fly was AM208, which went aloft on 13 November. AL975 featured a large air scoop under the Merlin 65 and was not a particularly attractive aircraft. Each Mustang X featured slightly different physical characteristic.

The nearly complete wing panels (including flaps, gear, ailerons, and stress doors) have been joined and moved into the production hangar.

Right P-51B wing panel on a floor dolly. Fuel tanks and gear were not fitted and this view shows how the interior of the wing was (or was not) finished.

As techniques improved and space became available, the P-51B wings had their own production line and at this stage the wings were at their aileron assembly stations. Note tires waiting installation on the left.

SPINNING THE P-51B

USAAF tests revealed the Merlin-powered Mustang had different spinning characteristics than the Allison aircraft.

ARMY AIR FORCES MATERIEL COMMAND
MEMORANDUM REPORT ON:
P-51B Airplane, AAF No. 42-12136
SUBJECT: Spin Tests   DATE: 30 April 1944

A.   PURPOSE

To report the results of spin investigations conducted on the P-51B airplane, AAF No. 42-12136.

B.   FACTUAL DATA

1.   Introduction

The airplane was spun by Maj. G. E. Lundquist, Maj. P. J. Ritchie, and Capt. W. A. Lien of the Flight Section. Completed spin forms were submitted by these pilots. A total of 30 spins were made in each direction with methods of entry from straight ahead stalls, turns, and snap rolls, power on and power off.

2.   Airplane Configuration

The gross weight of the airplane at takeoff was 9,130 pounds, with the CG location at 27.0 percent MAC, gear up. Spin chutes were installed on the tail. Spins were made with wheels and flaps up and with coolant and oil shutters in automatic.

3.   Spin Characteristics

A consolidation of the pilots' comments on the spin characteristics is as follows:

a.   Left spin (power off)

From a straight ahead stall entry, the airplane rolls sharply with the nose oscillating from 80 degrees below the horizon back to the horizon during the first turn. The oscillations dampen out considerably during the second turn after which the spin continues with the nose oscillating 30 to 40 degrees below the horizon. During the first two turns, the spin is very rough and as the oscillations dampen out the spin becomes more smooth. A slight rudder buffet occurs throughout the spin, seeming to buffet in phase with the oscillations of the spin.

When entering the spin from a left turn, a partial snap roll occurs, followed by falling with the nose down and a very slow rate of rotation. The nose gradually comes up into oscillation and the spin becomes identical in characteristics as above.

Recovery was made by applying full opposite rudder and moving the control stick slightly forward of neutral. Control movements were rapid. Upon application of opposite rudder the nose drops slightly and the spin speeds up from 3/4 to one turn after which the spin stops. It was noticed that recovery was quicker if opposite rudder was applied during the nose down part of the oscillation.

Approximately 3,700 feet was lost in a two-turn spin and 6,500 feet in a five-turn spin for the entire maneuver.

b.   Right spin (power off)

The right spin starts exactly the same as the left, but the oscillations continue without changing in magnitude with the nose approximately 40 to 50 degrees below the horizon. Recovery is affected more quickly, however, with the spin stopping in 1/4 to 1/2 turn after opposite rudder was applied. Approximately 3,000 feet was lost in a two-turn spin and 6,300 feet in a five-turn spin.

c.   Left spin (power on)

With the power on at 20-in. Hg./2,300 rpm, straight stall entry, the airplane oscillates in spin from 15 degrees above to 60 degrees below the horizon. When power is cut the spin becomes similar to the power off spin. With increased power the oscillations become so violent that power must be cut off and recovery affected, as the oscillations do not tend to decrease when the power is cut.

Recovery was made with the power off and was similar in procedure to that used in a normal power off spin. Power on spin recovery was not attempted. Approximately 5,000 feet were lost in a two-turn spin.

d.   Right spin (power on)

With the power at 20-in. Hg./2,300 rpm, straight stall entry, the first turn of the spin is flat and slow. The oscillation then becomes similar to the power off spin. With power cut off recovery was normal.

e. Recovery characteristics

There appears to be a danger of over controlling on recovery. Generally, there are two phases in the spin when recovery can be started, one being at the peak of the oscillation and the other when the oscillations have decreased to a minimum. If recovery is made at the minimum oscillating point, neutralizing the stick and rudder is sufficient to stop the spin immediately. If full opposite controls are used, a spin the opposite direction is apt to result.

If full recovery controls are applied at the peak of oscillation, no effect is obtained until the oscillation stops. At this point, recovery will occur and if controls are not neutralized immediately, a spin in the opposite direction will result.

In the dive recovery, the elevator force is very light and caution must be observed not to attempt too fast a recovery as over acceleration will result.

4. Effect of Spin Chutes on Recovery

Left and right spins were executed by Maj. G. E. Lundquist using the tailspin chutes to assist in recovery. When the chutes are opened after a two-turn spin, the nose of the airplane drops. The speed of the spin increases and oscillations decrease in magnitude. A normal recovery can be executed in 1/4 to 1/2 turn.

C. CONCLUSIONS

1. The spin characteristics of the P-51B are satisfactory for this type airplane, although there seems to be less consistency in regards to attitude in spin, oscillations, and difference between left and right spins, than was found in the P-51 or P-51A.
2. The danger of over controlling in recovery exists, for at the point of minimum oscillation opposite controls will begin a spin in the opposite direction.
3. Power should be cut immediately if a power-on spin is entered, as the power-on spin is very violent. Power off recovery can be easily executed.
4. Tailspin chutes are effective in assisting in recovery from spins on the P-51B, as control can be effected within 1/4 to 1/2 turn after the chutes are opened and recovery controls applied.

D. RECOMMENDATIONS

1. It is recommended that no intentional power-on spins should be attempted with this airplane. If a power-on spin is entered from any position, the power should be cut immediately and recovery controls applied.
2. It is recommended that the airplane be restricted from snap rolls as it does a very poor snap roll and usually ends up in a spin.

Firmly attached to a floor dolly, the P-51B wing section moved forward to receive final items.

Bill Lappin invited Lt. Col. Cass Hough (a USAAF technical officer at HQ VIII Fighter Command) to travel to Hucknall and fly one of the Mustang X aircraft. Hough would write, "General 'Monk' Hunter was reluctant to give me the okay because it was an experimental aircraft; but he did it, with the admonition, 'If you break your neck don't blame me!' I took my P-47 there for all the hands to see and fly while I was to have a go at the 'new' Mustang.

"I just assumed it would be a conventional airplane because nobody told me anything. The only information I got from Bill Lappin was that the first flights that had been made up at Hucknall resulted in the pilots being just delighted with the airplane.

"Flying a new airplane, I always put the power on easily at the start to get the feel of the airplane on the ground, then gradually give it power. When I got airborne, a couple hundred feet off the ground, I pulled the gear and decided then I'd see how it would climb from scratch. I poured the coal to it and the aircraft snap rolled! Rolls-Royce hadn't provided enough vertical fin area, and not enough offset.

"I was eager to get it to altitude and see how it performed because that was the critical thing then. I studied the fuel curves of the Merlin in several other airframes so I knew what the range of the airplane would be on internal fuel, but I didn't know how the airplane would actually handle at high-altitude because no one had ever gotten an Allison-powered Mustang above 24,000 or 25,000 feet.

"Ordinarily, the two-stage blowers, the early ones, were manually operated on the Spitfires. I had just begun to think it was time to change blowers—

Raised from the wing assembly area, a nearly complete wing is lowered to the factory floor.

I hadn't even inquired where the handle was for changing it—when all of a sudden I got this big 'chug' and a thump around 16,000 feet and of course it was then in high blower. But I was about ready to make sure my chute harness was okay, and wishing I could change my drawers! There was an automatic supercharger gear change and it was a complete surprise.

"I got up to about 33,000 feet with it and it was so maneuverable; and I could tell without making any speed runs, assuming the airspeed indicator was calibrated reasonably carefully, that it was performing wonderfully. I just couldn't believe some of the things I saw after doing a couple of speed runs with it."

Back in Inglewood, NAA and the USAAF had been kept informed of the British work and there was a great deal of interest. On 12 June 1942, a Merlin project was authorized by the USAAF and on 24 July, NAA submitted NA-101. The proposal featured a more sophisticated appearing aircraft than the Rolls-Royce modification. Contract W535 AC-32073 was signed on 31 July for the new aircraft, which received the USAAF designation XP-78. Since the P-51s were being built under Lend-Lease, it meant the aircraft were the property of the U.S. government and two aircraft were pulled from the con-

As the wings move down the line, complete P-51B tail sections were carried overhead en route to the assembly line.

tract. The aircraft were 41-37352 (the 33rd P-51, c/n 91-12013) and 41-37421 (the 102nd aircraft, c/n 91-12082). Designation was changed to XP-51B during September.

The extensive modifications were undertaken in a small room in the new engineering building. Packard would supply the V-1650-3 variant of the Merlin that had a two-stage supercharger for high-altitude performance. The engine weighed 335 pounds more than the Allison and it also had an intercooler for the supercharger. This meant that everything firewall forward would be new, while all the ducting and cooling intakes under the fuselage would also be new.

Packard and Rolls-Royce worked quite closely and Packard informed Rolls that the V-1650-3 would differ considerably from the Merlin 61. There were 18 major differences and these included a new carburetor, automatic supercharger speed shift, water-alcohol injection for emergency power, more durable ball-bearing water pump, new Delco magnetos, and a centrifugal separator to prevent the foaming of oil. Packard supplied thousands of engineering drawings to Rolls-Royce to document their various modifications to the Merlin.

Having visited aircraft companies in the United States, Germany, and Britain, Kindelberger was able to refine his concept of creating a production line that would be as simple as possible. One of his major contributions was the decision to build the Mustang fuselage in halves. This way internal equipment could be easily installed, rather than battling internally to finish the aircraft after the fuselage was basically complete. This portion of the P-51B production line comprised the right side of the fuselage.

Lowered onto individual floor dollies, the tail sections move toward final assembly. During this process, more items were added to each unit.

Brief Summary of Changes on Fighter Planes

This NAA document, centered on P-51B-5-NA production, illustrates the constant changes being made on the Mustang production line.

- A Type A-1 bomb gun sight head and periscopic mirror have been installed.
- A remote-reading compass has been installed in lieu of the Type B-16 magnetic compass.
- AAF Specification AN-C-80 has been complied with, covering the prevention of engine corrosion.
- An electric automatic coolant and oil radiator scoop activator has been installed, effective on P-51B-5-NA AAF 43-6513 and subsequent.
- Existing medium pressure hydraulic hose has been replaced with low temperature hose (-65 degreesF) meeting Specification AN-H-6 and having detachable end fittings.
- Amber, red, and green recognition lights have been installed on the underside of the right wingtip and a white light has been incorporated on top of the fuselage, effective on P-51B-5-NA AAF 43-6613 and subsequent.
- 1,000-ohm, 1/4-watt resistor has been substituted for the 4,000-ohm resistor in the SCR-522 volume control.
- Engine covers have been supplied to meet Specification 98-26751-F, Amendment No. 2, effective on P-51B-5-NA AAF 43-6513 and subsequent.
- Main landing gear struts have been reworked to improve cold weather operation. (Reference AAF Drawing X43B2292.)
- Vim leather packings (X43B2237-10-200) have been incorporated in the tail struts.
- Circuit protectors have been added in the generator circuit to back up the reverse-current relay, effective on P-51B-5-NA AAF 43-6713 and subsequent.
- The hydraulic hand-pump has been redesigned to incorporate O ring packings to improve cold weather operation effective on P-51B-5-NA AAF 43-6912 and subsequent.
- Wiring has been deleted for the battery-disconnect solenoid switch that was safetied through the ignition switch.
- A separate battery-disconnect circuit-breaker type switch has been installed.
- The ignition switch has been changed from Type A-9 to Type A-8, effective on P-51B-5-NA AAF 43-6713 and subsequent.
- A two-cell "Pen-lite" type flashlight has been provided for, on the left-hand underside of the instrument panel shroud, effective on P-51B-5-NA AAF 43-6413 and subsequent.
- A rheostat has been installed for use with the A-7 cockpit lights, effective on P-51B-5-NA AAF 43-6713 and subsequent.
- The pilot's wooden seat has been replaced by a magnesium seat, effective on P-51B-5-NA AAF 43-6713 and subsequent.
- To eliminate a fire hazard, the fuel tank bay has been sealed from the gun bay.
- The access hole in the front spar, inboard of rib station 75, has been provided with a cover, screwed to the spar, and sealed with vinyl adhesive resin.
- The SCR-535A Group A and Group B, including antenna, have been deleted.
- The ailerons were revised and strengthened to take the increased loads imposed as a result of the sealed balance aileron installation.
- One A-1 drop message bag has been installed in the cockpit. A phenolic sheet holder has been attached to the map and report case assembly, effective on P-51B-5-NA AAF 43-6513 and subsequent.
- Until the holder assembly was installed, the message bay was installed in the map case, effective on P-51B-5-NA AAF 43-6313/6512, inclusive.
- The clear vision panel has been deleted.
- A positive lock control has been added to the bomb rack solenoid, effective on P-51B-5-NA AAF 43-6613 and subsequent.
- The 75-gallon combat ferry tanks have been pressurized for operation up to 30,000 feet, effective on P-51B-5-NA AAF 43-6913 and subsequent.
- A fuel tank shelf has been provided above the 85-gallon fuselage fuel tank, effective on P-51B-5-NA AAF 43-6713 and subsequent.
- The fuel lines have been revised to accommodate the 85-gallon fuselage fuel tank, effective on P-51B-5-NA AAF 43-6913 and subsequent.

- The propeller anti-icing system has been deleted.
- Generator conduit has been removed and replaced with open wiring, effective on P-51B-5-NA AAF 43-6413 and subsequent.
- A new insignia has been provided to conform to AAF Specification AN-1-9A.
- Scraper rings have been substituted for boots on hydraulic struts, effective on P-51B-5-NA AAF 43-6513 and subsequent.
- All manufacturing dates have been removed from NAA manufactured and furnished parts, effective on P-51B-5-NA AAF 43-6513 and subsequent.
- A canvas cover over the engine cowling fixed front baffle has been deleted.
- In lieu of a carburetor heat rise installation, the following has been accomplished:
  - Carburetor rear duct has been revised to eliminate the mechanically operated door in the upper skin.
  - A spring-loaded icing air gate has been installed on each side of the duct.
  - The hot air scoop, located just aft of the exhaust stacks, has been removed and the opening closed with a coverplate.
  - The nameplate on top of the control pedestal has been revised to make the hot air controls inoperative.
- A filter has been installed in the hydraulic feed line to protect the automatic temperature control, effective on P-51B-5-NA AAF 43-6314/6512, inclusive.
- Provisions for carrying the AN-M-14 incendiary grenade have been deleted, effective on P-51B-5-NA AAF 43-6713 and subsequent.
- The oil dilution solenoid valve has been reworked. A rubber-insulated valve has been incorporated in place of the former type, effective on P-51B-5-NA AAF 43-6363 and subsequent.
- The hydraulic automatic scoop regulator has been relocated to a vertical position on the right-hand side of the fuselage, effective on P-51B-5-NA AAF 43-6317/6512, inclusive.
- Engine covers are no longer delivered as loose equipment, but are shipped separately.
- The AN-104-A antenna mast has been installed in lieu of the NAA furnished mast, effective on P-51B-5-NA AAF 43-6913 and subsequent.
- The coolant header tank has been redesigned to give increased performance at high altitudes.
- The radio antenna installation has been revised to accommodate the Detrola receiver only.
- An external power receptacle and an identifying stencil have been located behind the right-hand fuselage-to-wing fillet, effective on P-51B-5-NA AAF 43-6414 and subsequent.
- The antenna base has been grounded by removing the plastic block and mounting the mast on the removable inspection plate.
- Link ejection chutes have been redesigned to eliminate the jamming of links in the chute.
- A GFE [Government Furnished Equipment] charging handle has been permanently installed in each gun bay.
- Low-impedance headsets have been permanently installed in each gun bay.
- Provisions for the MC-385 adapter have been made effective on P-51B-5-NA AAF 43-6613 and subsequent.
- A Type 01-C rheostat has replaced the 01-B rheostat in the gun sight, effective on P-51B-5-NA AAF 43-6513/6712, inclusive.
- A Mazda 844 lamp has been installed in lieu of an RP-11 lamp, effective on P-51B-5-NA AAF 43-6513 and subsequent.
- Low pressure, low temperature hose in the instrument line has been changed to hose having a temperature range of -65 degreesF to +160 degreesF, effective on P-51B-5-NA AAF 43-6413 and subsequent.
- The Type N-4 camera was GFE and Government installed. It is now Contractor installed, effective on P-51B-5-NA AAF 43-6513 and subsequent.
- A spring-loaded high-blower test switch has been added. It is necessary to hold the switch in the high-blower position. The remote compass has been wired through the battery switch, effective on P-51B-5-NA AAF 43-6513 and subsequent.
- The wing structure has been reinforced to withstand the increased aileron forces.
- The T-30-P microphone and M299 microphone adapter have been installed.
- The pilot's wooden seat back has been reinforced to withstand harness loads in crash landings, effective on P-51B-5-NA AAF 43-6413 and subsequent.
- One set of sway bracing for the 75-gallon combat fuel tanks has been provided as loose equipment.
- Lord shock mounts on the remote indicating compass have been changed from 2 to 1 pound, effective on P-51B-5-NA AAF 43-6338 and subsequent.

- Fluorescent markers have been incorporated to indicate the operational limits of engine instruments in lieu of non-fluorescent paint.
- The oil dilution valve has been relocated to a point below the oil level in the oil tank.
- An AC770-2 petcock has been mounted on the firewall near the lower removable cowl and a drain line connected to the oil tank sump.
- A self-locking drain cock has been installed in the hole provided for the drain plug in the oil inlet line.

- Provisions have been eliminated for permanently installed oil immersion heaters.
- A loose baffle has been provided in the rear exit duct so that the engine and aftercooler radiator exit may be fully closed.
- The diaphragm oil pressure transmitter has been deleted and a return made to 1/4-inch line with gauge fitting, 43A14984, and check valve, 48A14985, effective on P-51B-5-NA AAF 43-6414 and subsequent.

A new motor mount cradled the Merlin and it was built out of aluminum alloy and box beam in construction. The mount was designed so that it could easily be removed with engine attached. To more efficiently absorb the Merlin's power, the engine would be mated to a Hamilton Standard propeller that was some 11 feet 2-inches in diameter. The new propeller was tested by Chilton on Mustang AL958 and few problems were encountered. However, the company's first V-1650-3 failed during ground running tests and a second engine was loaded in a C-47 and flown from Wright Field to Inglewood, arriving on 18 November 1942. Chilton got aloft in the first XP-51B (s/n 41-37352) on 30 November, but after about 45 minutes the gauges showed that something was going wrong with the Merlin as the oil temperature began to drastically rise while pressure dropped. Heading immediately back to the field, the Mustang

This view of a P-51B left fuselage half illustrates the relative simplicity of the Mustang's construction. The gear handle, trim console, and underwing stores salvo control are all in place as are the hydraulic lines for the retractable tail wheel. The large metal bar in the middle of the fuselage was part of the rollover structure to protect the pilot, while the circular opening to the rear was an access panel for the fuselage cables. The brown leatherette aircraft document case was immediately behind the rear viewing panel.

Right side of the P-51B fuselage showing considerably more wiring along with the oxygen bottles. The low-pressure oxygen system employed D-2 type low-pressure, externally reinforced cylinders. Note how the forward fuselage (the area forward of station 184, the second frame behind the cockpit), except areas between the radio shelf and the radiator air scoop not normally visible, were finished in Yellow Green, sometimes referred to as NAA Green. The rear section was left bare metal.

was trailing a telltale stream of white smoke. Chilton got the plane safely back on the ground, but the Merlin was finished. However, the USAAF had, this time, fully realized the potential of the Mustang airframe mated with the Merlin engine and even before the prototype had been flown, the original contract for the P-51A was modified to reduce the number of Allison machines and complete the contract with 800 P-51B-5-NA and 90 P-51B-10-NA aircraft (all under designation NA-104) while contract W535 AC-33940 was issued on 28 December for 1,350 P-51C-NT Mustangs (initial work had begun on 8 October) to be built at the new Dallas factory (NA-103). The contract for the P-51B-NA (W535 AC-33923, Model NA-102) covering 400 aircraft was not signed until 28 December. On 12 November 1942, Gen. Hap Arnold wrote to Pres. Roosevelt that some 2,290 Mustangs were now underway.

Arnold and other commanders realized that the war must be taken directly into Germany to bomb military and civilian targets into submis-sion. Obviously, an efficient escort fighter would be needed to protect the bombers from a very motivated Luftwaffe fighter force. On 20 February 1942, Arnold held a conference among his commanders on increasing the range of USAAF fighters. On 21 March 1942, a more extensive conference on this problem was held at the Materiel Division at Wright Field. A document *Case History of Fighter Airplane Range Extension Program* drawn up well after these conferences reported that, "Study and flight test of the fighter airplanes indicated that the P-51B consumed an average of 64 gallons of fuel in an hour, the P-38J an average of 144 gph, and the P-47D an average of 140 gph. The P-51 carried enough fuel for 4.45 hours and, therefore, needed an additional 112 gallons in order to meet the required 6 hours plus 30 minutes for reserve.

"By August 1943, there was already developed a leak-proof droppable fuel tank of 150-gallon capacity for the P-38 and a similar tank of 75-gallon

Complete P-51B motor mount on dolly and on its way to be mated with a fuselage firewall. Some early P-51Bs in combat had the motor mount tear away from the airframe. Bolts and nuts were found to be under strength and sometimes poorly installed. An urgent order to replace all bolts and nuts cured the deadly problem.

Rosie the Riveter torques exhaust stack bolts on a V-1650-3 as it rolls down the production line. Note the custom tool holders that would mount on the bare metal cowl former for easy access as equipment was installed. This photograph shows the header tank, which was a reservoir for engine coolant, and separated air from hot coolant exiting the engine. The header tank was a complex piece of equipment built by NAA and fitted with four Acme Aircraft castings (exit and filler nozzles).

MX-241: MUSTANGS AND BAZOOKAS

From battlefield to the sky, a ground weapon went airborne. It made sense to try to adapt this potent weapon to being carried aloft under the wings of an airplane.

General Dwight D. Eisenhower in his *Tools of Victory* included the bazooka (along with the atomic bomb, Jeep, and C-47) as one of the key items in America's World War II victory. The bazooka started out as a simple and effective shoulder-mounted rocket launcher that caused havoc among the enemy's armor forces (the actual concept for the recoilless weapon had been created by Dr. Robert H. Goddard, dean of America's rocket pioneers).

The somewhat unusual name is credited to stage comedian Bob Burns who, during the 1930s, created a tubular musical instrument to use in his act. However, there was also a bubble gum by that name along with a cartoon character.

"When we got the bazookas, our crew chiefs got busy installing them under the wings of our Mustangs [P-51As]," recalled former American Volunteer Group pilot Robert T. 'R. T.' Smith. "Once we figured out how to work those suckers, we really got down to business. One time I put three of the rockets through the front door of a Jap factory. Whatever was in there blew the hell out of the building and nearly flipped the Mustang over as I passed through the explosion."

Smith, who was flying with the First Air Commandos, and his fellow pilots, used the bazookas in daring attacks against Japanese targets. "One mission had us flying against a Jap airfield," stated the ace. "We got flying line abreast and salvoed the bazookas as one and it tore the hell out of the field. Plus, we were hosing the place with our machine guns on the entire run in to the target."

Today, the utilization of this effective weapon is not particularly well remembered as part of the Mustang's armament package. However, NAA engineers and the USAAF worked closely together to make the package particularly effective. At NAA, the bazooka project received the designation of MX-241 and extensive testing was undertaken. Bazooka units were shipped directly to the combat areas along with appropriate technical orders for installation and use.

P-51B-10-NA 43-7113 (first of the -10 block) was photographed on 31 August 1944 at Inglewood as tests were being carried out with the MX-241 system. In this portion of the flight tests, the aircraft was fitted with two M-14 steel three-tube launchers fitted to T-30 mounts.

For flight testing, the P-51B/Ds were not fitted with .50-cal. machine guns so that fine tuning could be done to the wiring. As can be seen, the wiring ran from the launchers up through the gun bays and into the cockpit.

The fittings for the M-14 tubes were placed outside the standard underwing pylon.

Plywood insets cover the rear of the tubes. Note the extensive clamping on the M-14 launcher. The Mustang could also be fitted with the M-10 launcher that was similar but built from strengthened plastic.

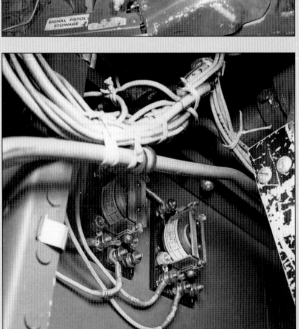

The MX-241 control panel was sandwiched between the throttle assembly and the signal pistol port. The rockets could be fired individually or in salvo. Also, the entire assembly could be jettisoned in flight.

Once attached, the MX-241 was a formidable piece of equipment. Each bazooka tube held a 4.5-inch M-8 rocket fitted with an M-4 fuse. Note the heavy steel strapping that kept the tubes together.

MX-241 wiring and relays running through the Mustang's wing and into the fuselage.

P-51D-15-NA 44-14886 on a test flight with the MX-241 system over west Los Angeles.

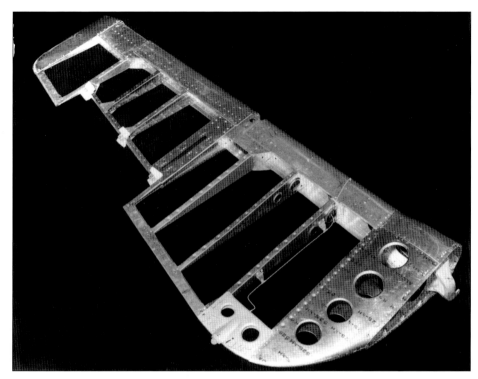

capacity for the P-51. At the same time, the Materiel Command initiated action to construct a paper tank similar to the British 108-gallon paper tank. Adequate production quantities of the various range extension tanks became available as a result of the decided increase in production after October 1943. The production schedule called for 22,000 tanks to be delivered during the month of November 1943. This monthly volume was not actually achieved until April 1944, when approximately 25,000 tanks were delivered. In June 1944, eleven prime contractors delivered over 48,000 tanks.

Simple yet strong P-51B rudder before covering. The recognition light and wiring are in place, but the large slot awaits installation of the phenolic resin trim tab. The aluminum skin retained its original stamping, and it is interesting to note the rudders did not receive a protective spray of zinc chromate. The rudder utilized a single spar with flanged Alclad ribs attached, a V-trailing edge piece and a beam for attachment of the trim tab. The leading edge of the rudder was cut out for the vertical tail's hinge fittings, the unit being hinged to the vertical tail with three sealed ball bearings. The rudder was dynamically balanced with a 16.6-pound lead weight fitted to the top, while an additional balance weight at the bottom of the leading edge helped reduce static unbalance. The trim tab was also hinged by three sealed needle bearings.

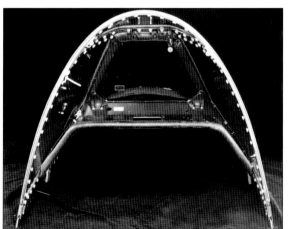
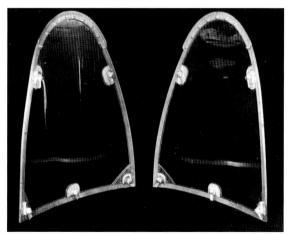

The P-51B's windscreen, canopy structure, and rear panel windows. Although it may look simple, the canopy framework was comprised of more than 1,200 pieces. The main portion of the canopy had a panel on each side that could be manually slid to the rear by the pilot via knobbed handles seen in the photo. The flat forward section of the canopy was 5-ply, laminated 1.5 inches thick, bulletproof, and slanted 31 degrees back from the vertical when installed on the aircraft. The windscreen's side and upper panels consisted of 3/16-inch-thick plexiglass.

Left console area of a P-51D-5-NA showing throttle and mixture control, bomb control and anti-salvo guard, landing gear handle and rudder, elevator, and aileron trim tab controls.

A Packard V-1650-3 is carefully lowered into the motor mount, which was now attached to the fuselage. At this point, the fuselage had been mated with the wing and tail section.

P-51B center fuselages turn at the north end of the fuselage line. More equipment was added to the fuselage as it moved forward.

"Additional fuel, it was believed, could be carried in the thin outer portion of the P-51B wing by means of a wing change. However, this change was not advised. It would require such redesign that production would be 'far in the future.' Moreover, the rate of roll of the airplane would be decreased and the additional weight caused by leak proofing the thin tanks would be uneconomical for the small fuel increase.

"But the internal fuel capacity of the P-51B/C was increased by the installation of one 85-gallon self-sealing fuselage tank. This increased the built-in fuel capacity to a total of 269 gallons and, at the same time, increased the weight, including fuel, approximately 650 pounds. As was to be expected, this weight increase resulted in considerably reducing the performance of the airplane. The rate of climb was reduced by about 470 fpm and the flying characteristics at altitudes above 25,000 feet were seriously affected. Furthermore, the airplane was sluggish and the acceleration obtainable without stall was very low. When the additional fuel tank was placed in the rear of the fuselage, the longitudinal stability was marginal until the rear tank was partially emptied." However, there was no doubt that the P-51B/C—combined with its superior airframe and relative thriftiness of the Merlin fuel consumption— would be the fighter aircraft that would take the war directly to the German heartland. The fact that the 85-gallon fuselage tank would cause problems did

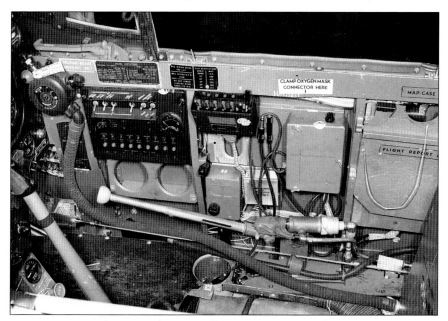

P-51B-1-NA *right console area illustrating engine limitations placard, SCR-522, and SCR-535 radio control boxes.*

Nearly fully equipped P-51B cockpit. Items of note include rear-view mirror mounted on the upper portion of the windscreen, a crash pad atop the instrument panel shroud, and basic flight instruments arranged in the central panel. The devices mounted to the lower right and left of the windscreen are movable fluorescent lights.

HOW DID THE MUSTANG COMPARE?

During summer 1943, the USAAF tested the P-51B against the P-51A, Thunderbolt, Lightning, Airacobra, and Warhawk.

Army Air Forces Board Project No. (M-1) 50
Tactical Employment Trials On North American P-51B-1 Airplane

Level Speeds

The P-51B-1 is capable of very high speeds at altitude. It is important in operations to keep the wing skin and the finish in good condition, free from rough spots, dents, and deep scratches. Airflow disturbances in the boundary layer region will materially affect speed performance. The average level flight maximum speed is about 435 mph at 30,000 feet at 3,000 rpm and 61-in. Hg. manifold pressure. Two 1,000-pound bombs reduce maximum speed by about 45 mph. The bomb racks alone cost approximately 15 mph loss in speed. From sea level to 11,000 feet the P-51B is 7 to 10 mph slower than the P-51A, which is the fastest fighter at that altitude.

Between 14,000 and 22,000 feet, the P-51B is about 15 to 20 mph faster; and from 22,000 feet up, the P-51B, in high blower, widens the speed advantage up to 75 mph true at 30,000 feet.

From sea level, the P-51B gradually gains on the P-38J and the P-47D until, at 16,000 feet, it has a speed of about 420 mph, which is about 10 mph faster than the P-38J and about 20 mph faster than the P-47D. Above 27,000 feet, the P-51B can no longer get War Emergency Power, but its speed of about 430 mph at 30,000 feet is equal to that of the P-47D and about 20 mph faster than that of the P-38J, both using War Emergency Power. The P-51B is capable of 400 mph at 40,000 feet.

Climb

The P-51B-1 is by far the best climbing of all current American fighter types, taking about 4.5 minutes to get to 15,000 feet, as against 5 minutes for the P-38J-1, and about 7 minutes for the P-47D-10. The P-51B maintains a lead of about .5 minute over the P-38J to 30,000 feet and reaches that altitude in about 11 minutes, which is about 6.5 minutes faster than the P-47D.

Zoom Climbs

In zooming the P-51B with the P-47D-10 from level flight at cruising and high speeds, and from high speeds out of dives, the P-51B gains speed rapidly and leaves the P-47D far behind. In zooming the P-51B with the P-38J, from level flight at cruising speed, the airplanes climb evenly at the start; however, the P-51B falls off while the P-38J keeps climbing. In zooms from high speeds (425-mph IAS), the P-51B pulls away from the P-38J and its zoom ends considerably higher.

Dive

The diving characteristics of the P-51B are superior to those of any other fighter type airplane. It is exceptionally easy to handle and requires very little trimming. The P-51B dives away from all other fighters except the P-47D, against which the P-51B jumps several hundred feet ahead in the initial pushover and then holds that position, apparently neither gaining nor losing distance.

Aileron Roll

With the new seal-balanced ailerons, the P-51B has a faster rate of roll at all speeds than any other fighter except the P-47D, the two being equal at cruising speeds.

Search View

The search view in the P-51B is better than in the P-51A, but is still obstructed above and to both sides and to the rear by the design and construction of the canopy. The view forward over the nose is considerably improved over the P-51A by the relocation of the carburetor air intake scoop, the elimination of the clear view panel on the left side of the windshield, and lowering of the nose of the engine 1.5 degrees.

Fighting Qualities

General

The fighting qualities of the P-51B were compared with those of the P-47D-10 and the P-38J-5 and, briefly, with the P-39N and P-40N (each aircraft carried normal combat load). The only maneuver the P-39 and P-40 have that is superior to the P-51B is a slight advantage in turning circle. In all other maneuvers, as well as performance, they are both far inferior. The P-51B has good performance at all altitudes, but above 20,000 feet the performance improves rapidly and its best fighting altitude is between 25,000 and 35,000 feet. The rate-of-climb is outstanding with an average of about 3,000 fpm from sea level to 25,000 feet. Above 20,000 feet, the overall fighting qualities of this aircraft are superior to those of all the other types used in the trials.

P-51B-1 Versus P-47D-10

The P-51B has a much smaller turning circle than the P-47D-10 and is able to get in behind the P-47D in 1.5 to 2 turns after a head-on approach. The war emergency speed of the P-47D-10 is comparable to that of the P-51B up to 30,000 feet, but above this altitude the speed of the P-51B increases rapidly over that of the P-47D. If the P-51B is jumped by the P-47D, it can turn into the P-47D and rapidly maneuver on to its tail. Dive, rate-of-climb, and acceleration of the P-51B are superior to those of the P-47D. The P-51B also holds its high speed longer than the P-47D in level flight after a dive, because it decelerates much slower.

P-51B Versus P-38J-5

The turning circle of the P-51B is smaller than that of the P-38J-5 at all altitudes. It has a far faster rate of aileron roll through all speeds. The P-51B accelerates rapidly away from the P-38J in a dive after reaching speeds of 325 mph IAS. When full power is applied, the P-38J will pull several hundred feet out in front before the P-51B can reach maximum acceleration and overtake the P-38J. If the P-38J has built up speed in a dive and is not seen in time, the P-51B can turn sharply into the P-38J and evades its fire. The P-38J cannot follow the P-51B at high diving speed at altitude, due to its lower limits of allowable diving speeds. At high speed, it is impossible for the P-38J to keep its sights on the P-51B due to the P-51B's rapid rate of aileron roll, allowing it to reverse its direction of turn faster than the P-38J can follow.

Escort

With its long range, high cruising speeds, and excellent fighting qualities, the P-51B airplane is very good for escort work. Pilot fatigue caused by poor cockpit ventilation and the not too comfortable seats are disadvantages for long-range flights.

Servicing

Complete servicing of the airplane with fuel, oil, oxygen, ammunition, radio check, and coolant for both systems requires approximately 18 minutes with a crew of nine men.

---

not matter in the face of the importance of the mission.

NAA had a huge amount riding on these new contracts and the first flight and engine failure with the XP-51B revealed, not surprisingly, cooling problems. Years later, Schmued wrote, "We opened up the whole [cooling] system, pulled out the radiator, opened the radiator header, and found that it was completely clogged up with corrosion particles that looked like popcorn. How did this happen? We did not know then that the Merlin engine had copper tubing embedded in its aluminum castings for the internal cooling circulation. Our aluminum radiator was not compatible with copper tubing. The cooling liquid provided an electrolyte and set up a battery, causing a very severe corrosion, aggravated by the heat of the system. We were really in trouble because aircraft were coming off the production line, and we had extensive cooling problems."

Since this was a problem that could throw the contracts into disarray, Schmued traveled to the Bureau of Standards in Washington, D.C., with plenty of paper work and photographs to see if the Bureau could help. Schmued recalled that this was on a weekend, he was afraid he would have to wait as the bureaucratic system took its weekend vacation. However, the Bureau fully understood the gravity of the situation and assigned a qualified employee to work with Schmued. The initial solution for the problem appeared quite simple: Slosh the radiator with Keg-Liner, as this was a lacquer liquid that was utilized in beer kegs to isolate the liquid from the metal.

Back at NAA, the Keg-Liner was used and the cooling problems stopped. Schmued later recorded, "It was a marvelous idea to invite the Bureau of Standards to help us solve our problems. I found that they are the most informed people on technical matters in the country. They can really help in problems that stump engineering departments. I must say that they were most obliging and helpful and deserve a great deal of credit for being there when we needed them."

Now nearly complete, the P-51B advanced on the line to receive its cowling and propeller. This view shows how the aircraft was supported on a dolly attached to the center rail of the production line. General, Firestone, and Goodyear all supplied tires for the Mustang production line.

The Mustang airframes move toward final completion. Of note is how random the primer has been added to the wings.

Overall view of the P-51B line illustrating how, on the left, various components were gathered to create the center fuselage and when the basic center fuselage reached the U-turn at the top right of the photo, the unit headed down the line with more and more equipment added, on the left, the fuselage was receiving its tail unit. Then it was time for another U-turn and the fuselage received the wing and the whole assembly moved toward completion at the left.

Once the P-51B was out of the factory building that did not mean the next stop was a USAAF unit—far from it. This early B was undergoing gear swing tests, with power being provided by a hydraulic mule, located under the propeller. The canopy had been removed and placed on the wing. Workers found that conducting line work under the camouflage netting worked well, since it helped diffuse the hot summer sun.

At NAA, work continued well through the night. P-51B-5-NA 43-6936 has its Merlin run-up under spotlights that were placed the length of the ramp.

Even though the nighttime ramp was well lit, it was still a dangerous place with all the whirling propellers. Mechanics fix a minor problem while the Merlin was running—with a complete lack of ear protection!

Obviously, something besides Keg-Liner had to be implemented as a permanent design solution so Bill Wheeler helped redesign the coolant system utilizing a new Harrison radiator and a new corrosion inhibitor: MBT. This inhibitor was developed by Union Carbide and rectified a problem that was created since Rolls-Royce utilized a mixture of 70 percent glycol and 30 percent water for coolant while Allison utilized only glycol. Wheeler would later recall that it took a year to make Wright Field change to glycol specification.

NAA also contracted with the Harrison Division of General Motors for a new radiator design and this unit had a frontal area of 2.7 sq ft. The scoop section had to be slightly redesigned for the extra weight, but the new radiator had a separate section for supercharger cooling, while the oil cooler was

P-51B has its Browning machine guns tested. Time would improve the firing pits, but this was a pretty basic structure with a re-enforced wooden structure and a pile of sand that had to be cleaned of lead slugs everyday.

At Inglewood, Mustang and Mitchell production was prolific, but a steadily increasing work force was capable of meeting wartime demands. The factory received constant changes from the military in regards to finish. Spec. 98-24105-Q Amendment No. 2, Paragraph E-6A dated 13 January 1943 read, "Each airplane shall have a radio call number painted on its vertical tail surfaces. The radio call number shall consist of at least four numerals and shall be determined in the following manner: The first number and the hyphen shall be omitted from the serial number of the airplane, using zero where necessary between the year designated and the serial number to make at least four numerals." The document continued, "For light colored backgrounds, the numbers shall be black in accordance with color chip No. 44 of AAF Bulletin No. 41, and for dark backgrounds, the numbers shall be yellow in accordance with color chip No. 48 of AAF Bulletin No. 41." Even with such precise instructions, mistakes were made at the factory and especially in the field.

Mustang Mk. III FZ149 receives a final check before a ferry pilot would take the plane to Newark, New Jersey, where it would be disassembled, covered in protective material, and shipped to Britain.

Buttoned up and ready to fly. Inspections completed, these P-51Bs await flight testing by factory pilots. Note how the gun ports had been crudely taped.

Bob Chilton points a P-51B directly at an NAA photographer ensconced in a company B-25.

mounted forward to the coolant radiator in its own separate scoop, with its own shutter.

This system was a high-pressure, liquid-cooling system that employed a closed circuit with a continuous flow from a centrifugal pump. The pressure system was similar to the conventional liquid-cooling system in that it used a radiator, header tank, and a centrifugal pump. However, unlike the conventional system, these units were constructed to withstand pressures up to 50 lbs/sq-in. The coolant liquid was pumped into the bottom of the coolant jacket on the lower exhaust side of each cylinder block and then passed to the cylinder heads through brass rubber-sealed transfer tubes, and out through a manifold attached to the intake side of each cylinder head

Firmly chocked, P-51B-1-NA 43-12342 is run-up by a mechanic prior to a test flight. Even though the aircraft had not yet left the factory, note how weathered the camouflage has become.

P-51B-1-NA 43-12408 displays the Mustang's broad and simple wing structure to advantage. The square tips bore some similarity to those of the Luftwaffe's Bf 109, and when the Mustang entered combat, distinguishing wing bands were required to hopefully prevent accidental firings on the fighter.

For engine runs, tie-downs had been fixed in the ramp's concrete and metal straps were attached to the hoist bar, which had been inserted in the rear fuselage.

This view illustrates how the entire radiator housing gracefully blended with the fuselage. Major Thomas Hitchcock, Assistant Attaché for Air in London, described the P-51B as "the world's outstanding fighter plane in 1943." Hitchcock, a prewar polo champion, came from an influential family and he used his position to promote the Mustang. Unfortunately, he would die when a wing separated from a Mustang he was piloting. His loss was a big blow to Edgar Schmued and the rest of the Mustang team.

UNDER THE HOOD

In aviation, the saying is "Speed is life." For surviving the rigors of aerial combat, that saying would be modified to "Visibility is life." Enter the Malcolm Hood canopy.

In order to improve visibility with early model Mustangs, a device called the Malcolm Hood was designed and manufactured. The hood comprised a bulged clear canopy that replaced the throw-over birdcage canopy. The reason for the name is the fact the unit was built by Robert Malcolm Ltd. The company specialized in plexiglass work and built Spitfire canopies (there is a misconception that Mustangs were fitted with bulged Spitfire canopies, but they were completely different). This was not just a simple switch—it was a relatively complex modification with many parts—of canopy, rails, hand crank, chain system, etc., but it did greatly improve the Mustang pilot's visibility. Testing with the hood started during December 1942. The basic hood design was undertaken by North American field representatives.

The basic hood was a frameless affair with the front and back rims left unpolished which sometimes gave the impression that the hood had metal straps. However, the plexiglass hood was devoid of these straps for a good reason—NAA wanted the hood to shatter if it hit the vertical while the pilot was attempting to escape. The bottom rim of the canopy did have metal strips to attach to the external runners mounted on the outside of the fuselage.

Once the prototypes had been built and tested, they were turned over to Robert Malcolm Ltd. for engineering and production. The company figured stress loads on the hood while designing the majority of the internal and external modifications needed for the hood. Complete Malcolm Hood kits were sent to modification depots and also directly to combat squadrons where the hood would be added by the ground crew. Malcolm Ltd. estimated that, in the field, installing the hood and its associated equipment would take about 135 man-hours.

Once production cranked up, the hoods were in great demand and the USAAF high command made it a priority to install hoods on as many European Theater of Operations (ETO) P-51Bs and Cs as possible. Of course, re-equipping all aircraft never took place, but by the end of 1944, a majority of Bs and Cs had the modification.

It is interesting to note that the USAAF ordered all ETO Tactical Recon Mustangs to have priority with the hood. As can be seen in one of our photographs, the Allison-powered Mustangs also had hoods. As time passed,

NAA engineers working closely with the USAAF were able to create the bubble canopy installation for the Allison Mustangs and P-51B/C in a very short amount of time. The 8th AF command gave the canopy the highest priority and Malcolm Ltd. worked three shifts producing the units. Technical orders were issued to combat units showing how the Hood was to be installed and it was a relatively complex modification, although orders stated it should not take more than 25 man-hours per airplane. P-51B 43-25050 of the 503rd Fighter Squadron, 339th Fighter Group, was photographed with a Malcolm Hood on 16 January 1945. All Malcolm Hood installations were done in the field and none in the factory.

Mustangs being issued directly to squadrons all had the Malcolm Hood fitted. For the first part of hood production, the company could not keep up with demand.

In the Royal Air Force, Mustangs IIIs could be delivered to operational units only after the Malcolm Hood had been fitted. The hood had been under testing since December 1942, but the first production hood was not fitted on a Mustang until February 1944 and we have no information on the large time gap. The aircraft was Mustang III FX893, but the RAF had tested the hood on Mustang I AG618 and, after flight trials, the following report was issued:

In accordance with instructions from Air Ministry (DAT) reference CS/11800, trials have been carried out on a Mustang I fitted with a sliding hood. This hood has been designed by North American representatives in this country and fitted to the aircraft at RAF Henlow and is merely an interim measure in order to ascertain the tactical advantages of having a sliding hood on Mustang aircraft.

The aircraft has been flown at Duxford for 5 hours and the following comments are forwarded:

Advantages

1) The view for takeoff and landing is considerably improved with the hood in the open position. Previously, pilots have felt a trifle cramped when landing the Mustang fitted with the standard hood as the long nose restricts forward view and the view to the side panels is poor when compared to most British fighters.
2) The aircraft has been flown at cruising and fast speeds with the hood open and the view for search was found to be greatly improved. Night flying was not actually possible on this aircraft as flame dampening exhausts were not fitted, but it is certain that the improved view would make this aircraft most suitable for night flying.
3) The view forward and sideward is now completely unrestricted and this gives much confidence to pilots when flying in bad weather.
4) It was found possible to fly with the hood open without using goggles, as apart from the slight eddy at the back of the cockpit, there is no draft.
5) With the sliding hood, entry and exit from the cockpit is much easier. It was found with the standard hood that it was advisable for a rigger to make quite certain that the hood was securely locked before taxiing out and with the sliding hood it was now unnecessary.

6) The aircraft fitted with the sliding hood was limited from diving, but maximum level speed runs have been carried out without any problems developing. The hood, although only a lash-up model, showed no signs of blowing away and stayed in the open or shut position at all speeds. It is necessary to use both hands to open or close the hood even at slow speeds and although at first this was found a little difficult, it became reasonably easy after practice. The hood has been opened at an indicated speed of 250 mph and closed again at 300 mph, though at these speeds the opening movement was found rather difficult.
7) Level speed runs have been made with this aircraft fitted with the standard hood and with the sliding hood. With the sliding hood there appeared to be a slight increase in speed, which is probably due to removal of the aerial mast and rear ventilators. It was also compared with a standard Mustang from an Army Co-operation squadron and again showed a slight superiority in speed.

Disadvantages

1) The radio mast has to be removed from its present position behind the cockpit to allow the hood to open. This will necessitate re-positioning the mast.
2) There is a very slight up draft through the cockpit when the inboard wheel fairings are open when operating the undercarriage, but this is not considered sufficient enough to worry about.

Conclusions

1) The tactical advantages of being able to open the hood of the Mustang in the air are very great and pilots have been most enthusiastic about the improved view, particularly during bad weather flying. This should be a great asset when carrying out Rhubarb operations.
2) The sliding hood will make the Mustang most suitable for night flying due to the view for search and night vision being greatly improved.

Recommendations

It is strongly recommended that as tactical advantages of having a sliding hood on Mustang aircraft have proved so great, a hood should be carefully designed and fitted to all Mustang aircraft as soon as possible.

CHANGE OF COLORS

The Mustang emerges from Olive Drab to bright bare metal. As continued allied victories became a harbinger to the war's end, the need for camouflage diminished.

On 1 January 1944, NAA issued a factory order regarding the deletion of camouflage paint from future fighter and bomber aircraft production. With the war advancing in the favor of the Allies, it was decided to remove the Olive Drab and Neutral Gray paint in favor of cost, simplicity, and performance. The removal of the paint on the Mustang gave the aircraft an entirely new look—the gleaming aluminum seemed to reflect the feeling of optimism that was taking hold across the country as the Axis powers began to retreat toward their respective homelands.

The NAA directive states: "At the earliest date, without delaying production, camouflage paint will be deleted from all spares delivered concurrently with airplanes without camouflage. Exterior surfaces such as fabric, plywood, magnesium, and dural will require protective primers of aluminized coloring. Alclad or stainless steel will require no covering. Antiglare paint will be on top of fuselage covering

P-51B-10-NA 43-7138 on the ramp at Inglewood—the aircraft in the foreground has just emerged from the factory in its new natural-metal finish while the Bs in the background were the last examples to receive the Olive Drab and Neutral Gray paint. The white cross on the aircraft to the right alerted ground crews that the craft was fitted with the 85-gallon fuselage tank. Regarding the tank, Louis Wait, NAA administrative test pilot, commented, "The first objectionable feature was that the weight without external tanks increased to about 10,000 pounds, which decreased the ultimate pullout factor from an original 12g down to 9.5g but this was not as serious as the fact that when the additional fuel was added, the airplane's center of gravity was placed so far aft that it became longitudinally unstable. This instability was particularly dangerous in that a pullout at high-speed was always accompanied by a stick force reversal which, unless opposed by the pilot, would quickly carry the airplane into an accelerated condition where the wings would fail at the inboard end of the gun bay."

forward vision areas to aid the pilot. The propellers will remain black with yellow tips.

"The wing leading edge of the Mustang will be smoothed and surfaced as outlined in the P-51B and P-51C Series Repair Manual Report No. NA-5741, with the exception that the camouflage coats will be deleted and aluminized lacquer will be applied over the surfaces. The deletion of the camouflage will eliminate approximately 42 pounds of finish from the B-25 Series Airplanes and 16 pounds of finish from the P-51 Series Airplanes. It is anticipated that the removal of the camouflage will also result in materially increased speed."

Camouflage at the factory was removed with a type of thinner that did not attack the gray airfoil smoother. However, thinners available in the field would damage and remove the important coating. Rivet heads, rough edges, etc., would be exposed and create an unwanted drag. To prevent this condition from occurring and to provide a timesaving method of accomplishing the elimination, NAA recommended that USAAF bases utilize the following procedure:

"In place of removing the camouflage from the airfoil smoother, apply additional paint to the area, which extends from the wing leading edge to approximately 40 percent chord. Use a mixture containing 8 ounces of aluminum paste to each unthinned gallon of clear lacquer (Spec. AN-TT-L-51) or clear varnish (Spec. AN-TT-V-118). This will allow the surface to assume the necessary appearance of unpainted aluminum or stainless steel. Any specified thinner may be used for the removal of camouflage from all other surfaces of the aircraft."

via two large ports at each end of the cylinder head and a small one at the center. These manifolds discharged into the header tank. From the header tank, the coolant liquid flowed to the radiator, where it was cooled by air flowing through the radiator, and then continued to the pump for another circuit of the engine.

The aftercooling system was provided for cooling the supercharger fuel/air mixture. The system consisted essentially of an expansion tank, heat exchanger, radiator, and aftercooler pump. The coolant liquid flowed from the expansion tank to the aftercooler pump, where it was pumped to the radiator and then back through the system to the supercharger case. The coolant passed through a jacket between the impeller, cooling the charged air as it passed into the second stage impeller chamber. The coolant then flowed into the heat exchanger where it cooled the charged air as it passed from the second stage impeller chamber into the intake manifolds. The coolant then returned to the expansion tank, completing the cycle. The system was of the low-pressure type incorporating a relief valve, which relieved at approximately 10 to 12 lbs/sq-in. The aftercooler radiator was constructed integrally with the engine coolant radiator.

On 4 December, Chilton had the XP-51B back in the air for intensive testing. Over the next couple of days, Chilton achieved a top speed of 441 mph at 29,800 feet with an initial rate-of-climb of 3,600 fpm. To show just how fast NAA could accomplish goals and just how important the P-51B was to the war effort, the second XP-51B flew on 2 February 1943 and the first production aircraft, P-51B-1 NA 43-12093, was flown by Chilton on 5 May and this machine was utilized to establish the official performance parameters. As more early P-51Bs came off the line, they were scattered to various USAAF test units and extensively flown—a big change from the XP-51.

Did taking an Allison airframe and sticking a Merlin upfront create the P-51B? Far from it. The P-51B was a vastly different aircraft than earlier Mustangs. The fuselage deeper, the cowling totally different, cooling system completely revised, wing

Gleaming in the morning sun, P-51C 42-103216 awaits a USAAF delivery pilot.

Royal Air Force Mustang Mk. III FX883 during a factory test flight. While in the States, aircraft assigned to foreign air forces had to be flown with American insignia.

P-51B-5-NA 43-7116 rolled out in the new natural-aluminum finish. Elimination of camouflage paint was a big time savings in Mustang production.

Dutch Kindelberger takes a moment from his hectic schedule to pose with a gleaming P-51B.

Late production P-51D wing showing many interesting details including missing stress doors, addition of most rocket stubs, and underwing pylons.

Line-up of P-51Cs at the Dallas (actually Grand Prairie) plant. The first Mustangs built at the facility were P-51C-1-NTs and were identical to the Inglewood aircraft. Unfortunately, it seems that the majority of Dallas negatives (along with masses of other data) were destroyed after the war.

The Dallas plant would build 1,750 P-51Cs.

Everything fully checked, USAAF ferry pilot Lt. Fred McConnell prepares to take a P-51C to a depot where it will be dispensed to an operational squadron.

The Dallas-built P-51Cs appeared to have used a darker primer on the wings (the primer extends to the fillets on this aircraft). Note how a portion of the anti-glare panel has been sprayed on without a sharp demarcation line. This would be changed before delivery.

Mustangs could be purchased by individuals or organizations wishing to make a patriotic gesture. These aircraft were called presentation Mustangs and usually had the name of the purchaser painted on the cowl. For some reason, Dallas seemed to have more presentation aircraft than Inglewood and P-51C 42-103644 carries the name The Spirit of Elks, Binghamton, New York.

A variety of aircraft were built at Dallas—Mustangs, Texans, and Liberators. A B-24 tucks up its gear before heading out on a test flight while P-51Cs in the foreground undergo engine checks.

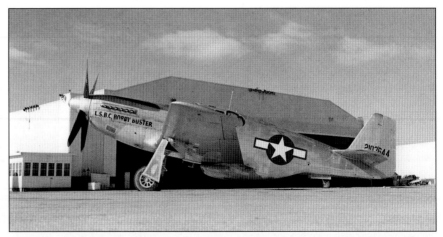

P-51C presentation Mustang L.S.B.C. Bobby Buster. Sometimes these markings would be left intact when the Mustang reached a combat unit.

Aircraft factories usually invited the local press to photograph presentation aircraft since they served as excellent morale boosters. This particular P-51C was named Brandeis Aza No. 533 B'nai B'rith.

Bob Chilton slides 43-12102 in next to the B-25 camera plane, showing the new bubble canopy to advantage.

Testing the bubble canopy in the NAA wind tunnel. Built of mahogany and metal, and costing $20,000, the quarter-scale model was hand sanded and given five coats of lacquer so that it shined like a fine violin. Weighing 400 pounds, the test model was firmly anchored to its support pylons, since the tunnel could produce speeds up to 325 mph. The model was adjusted for the first run at a zero angle-of-attack in order to initially get normal reactions, its final setting being accurate to within 1/100 of a degree. Allowing for the weight of the model, all scales were set at zero.

When 43-12102, the tenth P-51B-1-NA, was selected, the airframe was modified from the windscreen back to accommodate the bubble canopy and cut-down rear fuselage. These two photographs may represent the aircraft since it is surrounded by engineering drawings and a notice to keep off the aircraft.

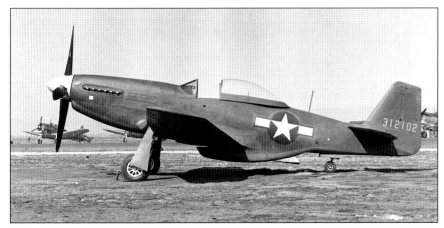

The installation of the bubble canopy gave the Mustang a completely new appearance.

The removal of the upper portion of the fuselage to accommodate the bubble canopy did result in a loss of keel.

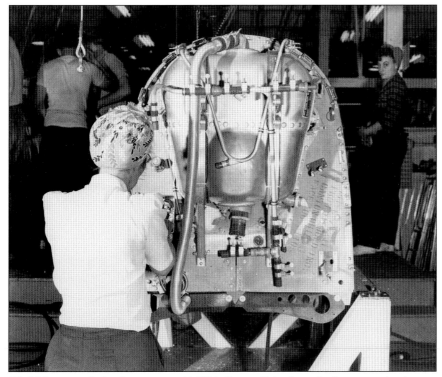

Finishing work is done on a P-51D firewall before being attached to a fuselage.

Oil tank is positioned on the completed firewall.

PLASTICS AND THE MUSTANG

Although thought of today as a space age material, plastics contributed to the fabrication of the P-51 Mustang and the survivability of its pilots in combat.

For the Mustang, plastics were essentially materials utilized for the flexible production characteristic of the NAA P-51 line. With few exceptions, these materials proved equal and often superior to light metals. As a result, plastics at NAA took the place of many materials for a great number of Mustang parts formerly made of metal.

Though often similar in appearance, plastics differed in composition and characteristics, depending upon the raw material and the adhesive agent. One type would shatter like glass when struck with a hammer. Another type, similar in many respects, but made from a different compound, could withstand severe blows without signs of damage.

For NAA, plastics were available in a wide variety—either in the form of molding compounds that could be shaped in dies, or in the form of sheets, rods, and tubes for conversion to the desired shapes by the application of moderate heats and pressures. In fact, there were more different types of plastics on the market than there were metals.

With so many types of plastics available to NAA, almost any physical characteristic could be obtained—such as the transparent covers for landing lights that conformed to the contour of the wings of the P-51 (before the light was located in the gear well). These Plexiglas or Lucite covers combined strength and rigidity with exceptional heat resistant properties, but they were also easily molded.

In building the P-51, one of the most trying problems was that of weight control. Since plastics weighed some 30 to 40 percent less than aluminum, NAA engineers were able, with the substitution of plastic components, to create a 55-pound weight savings for the P-51D. Important features in the utilization of plastics on the production line included a reduction in man-hours along with a drop in production costs. At the NAA Texas facility, instrument vacuum manifolds made of plastic could be manufactured at the rate of two per minute. When built of aluminum, it took nearly an hour of machine time to create one unit.

One of the greatest wartime advances in plastics was the manufacture of phenolic plastic parts by the thermo-elastic process, which was developed at the NAA Inglewood plant. In this process, the laminate sheet was heated and put into a form die; then pressure was applied and the sheet was formed to the contour of the die. These sheets, generally the color of fine malacca cane, were used in the making of such items as trim tabs, ammunition boxes, and chutes. The chutes weighed approximately 30 percent less than when made of stainless steel and they also required considerably less production time and material.

The NAA-patented thermo-elastic process made possible the use of high-strength material in short production runs with very low tooling costs. From 80 to 90 different types of parts were formed from plastic sheets by this process, many of the pieces being produced in hand-operated molds or dies.

As stated, certainly the most recognized piece of Mustang was the famed bubble canopy. Its contribution to pilot survivability in aerial combat was simply incalculable. There were at least five variations of the bubble shape.

Perhaps the most striking example of NAA plastic work was the one-piece teardrop canopy of the P-51D. This canopy was 5 percent more transparent than the best grade glass and was the first free-blown enclosure of its type. The process for blowing the canopy was developed at NAA's Texas facility where the bubble die (generally referred to as the bubble tub because of its appearance) was built.

The V-1650-7 Merlin is mated to the P-51D fuselage. Finished as a complete unit, the entire engine installation was a masterpiece of simplicity, and an engine change could be done in the field in less than 24 hours.

Complete Merlin powerplants fitted in their motor mounts are moved via an overhead railing and head toward the fuselage line.

Adjustments being made to the spinner back plate before the entire unit was attached to the Merlin.

Production of the new Ds had benefitted from lessons learned with the B. This fixture held dozens of Hamilton Standard propellers and when units were required, they were raised with an automatic lift. Note that the spinner back plates are already attached. As with virtually every other major D component, the propellers were moved via overhead lifts. Note the stout metal and canvas strap for lifting the heavy unit.

Worker carefully guides the Hamilton Standard propeller onto the Merlin's driveshaft. Note the lightening holes that have been drilled into the spinner's back plate.

Veritable sea of P-51D tail cones, horizontal stabilizers, and rudders all came together to complete a rear fuselage (complete with dorsal fin) and then moved via the overhead line to the main fuselage sections.

structure changed, and landing gear geometry changed. However, the basic design and construction concept remained the same. It was during this time of creative development that the radiator intake began to evolve into its final configuration.

As there had been aerodynamic problems with the Allison Mustang's carburetor air intake, a similar problem developed with the radiator intake. In its original state, the aircraft did not have a gutter between the intake and the fuselage. Instead, Schmued had the variable area entry panel on the forward portion of the intake. Various problems were encountered with this configuration, most notably a very loud banging noise that was coming from the duct and traveling upward to probably terrify the test pilots. Irv Ashkenas got to work on this problem and discovered that the banging was caused by the duct intermittently ingesting the turbulent boundary layer of air that was moving closely across the skin of the Mustang. There were many minor variations in the early Mustangs to eliminate the problem (by the A-36A, the adjustable intake was gone), and Ashkenas discovered that he should

MODIFICATION CENTERS

As mentioned several times in this volume, the Mustang production line was a nearly organic, constantly changing wonder. However, as the hundreds of various modifications to the airframes moving down the line were required it was unwise to keep stopping the line so changes could be instigated. Virtually all combat aircraft plants decided not to incorporate on-going modifications into the line—rather, after the aircraft was completed it was flown to a modification center where the various improvements or corrections could be undertaken without sapping the energy of the line.

The mod centers, while very effective, also increased cost, utilized vital manpower, and delayed the combat aircraft reaching the front. Also, the result of rework at mod centers was an excessive use of materials. The scrap or recycle pile of metal and parts ruined or discarded at mod centers was sizable. Fitting had to be changed, tubing cut, perhaps control cables cut and rerouted, different armaments installed, etc. When America first went to war, the modification center was the answer to a critical need and it was also a shining example of American ingenuity. To attempt Mustang modifications on the line would have been disastrous. The USAAF was rushing to get everything flyable equipped for combat. The job of the mod centers was to prepare Mustangs, already constructed, to fight without regard to appearance.

When an order for Chinese P-51Cs was received, these aircraft were to be fitted with special equipment for the China-Burma-India (CBI) Theater. Without a hold-up, the aircraft were slotted into the normal production line and the USAAF order was fulfilled ahead of time.

The development of NAA's skilled production know-how and the increased versatility and skill of the men and women who built the Mustangs made possible the successful system of modification in production. At the Dallas facility, a group of employees from all departments had a hand in the modification work. Thus the people who would actually do the work thrashed out particular problems ahead of time. The plan that evolved was to feed modified/upgraded Mustangs from a particular allocation into the line at intervals between unmodified, standard production Mustangs from another allocation. Thus the extra elapsed time needed on the modified P-51s could be balanced by temporarily intensifying work on the standard Mustangs.

At Dallas, the Mustang line would never be completely filled with Mustangs of a particular type. Within a short time, high-priority P-51s could be rushed into the line by pulling out Mustangs of lower priority. Meanwhile, pooled in reserve at all times were enough major P-51 components of the various modification types to take care of all emergency changes. Basic changes, such a leaving a space unriveted on the skin for special access doors, were made in the earliest production stages possible in order to hold to a minimum extra work in final assembly. Key to the success of the concept was a constant coordination between all departments concerned with the particular modification.

The Dallas plant also employed a skilled wood shop whose workers undertook projects from crating to creating tooling dies. In order to make the modification process more effective on the production line, the wood shop completed a magnificent full-size wooden Mustang that was complete in every detail, but was left unskinned. Engineers could utilize the mockup to check equipment that would be added to the production line aircraft and this greatly reduced time as well as possible confusion.

During May 1944, there were six different modification variants on the Mustang line, and the next month this built to nine—additions included cameras, specialized navigation aids and instruments, and other equipment specified by the USAAF. During March 1944, the USAAF placed an emergency allocation for 176 standard P-51Cs to be delivered within a month. By adjusting the line to deliver just stock P-51Cs, it was only two weeks until aircraft from this order were emerging from the factory door and just six weeks later these aircraft were reaching the desired combat units.

The P-51D production line had a surprising amount of automation. Note how stabilizers, rudder, and dorsal fin came together into one unit.

Complete set of P-51D self-sealing fuel tanks.

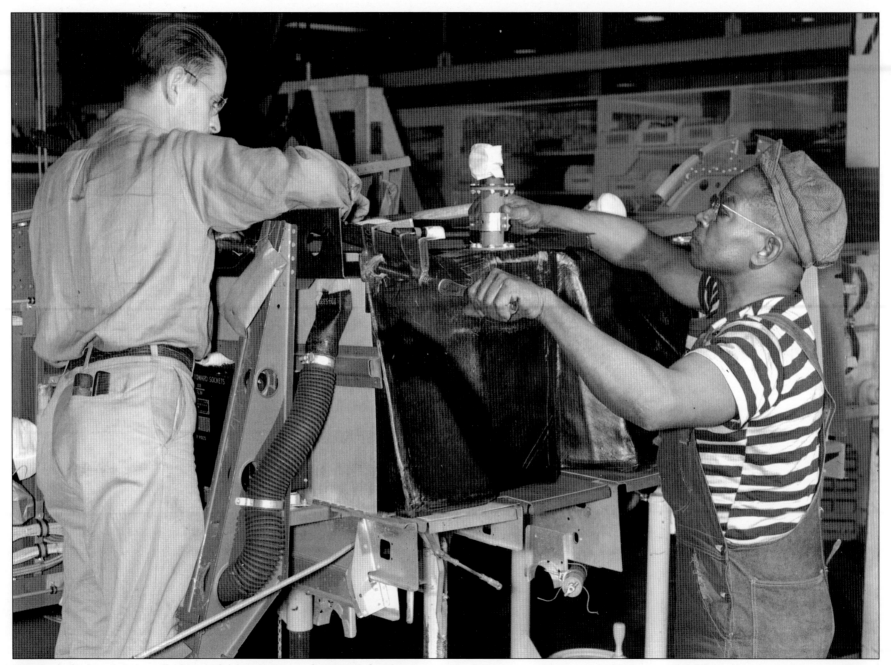

Fuselage fuel tank is installed into the beginnings of a P-51D fuselage.

As floor space increased, the production moved around a bit to take advantage of the extra room. Self-sealing tanks await installation in wings moving down the conveyor line.

Bare wing sections moved down a narrow aisle where plumbing and other components were installed. Note how the shelves held each station's needed components.

Before more interior space became available, these P-51D wings were completed in the open. These views give a good idea of the top and bottom finishes for an average wing.

BRIEFING FOR P-51 PILOT INSTRUCTORS

8 AUGUST 1945
BY LOUIS S. WAIT
ADMINSTRATIVE TEST PILOT
NORTH AMERICAN AVIATION, INC.
INGLEWOOD, CALIFORNIA

Early P-51 types were designed for a combat weight of 8,000 pounds, good for an ultimate pullout factor of 12g, with a pilot allowable applied factor of 8g. As a result of equipment and fuel tank location, the airplane was positively stable under all conditions of flight; the pilot always had to pull more pounds on the stick to produce more g in a turn; when this force was released the airplane immediately stopped turning. The same was true of the aileron and rudder forces. The changes in trim tab setting for climbing and diving were negligible.

The new, heavier, more powerful Packard-built Rolls-Royce engine made necessary a heavier radiator for proper cooling, and a heavier four-blade wide-chord propeller to utilize the increased engine power at altitude. The P-51B/C, as the result of these modifications, was an overloaded airplane since the combat weight was increased from 8,000 to slightly over 9,000 pounds. As later results demonstrated, the decrease in g factor alone was not a serious complication.

However, other adverse characteristics did become apparent. The increased engine power and four-blade propeller caused a marked decrease in directional stability. Whereas the pilot previously had to use increasing rudder pressure for increasing sideslip or yaw angles, the rudder forces now tended to decrease at yaw angles greater than 10 degrees, and if the pilot did not apply sufficient opposite rudder, the airplane tended to increase the skid or sideslip all by itself, eventually resulting in an unintentional snap roll or entry into a spin.

This condition became serious at high speeds, as the snap maneuver resulting from excessive skidding imposed a higher unbalanced load on the horizontal stabilizer than that for which it was designed. Horizontal stabilizer failures began to occur, and since the highest incidence was in slow roll maneuvers, slow rolls were immediately prohibited. Even though the P-51B/Cs were cured by reworking the tail surfaces and strong enough to take very high speed snap maneuvers, slow rolls were still prohibited because the inverted snap maneuver that often occurred...was catching the pilots unaware. It became necessary to increase the directional stability of the airplane by adding a dorsal fin, and by rigging the rudder trim tab to give opposite boost.

As an interesting sidelight, many pilots flying the P-51B/C in combat had discovered an excellent use for the directional instability just mentioned. The first well-described use came about when a P-51 pilot following an enemy airplane in a steep dive glanced in his rear-view mirror and mistook his wingman for a Bf 109. Since evasive action was apparently mandatory, the pilot proceeded to push all the controls into the northwest corner of the cockpit, and the consequent series of inverted snap rolls, entered at over 450 mph indicated, separated subject P-51B pilot from his target, his wingman, and almost from his airplane. The fact that the stabilizer fell off in the hands of the crew chief during inspection after the airplane had flown to its home base did not deter other pilots from using the same tactics when necessary.

Although several pilots who had used the above-described maneuver complained that they could not any longer obtain their usual evasive action because of the addition of the dorsal fin and change in the rudder boost tab, it is believed that the increased directional stability overcame all of the difficulties previously encountered.

The first objectionable feature [of the 85-gallon fuselage tank] was that the weight without external tanks was increased to about 10,000 pounds, which decreased the ultimate pullout factor from an original 12g down to 9.5g, but this was not as serious as the fact that when the additional fuel was added, the airplane's center of gravity was placed so far aft that the airplane became longitudinally unstable. This instability was particularly dangerous in that a pullout at high speed was always accompanied by a stick force reversal, which, unless opposed by the pilot, would quickly carry the airplane into an accelerated condition where the wings would fail at the inboard end of the gun bay.

With full fuselage tanks and two 110-gallon external tanks, the gross weight of the P-51D is over 11,600 pounds, nearly 50 percent more than the design weight of the airplane. The pilot's allowable pullout factor is 5g and the ultimate wing failure load occurs at 7.5g. Although additional weight has been added to the P-51, the ultimate and allowable load factors have not been decreased sufficiently to prevent the pilot from accomplishing any combat maneuver.

The only way to obtain increased strength or any substantial amount of increased stability is to start from scratch and design a new airplane. This has been done in the P-51H. Actually, the model designation of this airplane is somewhat confusing because the airplane is structurally no longer a P-51—it's a brand-new airplane. The P-51H is designed to develop over 11g ultimate pullout factor at a design gross combat weight of 9,600 pounds. Further, the arrangement of the airplane has been changed slightly so that it is always stable, regardless of the disposal of fuel or armament load. The P-51H is a truly worthy successor to all previous P-51 Series airplanes.

With many of the interior items now added, wings received final detail work.

With control sticks installed, this view of the top wings for P-51Ds shows the unevenness of primer application along with bare metal flaps and ailerons.

When Mitchell production moved, the additional space was given over to the Mustangs. Very basic wing sections on the left worked themselves to relatively complete wing frames on the right.

Bottom view of nearly completed wings with the landing gear legs attached to their fittings. The huge bare-metal stress doors not only covered the fuel tanks, but also proved a good portion of the wing's integral strength.

At this stage, tires and wheels had been added while attached clipboards list what still needed to be done. There was an overall standardization to the production line, but there were also many small differences. For example, sometimes interior areas received their assigned paint covering, sometimes they didn't.

move the duct further from the bottom of the aircraft so a stream of smooth high-speed air was able to enter the inlet. However, this took quite a bit of experimenting to find the exact distance that would optimize airflow.

Ed Horkey recalled, "The boundary-layer bleed wasn't all that simple. If you drop the radiator inlet down far enough to get rid of all of the turbulent boundary layer, the drag would be too high; so it ended where it was a compromise of the bleed depth to get an acceptable cooling performance with minimum drag.

"It so happened that later on when we started the P-51B project, we got the boundary-layer bleed a little too small. What would happen was that it caused a duct rumble. Chilton described it to us as somebody pounding on a locker. The boundary layer would build up, and airflow would go around the duct inlet, and then it would all of a sudden go inside again, and this would create a large impact load. We did two things: We got the model out again and started checking the bleed. We also took an actual XP-51B up to Ames

Out of the jig, the wing received final attention as it moved toward the fuselage line.

Before the wing was attached, this photo was taken looking up into the Mustang cockpit showing the rudder pedal assembly and the maze of tubing and wiring.

The Harrison radiator is aligned into position...

Aeronautical Lab and cut the wingspan down a little and mounted it in the 16-foot high-speed wind tunnel.

"I took the first ride, and when we got up to 500 mph in the tunnel, we got the rumble. It was quite a thrill… we lowered the top inlet of the radiator duct a small amount and also went to the cutback, or slanted, inlet shape and solved the problem on the P-51B. I am absolutely certain, having been there, that the boundary-layer-bleed solution credit should be given to Irving Ashkenas."

Moving the P-51B inlet to where it was about 1.5 inches away from the belly skin created the gutter needed to carry the turbulent, low-energy surface boundary layer air clear of the inlet. This allowed the variable inlet to be eliminated and an adjustable chute at the end of the ducting would control the volume of air flowing through the system. Thus, cold air would enter the inlet and

...and then jacked into place where it will be secured to the airframe. The radiator had 2.7 sq ft of frontal area and contained a separate section for supercharger cooling, while the oil cooler was fixed forward of the coolant radiator in its own channeled scoop with shutter.

THE PHOTO FIGHTER

Never before had there been such a successful combination of the photo recon mission with air-to-air combat capability.

One of the great, and often overlooked, strengths of the basic Mustang design was its ability to carry photoreconnaissance cameras into combat. During World War II, a variety of fighter aircraft were fitted with cameras—the most notable being the F-4/F-5 conversions of the Lockheed P-38 Lightning. However, the Lightning had one great drawback. It was unarmed, and if engaged by enemy fighters, the pilot had little choice but to ram the throttles all the way forward and hope to head back to safe territory. The photo recon Mustangs, however, carried their full compliment of armament and could engage the enemy on very equal terms. In fact, several Mustang photo recon pilots became high-scoring aces.

With the Royal Air Force's early aircraft, a Williamson F.24 camera with an 8-inch focal length lens was mounted behind the pilot and was fixed to shoot to the left. However, this installation could be reversed. Simplistic but effective, USAAF Mustang photo recon variants would soon become more sophisticated than the RAF aircraft. A great deal of the P-51's effectiveness as an aerial camera mount was due to one man—Sherman Fairchild. Coming from a wealthy family, Fairchild was a retiring individual who attended Harvard for one year but had to drop out after contracting tuberculosis. However, he utilized his wealth to create numerous companies and pursue his varied interests. In the aviation world, he is best known for Fairchild Aircraft—a company that produced a wide variety of military and civilian aircraft. He had a real passion for cameras and soon developed numerous cameras for aerial photography (achieving several patents along the way).

Founding Fairchild Aerial Camera Corporation, among Fairchild's many accomplishments, was inventing a large, high-speed, between-the-lens shutter that was ideal for aerial mapping. In 1920, Fairchild supplied Gen. Billy Mitchell with a camera to record his history-changing aerial bombing attacks on a captured German battleship—a mission that would change the course of bombardment aviation.

During World War II, Fairchild's cameras became standard equipment for the USAAF and USN. The aircraft we will examine in this section is the F-6D/K. The modifications for the new mission were relatively simple with the work taking place in the rear fuselage with the internal addition of

mounts, ports, and wiring for the cameras. The F-6D/K usually carried two cameras—a K-17 and a K-22. One camera aimed almost horizontally to the left while the other looked down at an oblique angle. Most of the aircraft were fitted with a direction finding receiver that had a rotating loop antenna mounted atop the fuselage. Some 163 P-51Ks were completed as F-6Ks while 126 P-51Ds (from the -20, -25, -30 blocks) became F-6Ds (it should be noted that there were also random conversions that increased the total number). In the field, these aircraft were in very high demand due to their ability to range far into enemy territory and rapidly return to base with their results.

Completed P-51K-5-NT 44-11554 (on the data block, the aircraft's designation had not yet been changed to F-6K) is shown raised to flight level for final calibration. The stripes on the wing upper surface were for the pilot to use as reference points for photography and bombing. As can be seen, the hoist bar was directly next to the upper camera port. The F-6K was fitted with a four-blade Aeroproducts A-542-A1 Unimatic propeller that had a diameter of 11 feet 1 inch.

A nearly complete photo fighter coming down the line, strangely all by itself. At this late point in the Mustang's production life its seems (from examining other photographs) that the custom of having the national insignia and other markings painted on the airframe had been dropped and that a simple stencil marking had been applied with final markings to be added when the aircraft was completed.

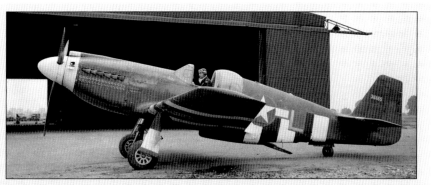

Even though this book does not cover the operational aspects of the P-51, we wanted to use this photo to illustrate the importance of the Mustang as a camera platform. F-6A 43-6165 was converted from a P-51A-10-NA and was being used for aerial reconnaissance during and after D-Day (hence the invasion stripes). Even though Merlin-powered Mustangs were available in large numbers, the low level performance of the F-6A made it ideal for the mission. Major Boardman C. Reed was photographed preparing to start the V-1710-39 at Chalgrove Airfield, Oxfordshire, England.

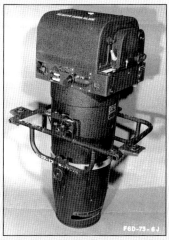

For the F-6D/K, NAA developed an ingenious internal mount that could hold a variety of Fairchild K-series cameras.

The aircraft's mounts were built to withstand high g forces, but shutters could jam if the camera was operating during a moment of high stress. Depending on the mission, each camera could be fitted with a variety of lenses.

The Fairchild intervalometer with which the pilot would control operation of the cameras.

With all cameras in place, the F-6D/K could easily operate with a full load of ammunition, bombs, and rockets.

The cockpits of the F-6D/K series carried various placards relating to the operation of the cameras, such as this one next to the pilot's left shoulder that gave specific camera operation instructions. A point of note is that the manufacturer's data plate refers to the aircraft as a P-51D-5-NA. Some aircraft, especially Dallas-built F-6Ks, had the plates labeled as F-6K.

The intervalometer in place on the cockpit floor by the pilot's left leg where it could be reached with relative ease.

This large panel on the right side of the fuselage allowed access to the cameras and ADF. The placard notes that if cameras and MX-241 were installed, then the fuselage tank had to be empty.

Parked under the camouflage netting at Inglewood (the more subdued light shows how different types of aluminum contrasted with each other). The aircraft's wing was still in primer finish and national markings and serial had yet to be applied. The Automatic Direction Finder (ADF) was directly above the camera port. ADF is a radio receiver equipped with direction-sensing antenna used to take bearings on a radio transmission.

F-6K 44-11907 awaits delivery on the broad concrete ramp of the Dallas facility. Note how the national insignia wrapped around the camera port. Although difficult to see, the third camera port was located directly in front of the tail wheel doors.

The P-51D fuselage was carefully lowered onto the wing. Note how following wings were moving along with leading edge down.

With the wing now attached, the radiator installation received a final inspection. Note the large bands holding the unit in place.

Inspector gives the radiator scoop a final look. Small rubber stamps with the inspector's personal codes were stamped onto components that had been satisfactorily inspected.

With wing and radiator installed, this F-6D continued down the line for the addition of more components. Note the canopy on the left wing panel awaiting installation.

Protective film still in place, the canopy is prepared to be attached to its rails. Note the filler cap for the fuselage tank.

expand rapidly and reduce its velocity before traveling through the hot radiator. This flow of air provided an efficient transfer of heat. The movable flap would then control the exit pressure and the entire system would offset the radiator drag by approximately 90 percent. There were two adjustable outlet scoops for both the oil (NA 102-31023) and coolant radiators (NA 102-31025) and these were hinged to the fuselage just aft of the oil radiator and the coolant radiator. These scoops were operated by means of thermostatically controlled hydraulic struts. However, some of the P-51Bs (42-10309 to -103378 and 43-6513 to -6712) were fitted with adjustable oil and coolant radiator scoops that were electrically operated.

The wing was set at a 1-degree angle of incidence with a dihedral angle of 5 degrees. A tank bay at the inboard end of each wing panel provided space for a 92-gallon self-sealing tank and housed two .50-cal. Browning M2 machine guns (as a point of interest, the AAF decreed that this was the minimum allowable armament for a fighter). The landing gear consisted of two retractable main gear assemblies with disc-type brakes and 27-inch smooth-contour wheels, installed in the main wings, and a retractable tail gear assembly with a 12.5-inch smooth-contour wheel installed in the tail cone.

With the massive increase in Mustang production, Dutch and his staff worried about maintaining the metal quality NAA had become known for. Particularly vexing was the laminar flow wing. Ongoing studies indicated that a theoretical laminar flow could be extended as far back as 60 percent of wing chord. However, wind tunnel testing showed that this figure could actually go to 70 percent, but these wind tunnel tests used absolutely pristine laminar flow models. It became increasingly known that such a wing could be built in theory under very controlled conditions, but in mass-production could such inaccuracies such as joined rivet heads, waviness due to manufacturing limitations be controlled? These types of imperfections could be sufficiently large so as to induce a permanent transition from laminar to turbulent flow further forward on the wing chord locally increasing profile drag. Further research revealed that the laminar flow wing profile contour over the leading edge portion of the wing chord had to be within plus or minus 1/1,000 inch of the specified airfoil dimensions to achieve very low drag coefficients. This tolerance could be relaxed farther aft on the chord. Unfortunately, even for a company as dedicated to quality as NAA was, this meant that the theoretical drag advantage of a laminar flow wing could not be achieved with standard production methods.

With the P-51D nearest to the camera fitted with prop and spinner, the row of Mustangs in the background shows varying stages of completion as they had components added at each station. To the right, fuselage center sections moved down the line to where they would be joined with wings (barely seen on the far right).

This view shows how each P-51D nested in its individual dolly and how that dolly was attached to the center railing and moved down the line.

MUSTANG VERSUS ZEKE

Utilizing a captured Mitsubishi Zeke, the USAAF compared the enemy's top fighter with a P-51D.

April 1945
AAF Proving Ground Command
Eglin Field, Florida

Comparative Performance Between Zeke 52 and P-51D

PERFORMANCE

Airplane	Altitude	MP	RPM	Results
P-51D-5-NA	10,000 feet	62.5-in. Hg.	3,000	Approx. 80-mph true airspeed faster than Zeke
Zeke 52	10,000 feet	38-in. Hg.	2,750	
P-51D-5-NA	25,000 feet	62-in. Hg.	3,000	Approx. 95-mph true airspeed faster than Zeke

Combat Comparison Zeke 52 versus P-51D

Level Turning Circle

10,000 feet. The run was begun from a line abreast formation at 200 IAS. At the end of 1 minute at full power, the P-51D had an estimated lead of 400 yards. After 2 minutes, the lead had increased to 1,500 yards.

25,000 feet. The run was begun from 190 IAS. Estimated lead for the P-51D was 300 yards after 1 minute and 1,000 yards after 2 minutes at full power.

Dive Acceleration

10,000 feet. Dives were begun from level flight line abreast formation at 200 IAS, with full power applied as the dive was entered. The P-51D began to pull ahead immediately. The selected red line airspeed (325 IAS) of the Zeke was reached after 27 seconds. At this time, the P-51D had a lead of approximately 200 yards.

25,000 feet. Results were much the same as at 10,000 feet. The Zeke reached 325 IAS after 20 seconds, and the P-51D was rapidly widening a lead begun shortly after the dive was entered.

Aileron Roll

At both altitudes, the rolling ability of the Zeke was slightly better than the P-51D IAS. At speeds above 220 IAS, the P-51D was superior, due to increasing control forces in the Zeke.

Zoom From Level Flight

10,000 feet. The P-51 gained an advantage of approximately 500 feet above and ahead of the Zeke after a zoom from a shallow dive, applying full power when the nose passed through the horizon.

25,000 feet. Results were the same as at 10,000 feet.

Spirals

Climbing and diving spirals were executed at 10,000 and 25,000 feet, with either airplane alternately leading in a line astern formation. Results were the same at both altitudes. The Zeke could stay in range within the P-51D's turn during either a climbing or diving spiral. With the Zeke in the lead position at the start of a spiral, the P-51D could hold the initial advantage for only a short time.

Combat

Results were essentially the same for the two individual combat comparisons at 10,000 and at 25,000 feet. The following three initial conditions were checked:

- Head-On Approach. The two airplanes approached each other on the same level approximately 500 feet apart. As they came abreast to each other, the Zeke immediately turned onto the P-51D's tail, but was unable to close range as the P-51D dove away. The P-51D was able to gain altitude after the dive and make repeated passes from above, for which the Zeke's only defense was turning to face the attack and firing a snap shot.
- Zeke 2,000 feet Above and Directly Behind. When the Zeke started a pass from above, the P-51D could dive away out of range and use excess speed to climb to a favorable attack position. The P-51D's

higher climbing airspeed and superior climbing ability aided in keeping out of range until in position for a pass. The Zeke was able to turn into each attack for a short burst, but never gained the initiative.

- P-51D 2,000 feet Above and Directly Behind. The P-51D was able to climb for continued attacks after the first pass, and the only firing opportunity for the Zeke when attacked was to run into the P-51D for brief bursts.

Conclusions

The P-51 is greatly superior to the Zeke in maximum level flight speed at both 10,000 and 25,000 feet. Due to advantages in speed, acceleration, and high-speed climb, the P-51D was able to maintain the offensive in individual combat with the Zeke 52, and to break off combat at will. The Zeke 52 is greatly superior to the P-51D in radius of turn and general maneuverability at low speeds.

Recommendations

The pilots of AAF fighter aircraft should take advantage of high-speed performance superiority when engaging the Zeke 52 in combat; speed should be kept well above 200 IAS during all combat; *hit and run* tactics should be used whenever possible, and following the Zeke through any continued turning maneuvers must be strictly avoided.

The factory production was one thing, but use in the field was entirely something else, as the wing would be subjected to all forms of indignity. However, NAA went as far as they could in guaranteeing that the Mustang would see some form of benefit from their wing production system.

The identical external removable bomb racks could be installed on the lower outer panel of each wing. Each one of these racks could accommodate any one of the following loads:

- 100-pound practice bomb (N38A2)
- 100-pound demolition bomb (AN-M30)
- 250-pound demolition bomb (AN-M57)
- 300-pound practice bomb (Mark I)
- 300-pound demolition bomb (Mark 1M1)

To build worker morale, military and political figures often visited the production lines to view progress. Here, General Carl Spaatz admires the handiwork of aircraft engine assemblers during a tour at the Packard Rolls-Royce V-1650 division. Women workers undertook a good deal of Merlin production.

British cabinet member and Supply Council Director Col. J. J. Llewellin (right) and Packard Vice President W. M. Packer inspect the two-stage, two-speed impeller assembly for the V-1650.

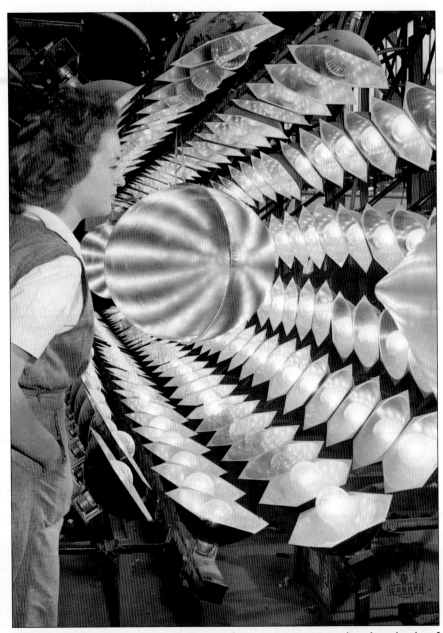

At the Weber Showcase and Fixture factory in Los Angeles, hundreds of drop tanks passed through an infrared paint drying system while a female worker kept an eye on production in this 5 August 1944 photograph.

- 300-pound demolition bomb (Mark 1M11)
- 300-pound demolition bomb (Mark 1M31)
- 325-pound depth charge (AN-MK17)
- 500-pound semi-armor piercing bomb (AN-M58)
- 500-pound demolition bomb (AN-M43)
- 588-pound chemical tank (AN-M10)

When neither bombs nor other special equipment was carried, a 75-gallon metal combat fuel tank or a 150-gallon ferry fuel tank could be installed on each wing rack. These tanks could be dropped by the normal operation of the bomb control system.

With the P-51B, the cowling for the Merlin lost some of the racer-like sleekness created by Art Chester on the earlier airplanes. However, the cowling was still quite close fitting and streamlined. The engine cowling consisted of readily removable panels, which were held by Dzus fasteners to the cowl formers. Access to the coolant tank filler plug was gained by removing a small panel on the forward end of the top left cowl. Two hinged doors near the aft end of the top cowl offered access to the aftercooler tank plug and to the oil tank filler neck. P-51B-5s and P-51Cs had two ground handling doors in the cowling: One below the engine reduction gears and the other at the bottom of the accessory compartment. These aircraft were also equipped with removable louvers that provided access to the carburetor air filters. All

Completed instrument panel of a P-51D-10-NA.

Completed P-51D-5-NA left side console.

Looking up into the left side of a P-51D-5-NA fuselage before the unit was completed.

SUMMARY OF CHANGES

*U*nless otherwise noted, all changes noted herein begin with the first P-51D airplane of block 20 and continue through all subsequent contractor's blocks at Inglewood and Dallas.

Block Description for P-51D-20 Airplanes
Serial Number
P-51D-20-NA	AAF 44-63160/64159, Inclusive
P-51D-20-NA	AAF 44-72027/72626, Inclusive
P-51K-15-NT	AAF 44-12553/13252, Inclusive

MCR C-311-5
Gun Sight Spare Lamp Holders Addition

In compliance with an AAF request, a three-clip bracket was designed to support the three spare gun sight bulbs, a spare fluorescent lamp bulb, and two other spare bulbs. This bracket was installed under the instrument panel shroud on the left-hand side where all the bulbs are easily accessible to the pilot during flight.

MCR C-359-1
Priming of Metal Surfaces

Because of corrosion difficulties, a minimum of one coat of zinc-chromate primer was applied to all interior metal surfaces of wings, fuselages, and control surfaces. This change became effective in production on and after Airplane P-51D-20-NT AAF 44-12553 (P-51D-20-NA Airplanes not affected).

MCR C-364-1
Carburetor Engine Compartment Preheat

This change was designed to permit the utilization of heated air within the engine compartment in the carburetor air intake duct as required under icing conditions. To accomplish this, a butterfly valve was installed in the top of the carburetor air duct forward of the elbow assembly. The butterfly valve is pivoted off-center and spring loaded to allow automatic opening in case the forward section of the duct is obstructed by ice.

MCR C-402-1
Oil Tank Changes

The oil tank was revised to include a removable top as well as a removable sump, which permits removal of the internal hopper and provides access to the warming chamber as well as the area surrounding the warming chamber.

Change of the tank assembly required extension of the forward area of the stainless-steel dishpan. The hopper assembly was revised to exclude the bottom, which was replaced by a revised baffle. The skins for the oil tank assembly were changed in contour around the inlet and outlet castings to utilize bolting the flanges, which replaced the welded flanges.

MCR C-402-2
Oil Tank Dip Stick Installation

A dipstick was provided in the oil tank so that the level of the oil could rapidly be determined. The access door was enlarged to provide suitable access to the dipstick.

MCR C-411-4
Landing Gear Door Locking Cable Spring

The landing gear fairing door retracting cable was revised to incorporate a spring-loaded device to maintain tension on the cable during all cycles of the landing gear operation. This involved the installation of a bracket on rib station 0 that supports a bell-crank to which the door retracting cable attaches. A slotted rod was attached to the bell-crank. This eliminates the necessity of the springs in the door to move the cable in the wing and eliminates any restrictions on the door hooks. The installation also prevents the cable from catching on any objects during the gear cycles. This change became effective in production on and after airplanes P-51D-20-NA AAF 44-63161 and P-51D-15-NT AAF 44-11953.

MCR C-429-3
Gun Sight—Installation of K-14 Computing

Installation of the K-14 gun sight became effective in production on and after airplanes P-51D-20-NT AAF 44-12853 and P-51D-20-NA AAF 44-72227.

MCR C-432-2
Fuel Tank Hanger Fitting Revisions

It was considered advisable to have the hanger support somewhat weaker than the fuel cell fitting so that it will tend to fail before the fuel cell itself fails. The hanger fitting was changed by increasing the thickness of the boss pad by 1/32 inch and by increasing the interior fillet radius from 1/16-inch radius to 1/8-inch radius.

MCR C-444-2
Gun Camera Opening Automatic Cover

A metal door cover was installed in the gun camera leading edge cutout. The function of this door is to prevent damage to the lens by rocks and mud splashing on the lens during takeoff.

The automatic door replaced the glass window forward of the lens. A cable to actuate the door attaches to the left main gear and holds the door in a closed position when the gear is extended. Retraction of the gear allows a spring to open the door.

MCR C-445-1
Flap Actuating Strut Redesign

The hydraulic wing flap actuating strut was redesigned to facilitate installation and service. This change was necessary since the installation of the fuselage fuel cell covered the two access holes in the radio shelf, which were previously used in mounting the actuating strut.

The new installation required a new hydraulic actuating strut, three new hydraulic lines, a new support bracket, a larger cutout in the beam at fuselage station 168, and a change in length of the connecting links between the torque tube bell cranks and the attachment of the flaps. It will be noted that the actuating strut was designed with a chrome-plated steel piston operating in a 24ST aluminum alloy cylinder.

The actuating strut was attached to the lower right-hand longeron by means of a cast aluminum alloy bracket, allowing the strut to rotate in a vertical plane and attach directly to the torque tube bell crank. The phenolic fiber fairlead is no longer necessary since this type of mounting eliminates all side loads in the actuating struts.

MCR C-463-1
Magnetic Inspection of Bolts and Screws

All important parts or assemblies, including bolts, screws, and nuts 1/4-inch diameter or over, fabricated of magnetizable ferrous materials, and involving safety of the ultimate part, are magnetically inspected per AAF Specification AN-QQ-M-181.

Inspection of bolts, screws, and nuts includes in excess of 78 percent of the total number in the airplane. All bolts, screws, and nuts of 1/4-inch diameter and larger are 100 percent magnetically inspected. Bolts, screws, and nuts of 3/16-inch diameter are 4 percent magnetically inspected.

MCR C-467-1
Electrical and Radio Wiring Identification

In compliance with AAF Specification AN-W-14, each cable is identified by a combination of letters and numbers to represent the circuit, wiring identification, and size of cable on all open wiring installations. Each cable is identified at not more than 3 inches from the end of the terminals and at not more than 15-inch intervals. Cables, encased in nontransparent conduit only, required markings at not more than 3 inches from terminals.

MCR-469-6
Message Bag—Type A-1 Deletion

The Type A-1 drop message bag (AE-45-200) was deleted. This change became effective in production on and after airplanes P-51D-20-NA AAF 44-63400 and P-51D-10-NT AAF 44-11774.

MCR C-470-1
Zero Rail Launcher Installation

Installation of electrical and structural provisions for the zero rail rocket launchers were made a permanent part of the airplane. This installation permits a total of 10 rockets to be carried. An alternate arrangement, made possible by the removal of the mounts for the two inboard rockets and addition of bomb racks, allows either two 500-pound bombs or two long-range fuel tanks to be carried.

For firing the rockets, a firing button is mounted on the control stick. A Type A-1 control box assembly is mounted flush in the pilot's front switch box below the instrument panel. A four-provision selector switch, with contacts for Safe, Rockets, Both Bombs, and Bombs Train, is provided. The wiring is arranged so that the rockets fire alternately from one side and then the other beginning with those outboard.

The forward center rocket mount on each wing covers the airplane jack point. It will be necessary, therefore, to remove these two mounts to jack up the airplane. The jack point at the airplane centerline may be used without removing the mounts.

The center of gravity is kept forward to prevent an adverse movement of the airplane center of gravity with the ten 5-inch T-64 rockets in position. When mounted, the rocket fins clear those of adjacent rockets by about 1.5 inches.

This change became effective in production on and after airplanes P-51D-20-NA AAF 44-14434 and P-51D-20-NA AAF-12553.

MCR C-479-3
Cowling—Fuel Drain Access Door Change

A fuel drain access door was provided under the fuel strainer and in the engine removable rear cowling to permit drainage of water from the strainer without removing the cowling. This change became effective in production on and after airplanes P-51D-15-NT AAF 44-11953 and P-51D-20-NA AAF 44-63160.

MCR C-479-8
Carburetor Hot Air Control Handle Design

The hot air control handle was redesigned to permit the use of the flat pattern identical with the cold air handle. To accommodate this new design, the hot air control handle was relocated in its assembly. Provisions were made to install a new fairlead assembly support of ram and hot air controls rods on the front cockpit floor assembly. Clearance was allowed between the ram air, control rod, and the carburetor boost mixture overboard drain line, and between the hot air control rod and coolant lines.

Detail of a P-51D-10-NA armament panel.

Completed right side console of a P-51D-10-NA. Even though aircraft were of the same block number, this did not mean that every bit of equipment inside the cockpit was standardized, for it often depended on what was available on the production line.

Every P-51D had to undergo a full armament check. As production progressed and modernized, this special rig was built to test the six Brownings and it was a big improvement over the pile of dirt utilized for earlier aircraft weapon testing. As can be seen, the Mustang could accurately be placed within the rig, and after firing the spent lead could easily be collected.

cowling panels were constructed of aluminum alloy except sections that were adjacent to the exhaust stacks. Those panels were made of corrosion-resistant stainless steel.

Even given the significant differences between the Allison and Merlin Mustangs, the assembly line changed to the new aircraft in a typically efficient NAA manner. However, NAA and the USAAF had seriously considered the implications of mass-producing the new B model alongside the huge order for 1,200 P-51As and, accordingly, a simple and efficient production line was designed and implemented that could accommodate the delivery of 20 Mustangs per day. After reconsideration and the obvious advantages of the P-51B, the P-51A was slashed, but the assembly system was ready to go and easily accommodated to just the P-51B. As P-51B/C aircraft began to flow to the combat units (peak production rose from 20 aircraft accepted in June 1943 to 763 aircraft in October 1944), numerous suggestions and modifications were incorporated into the production lines. The British had originally planned to receive engineless P-51B/C aircraft, but with so many changes incorporated by Packard, it made more sense to receive the whole aircraft. On 26 August 1942, the British placed an initial order for 400 Merlin aircraft as Mustang IIIs (the RAF would eventually receive 308 Bs and 636 Cs under the terms of Lend-Lease and both would carry the Mk. III designation).

With production in full swing on the B/C, constant improvements and modifications were undertaken as reports came back from test pilots and combat fronts. As can be seen elsewhere in this chapter, virtually every high-ranking USAAF officer wanted more range from the Mustang and Gen. Hap Arnold wrote of the, "...absolute necessity for a fighter that can go in and out with the bombers." He wanted aircraft with such range by January 1944, but this schedule was quickly tightened as bomber losses began to mount. After a phone conference between Arnold and Kindelberger, Dutch made the engineers get busy over the 4th of July weekend with orders to give Arnold what he wanted. The aircraft already could fly 4.75 hours with two 75-gallon drop tanks.

Schmued wrote, "We ran into problems getting enough fuel in the airplane until the idea to install an 85-gallon tank behind the pilot came up." This would give the aircraft an overload condition and would have troubling effects on the center of gravity. Even on paper, it was obvious the pilot would have to handle the Mustang gingerly until most of the fuselage tank's fuel had been consumed.

As with so many other projects, Bob Chilton took on the testing with the new tank. "I did those first long-distance flights before NAA would approve the tank for production. I was sitting there 7.5 hours. It was horrible. I simulated the route to Berlin by going to Phoenix and then heading back over the ski resort at Palm Springs," recalled Bob. "At 30,000 feet over San Jacinto, I started to dogfight with myself, roaring around the sky at full throttle for 5 minutes. I went up and down California a few times—Santa Barbara to San Diego and back, over and over. In the Mustang, 7.5 hours [of flying] is brutal." Dutch reported to Arnold during mid-August 1943 on the fuselage tank and

In order to improve safety on the P-51D ramp, these rigs were constructed that would prevent workers from accidently coming into contact with the propeller while the Merlin was running.

A completed F-6D photo-recon Mustang just after emerging from the factory.

Although not a true TP-51D conversion, 44-13809 was fitted with a basic instrument panel behind the pilot. The aircraft, named Joe's Baby, was used by Bob Chilton to give VIPs and members of the press a taste of what it was like to fly in a Mustang. However, in this photo Joe's Baby has come to grief in an unscheduled meeting with a B-24 Liberator.

NAA, as well as the USAAF, carried out extensive weapons testing with the Mustang. P-51D 44-13594 was fitted with a most impressive load of six .50-cal. machine guns, six 5-inch HVARs, and two 1,000-pound bombs.

Utilizing an underground reservoir, oil was pumped into the Merlin's tank before engine tests. Note the custom heavy-duty wheel chocks utilized when the engine was being run.

The national insignia was precisely aligned with the centerline thrust of the Mustang.

CHASING THE STORMBIRDS

During the late 1930s, Germans had an extreme interest in advanced aircraft that could have military capabilities. Heinkel had flown the He 176 on 1 June 1939. Powered by a rocket, the aircraft was revolutionary, but it was followed by the first flight of the He 178 on 24 August—the world's first turbojet. Both planes held great promise for the Luftwaffe but the Nazi government did not have the vision to quickly bring these aircraft to production.

Messerschmitt was doing similar important advanced research with their rocket-powered Me 163 Komet point interceptor and Me 262 twin-turbojet fighter. Delays meant that when these advanced machines did finally start front line service, it was too late. These aircraft could prolong, but not change the outcome of the war in Europe. However, when the rockets and jets engaged the 8th Air Force bomber formations, there was havoc. With their high speeds, bomber gunners could not track the speeding aircraft.

Over 100 mph faster than the Mustang, P-51 pilots began to develop tactics to intercept and destroy the Me 262s. By this time, the Allies had control of the air and the best way to get at the Me 262 was when the aircraft was vulnerable taking off or landing. The Germans knew this and would usually have a standing fighter patrol over the airfield during Me 262 operations.

Still, this was not an ideal situation and introduction of a first-line jet fighter into USAAF service was a long way off. Accordingly, NAA and the USAAF attempted to come up with various stopgap measures. One of these involved P-51D-25-NA 44-73099 that was modified to house an Aerojet rocket motor and associated systems.

The rocket was fitted behind the radiator and the nozzle was just in front of the tail wheel. To feed the motor, two streamlined pressurized tanks were mounted below the wings. These two 75-gallon tanks held the rocket's

In flight attitude and firmly chained to the ground, Bob Chilton fires the Aerojet rocket.

fuel—red fumaric acid in one and aniline in the other. Both were extremely flammable and highly corrosive.

Bob Chilton took the modified aircraft up for the first time on 23 April 1945. Taking the Mustang up to 21,000 feet, Bob stabilized the airspeed at 429 mph. Taking a deep breath, he ignited the rocket and the Mustang surged forward—the speed going up to 513 mph. The fuel tanks were good for just 1 minute of operation, but in that time the P-51D gained almost 100 mph. This would give the piston-engine fighter an advantage—albeit a very brief one—in dealing with the enemy jets. Chilton recalled that, "...a big part of the problem was that Horkey could not design an underwing tank that did not induce considerable drag. So, we had a very brief but notable increase in speed, but that was it."

The rocket Mustang made several more flights, but by the time the USAAF took delivery of the machine for more testing, the war in Europe was over and it is not known if further testing was ever undertaken.

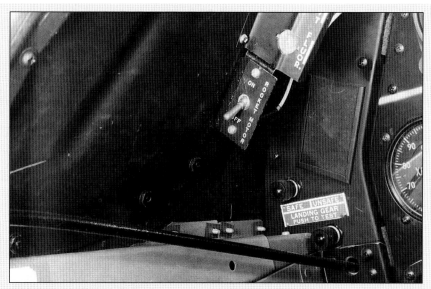

Simple on/off switch for the rocket motor was located just under the left side of the glare shield.

In flight Bob fires the rocket, which was recorded from a P-51D chase plane. Note how the bottom of the rear fuselage had been painted with a reflective material in an attempt to prevent damage from the rocket's white-hot flame.

This extremely rare photo shows the Mustang with the rocket on, rapidly pulling away from the chase plane, which was at full power at the time.

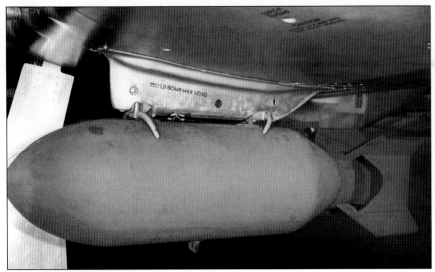

For test purposes a 500-pound general purpose bomb had been attached to the left underwing pylon of P-51D-5-NA 44-13553. As can be seen, the pylon had been stenciled for a maximum load of 550-pounds when photographed on 20 May 1944, but testing would increase the load to 1,000 pounds.

A day's work on the Inglewood P-51D ramp. Mustangs are prepared for engine tests and when those were successfully completed, the aircraft on the left were ready for flight test.

The air over Inglewood was alive with the bellow of the Merlin as P-51Ds underwent constant flight tests. The weather was generally good at Mines Field, but proximity to the ocean sometimes meant that a thick marine layer sometimes interfered with operations.

With cowlings neatly stored aboard the Wabash Cannon Ball, a factory-fresh P-51D had its Packard fired up for the first time after being attached to the airframe.

told him that it would take around 2.5 months to produce deliveries while also telling Arnold that there would be a loss in longitudinal stability. Aircraft already in production, such as the P-51B-10-NA, would be built with the tank while tanks could be shipped to Britain for field installation.

Inglewood would complete some 400 P-51B-1-NA and 800 P-51B-5-NA aircraft (these aircraft became P-51B-7-NA when the 85-gallon tank was field installed). As mentioned, the P-51B-10-NA would have the tank factory installed and the company built some 398 of this variant. Toward the end of this production run, Packard began deliveries of the V-1650-7 that had more power at lower levels and this engine went into 390 P-51B-15-NA Mustangs for a factory total of 1,988 P-51Bs.

While all this was going on, the modern new NAA facility in Dallas began Mustang deliveries beginning with 350 P-51C-1-NTs (-3-NT with field added fuselage tanks) and this production quickly increased to include 450 P-51C-5-NT and 950 P-51C-10-NT for a total of 1,750 P-51Cs.

The B/C Mustang, as well as the majority of Allied and Axis fighters of the period, had canopies constructed from metal-framed plexiglass. While efficient in protecting the pilot from the elements, on some early war Italian fighter aircraft, pilots demanded the canopies be removed since they thought the open cockpits would greatly improve their chances of seeing enemy aircraft. The Malcolm hood (see sidebar "Under the Hood" on page 128) was a huge improvement, but this field modification was only an interim measure.

The primary reason for the lack of one-piece, clear-vision canopies in the early war years was that the technology required to create a large blown plexiglass transparency simply did not exist. The incredible pressure of wartime development saw such technology and machinery quickly developed that ensured a bubble canopy could be created that would take the pressure of high-speed flight and the stress of combat maneuvering. Thus, NAA engineers began sketching out a drawing of a P-51B with a bubble (or teardrop, as the unit was often called) canopy, and the paper results produced a sleek looking aircraft with virtually unprecedented visibility.

The next step was to create a beautifully crafted wind tunnel model so that the bubble concept could be tested. Using lift and drag data, engineers could take the results of wind tunnel tests and closely determine what a completed aircraft could offer. Without the tunnel, if it had been necessary to change an actual aircraft and fly it to correct each fault or error, the expense and time would have been prohibitive during wartime.

NAA tested the model and found that such a modification would be perfectly acceptable. The disturbed air flowing from the bubble did not adversely affect the tail surfaces, but the removal of the upper portion of the fuselage did result in a slight loss of keel, and engineers calculated that the bubble top Mustangs would be that much more directionally unstable than current variants.

P-51B-1-NA s/n 43-12102 (the tenth such aircraft) was chosen for modification and redesigned from the windshield back to accommodate the canopy

Hands in his pockets, the factory test pilot was probably wondering how P-51D-5-NA 44-13471 would handle with the fully loaded extended range tanks in place. These huge tanks were seldom used. Note the tank/wing fairing on the ground.

Pulled from the flight-test line, this Mustang was having hydraulic issues that required extra repair time. With gear fully retracted, underwing jacks supported the Mustang.

OPERATIONAL MERLIN MUSTANG MODIFICATIONS

When the Mustang was shipped overseas, it was deemed not acceptable for combat without the airframe undergoing a series of modifications (in a way, this was the overseas variant of the stateside *mod center*). These modifications brought the Mustang up to the latest combat standards (many of these items were later incorporated into the Inglewood/Dallas production lines).

Since the ETO had the largest number of Merlin Mustangs, the most comprehensive modification program was developed for the type. The USAAF's Base Air Depot Area in Britain created a listing of modifications and servicing requirements beginning in November 1943 with periodic updates being issued. More than 70 different items were listed by V-E Day and, as a point of interest, this was less than required for other fighter types entering ETO service. The most comprehensive list was issued on 5 August 1944 and gives an inside look at problems incurred during nine months of Merlin Mustang operation. This listing was divided into two stages: Stage I detailed items that had to be completed before a Mustang was classified operational; Stage II comprised priority modifications considered absolutely essential for combat.

Stage I

Form 1A inspection (normal pre-delivery check covering all aspects of airframe, engine, and accessories).

- Change boost control to provide 61 inches at gate and 67 inches through gate.
- Modification of the mixture control lever operation to eliminate Full-Rich and Auto-Rich positions (this prevented the lever from being moved to an over-rich fuel mixture that was deemed not necessary in the ETO).
- Replacement of the enrichment jet and resetting of operating valve (a smaller water-injection valve was installed, as the original was considered too large for the higher air humidity of the ETO and could have an adverse effect on engine performance).
- Aircraft markings (a directive to add identity markings consisting of a white spinner, nose band, and single band across each wing and tailplane surface on camouflaged aircraft, or black on natural metal aircraft—an aid to prevent confusion with the Bf 109).

- Pressurized 75-gallon combat wing tanks, except on tactical reconnaissance versions (only early P-51B/C variants arrived in the ETO without this feature).
- Rework or replacement of exhaust stacks (early combat showed that many individual stacks developed serious cracks that could create a fire hazard. Until stronger stacks became available, a quick fix saw stacks strengthened by welding a metal strip on both sides).
- Inspect empennage attachment bolts (fatal accidents had occurred when tails separated in flight. During February 1944, P-51Bs were grounded for inspection, which revealed that bolts holding the tail were improperly tightened and often of insufficient length to allow required tightening. The grounding lasted just a few days until the emergency inspections could be completed).
- Full power check (standard operation to ensure engine was functioning correctly. When this was done, it was found the early Merlins had considerable power variations).
- Swing compass.
- Reinforcement of horizontal stabilizer (as highlighted in the Louis Wait sidebar, tail failures were taking place. A temporary fix was adding a doubler plate to the tailplane spar).
- Inspection of engine mounting bolts (a series of accidents in early 1944 saw the Merlin separate from the airframe during maneuvering. Inspection revealed the bolts and nuts were of insufficient strength and this was corrected by adding much stronger nuts and bolts).
- Install Zerk fitting on coolant pump (engine coolant pump bearings were more durable because the Zerk fitting provided better greasing. The Zerk fitting is a registered trade name for a type of fitting used to put grease into a bearing. A Zerk fitting has a ball-shaped top that is gripped by the nozzle of the grease gun when pressure is applied. Grease is pumped through the fitting into the bearing until it flows out between the surfaces of the bearing. When the grease gun is removed from the Zerk fitting, a check valve inside the fitting prevents grease leaking out, and prevents dirt getting into the bearing through the fitting).
- Remove bomb racks on tactical reconnaissance aircraft only (it was considered that the Mustang had enough internal fuel for the tac-recon mission and removal of the racks would increase speed).

- Replacement of left aileron counter-balance assembly.
- Inspection and rework of coolant header tanks scroll tubes (internal tubing assembly in the coolant header tank crank caused it to vibrate and wear a hole through the tank wall resulting in loss of coolant. The original fix to strengthen the scroll tubes did not work. Even with a newer fix, the problem kept happening until V-E Day and was not cured until a new and stronger tank was supplied from the factory).
- Modification of the supercharger volute drain valve assemblies.
- Rework of generator conduit (electric generator wiring harness impeded servicing and was also exposed to possible damage).
- Reposition of SCR-522 radio, battery, and dynamotor (repositioning reduced maintenance since the armored pilot's seat no longer required removal).
- Remove first aid kit (installed behind and above the pilot's seat by manufacturer and deemed unnecessary since all pilots carried such a kit in their personal equipment).
- Installation of sway brace for 108-gallon wing tanks (British manufactured paper or steel tanks required a special brace to prevent oscillation).

Stage II
- Downward identification lights (original wing leading edge light covers cracked because of wing flex during heavy maneuvers. Cover removed and covered with thin aluminum sheet. Lights were repositioned under the wing).
- Installation of sliding hood (this is the Malcolm Hood detailed elsewhere in this chapter).
- Installation of gun camera overrun (allowed gun camera to operate after guns ceased firing for better assessment of target damage/destruction).
- Replacement of operating solenoid on all .50-cal. Browning M2 weapons (G-9 fitting as used on the P-47 was considered better).
- Installation of selective bomb release (enabled pilot to release right or left bomb/drop tank individually).
- Rear-view mirror on bubble canopy (with the P-51D, rear-view mirrors were no longer deemed necessary. However, pilots disagreed and a variety of mirrors were installed on the windscreen frame).
- Reinforcement of the hydraulic hand pump mounting (the lever sometimes failed while being heavily pumped).
- Rework propellers due to oil leaks (early P-51B/C props had poor seals that allowed oil to escape and be thrown on the windscreen).
- Removal of carburetor heating system (applied only to P-51C).
- Replacement of phenolic canopy guide blocks (found to cause problems opening and closing canopy).
- Replace non-reinforced oxygen bottles with reinforced type (higher safety factor).
- Rework coolant pump (kit supplied to increase reliability).
- Installation of BC-608 contractor unit (for radio).
- Installation of safety bolts for canopy side panels (small panes of the P-51B/C canopy situated to the rear of the pilot were secured by spring clips. These could become dislodged in flight and a bolted assembly was created to hold panels).
- Rework rigging and testing of bomb rack assembly (to counter frequent complaints of mechanism failure).
- Fuel gauge rework and modification of scupper at fuel tank vent outlet (to correct fuel being lost from fuselage tank).

and cut-down fuselage. Fuselage formers were redesigned and built to create the sleek fuselage, the remainder of the craft was stock B. Chilton took the plane up on 17 November 1943 and told Dutch that the modified plane was just what the USAAF needed. This would lead to the most important of all Mustang variants. Model NA-106 (contract AC-30479) was assigned for the conversion of the 201st (42-106539, c/n 106-25341) and 202nd (42-106540, c/n 106-25342) P-51B-10-NAs that would be utilized as engineering test units for the new version of the Mustang—the NA-106, or P-51D.

Besides the bubble canopy, the new variant would have many other changes. The cowling was revised, as was the wing structure in order to accommodate two extra .50-cal. Brownings, while the landing gear geometry was changed. The fuselage fuel tank was installed in all Ds and the V-1650-7 was fitted as the standard powerplant. The Dash 7, as it was commonly known, was a reliable engine (see sidebar "V-1650-7 Engine" on pages 102 and 103 for performance statics). Once in frontline service, it was not uncommon for engines to be interchanged and earlier model Mustangs could be found with Dash 7s while later variants could be mounting a Dash 3. Overhaul time was determined to be 300 hours flying time for either variant. Besides some of the early Ds, the elevators finally had their fabric covering replaced with metal, but the rudder remained fabric-covered throughout D-model production.

Some attention was paid to improving the P-51D's aileron effectiveness, with seals being attached to the aileron balance strip's leading edge. This

Various dorsal fins were tested on the Mustang in order to strengthen the tail assembly. This slightly non-standard unit was fitted to 44-13255, photographed on 10 May 1944.

Each Mustang was issued with its own kit of protective canvas covers.

This one photograph illustrates how the fate of the Axis had already been determined—a couple days worth of Mustang production awaits delivery to combat units.

What it was all about—production and flight tests completed, plain vanilla P-51D-20-NA 44-63406 glistens in the afternoon sun.

MYSTERY MERLIN MUSTANGS

In wartime, speed is the essence and sometimes facts were not recorded where they should have been. Also, in the many years since the P-51 was designed and built, tons of documents and photographs have been destroyed—some accidentally, most on purpose. One of the small mysteries of Mustang production is an order for Australia. One hundred P-51D-1-NT aircraft came under Model NA-110 that went into effect on 23 April 1943 (ahead of NA-106) and the customer was listed as the USAAF under contract AC-389. These aircraft were not assigned USAAF serials and do not seem to be associated with any form of Lend-Lease agreement. Identity comprised NAA construction numbers 110-34386 to 110-34485 and it has been stated that these aircraft were shipped unassembled.

From this group, it has been stated that the Australians built up 80 aircraft under the designation Commonwealth Aircraft Corporation (CAC) CA-17 Mustang Mk. 20 and the planes were allocated Australian Air Force serials A68-1 through A68-80. One source has stated that these parts were poorly made and/or damaged in transit and that CAC had to remake/repair components to meet the contract. It would not make sense that NAA would supply poorly made parts, as this would indicate the company went to some effort to make inferior parts for the Australians.

Now comes the confusing part, some historians have stated that the first few of these machines featured P-51B/C canopies and that would seem to indicate they were complete B/C airframes for it would make no sense to go to the extra work to modify a few D wings to fit on B/C fuselages. Or would it? Researching archival photographs unearthed a cockpit shot of what first appeared to be a standard P-51B. However, since these photographs were taken with 4 x 5 negatives a great amount of detail could be examined under magnification. Both factory and USAAF nameplates were quite clear and the USAAF plate reads: P-51D-1-NA, s/n 42-106540, order no. AC 30479 and the NAA plate states AC 30479, s/n 25342. This identifies the aircraft as the second P-51D, which would make it logical that the first P-51D also had the built-up canopy. Also, looking out the right sliding window, it appears the wing is fitted with three machine guns and the airframe is camouflaged in Olive Drab and Neutral Gray. Also, there is a non-standard black bar mounted on the canopy frame that appears to be some sort of leveling device. Was this checking for alignment for a future bubble canopy?

Our second mini-mystery concerns an underwing photo of a Mustang fitted with an HVAR 5-inch rocket installation. Once again, it is of note that the craft has a six-gun wing and is also camouflaged. Could this be one of the two first P-51D-1-NAs?

On the engine test ramp, part of a day's production of P-51Ds awaits engine tests. Note that each aircraft had its own crew shack where tools could be stored and reports filled out.

USAAF ferry pilots began to mount up for a delivery flight. If the aircraft were going to Britain, they were usually flown to Newark, New Jersey, where Dade Shipping would prepare them for the ocean crossing on a ship.

Wonderfully detailed view of a P-51D-20-NA wheel well that illustrates the various tubing, landing light, gun camera installation, and the very smooth condition of the wing—something that would change, and not for the better, once the plane began operations with a combat squadron.

Fitted with overload underwing tanks, a factory pilot runs the Mustang's engine prior to a test flight to check out flight conditions with tanks attached. The spinner on this aircraft had been painted red; probably meaning the aircraft was assigned to NAA for test purposes.

With very little fanfare, the 10,000th Mustang is pulled from the assembly building.

Covered in the signatures of workers, the 10,000th Mustang prepares to depart its birthplace for a USAAF unit.

High over a coastal undercast, a Mustang is put through its paces. Flying only stopped if the weather turned really ugly.

As P-51D/K production ramped up at NAA's Dallas plant, operations were basically similar, but as can be seen in this view of the engine run-up area, AT-6s were mixed into the equation.

The Dallas plant enjoyed quite a bit more ramp space—the extent of which can be seen in this public relations photograph of a Soviet Texan and Mustangs for the Free Netherlands Air Force, Royal Australian Air Force, USAAF, and RAF.

Dallas also offered very good flying weather for most of the year and the flat countryside surrounding the NAA plant was relatively unpopulated.

High-angle view of the engine test area shows the railings to which the aircraft were attached. With the end of the war, the huge plant became almost a ghost town.

THE MUSTANG TRAINER

The dual-control TP-51D was produced too late and in too few numbers to have any real significant effect on Mustang flight training.

It seems to be a curious axiom that most dual-control versions of World War II single-seat fighter aircraft were produced near the middle or end of the particular aircraft's combat life. This certainly held true for the Mustang. In Britain, numerous P-51B/C aircraft were field-modified to carry a second seat behind the pilot. These conversions were usually carried out by crew chiefs and each conversion had considerable variation. Often, Mustangs used for such conversions had been classified as war weary but these modifications served a number of purposes. Some were used as high-speed transports while others were utilized for fun flying—giving rides to the ground crew. Many of these modified aircraft received unique color schemes, but usually carried the unit codes of the squadron or group that did the conversion.

However, none of these two-seat aircraft had dual controls—a modification that was complex at best. Well into the production run of the P-51D, North American received a USAAF contract to convert 10 aircraft to full dual-control configuration. This was a lengthy modification. The rear fuel tank was removed and engineers then completely redid everything behind the pilot's seat. They managed to squeeze in a full instrument panel, stick, rudder pedals, and throttle along with the second seat. What is interesting is that this work was undertaken in the standard cockpit space and under a stock D canopy. As can be seen in the photographs, North American would go from a stock

canopy to one with a more bulged configuration. The second seat would still be an extremely uncomfortable and cramped position for the instructor/ student and visibility over the nose would have been almost non-existent. Also, being over the radiator the position would have been very warm. Ten TP-51D conversions were undertaken (comprising Inglewood-built P-51D-25-NA 44-84610/-611; Dallas-built P-51D-25-NT 45-11443/-450) and most seemed to have been utilized with the 3615th AMB, 3616th AMS at Craig AAFB, Selma, Alabama, but the aircraft were also shuffled between various stateside bases where they were used for indoctrination or recurrence training.

It was not until after the war that a much more satisfactory TF-51D was built—and this was not done by NAA, but rather by Temco in Dallas. Temco—Texas Engineering and Manufacturing Company—had taken over a good deal of the former NAA plant and was engaged in a number of military

USAAF 44-84610 was the first TP-51D conversion and this view illustrates the stock D model canopy. Armor plate had been removed from the pilot's seat and the top of the second instrument panel is clearly visible. It is interesting to note that the data block on the fuselage had already been changed to TP-51D.

In order to make the second seater a bit more comfortable, a higher and more bulged canopy was added to the TP-51D, but this was still not an ideal solution.

and civilian projects. Temco approached the conversion in a much more logical manner by removing part of the rear fuselage deck to create a much larger cockpit that would more easily accommodate the rear seat, panel, and associated controls. A new and larger canopy frame was built for the greatly extended canopy. Some 15 TF-51D Temco conversions were undertaken and the trainers were in high postwar demand. As a point of interest, the airframes were new six-year-old P-51Ds that had been stored (along with hundreds of other Mustangs) at Kelly AFB.

After the war, many Air National Guard units were equipped with Mustangs and it was not uncommon for the TFs to have served with several ANG units where they were utilized as valuable trainers for the weekend warriors. Also, many Mustangs had been supplied to friendly foreign nations that also requested TFs for training. Some of these limited edition former ANG machines were passed to Latin American air forces after being phased out of USAF service.

With the start of the Korean War and the equipping of the Republic of Korea Air Force (ROKAF) with Mustangs, an extremely high accident rate saw several of the TFs transferred to South Korea where they helped reduce the ROKAF accident rate.

Carrying TF buzz codes, 44-84662 was photographed over Los Angeles while on a visit to the North American factory. The well-used Temco aircraft had the tail wheel fixed in the down position. The postwar USAF was having a problem with the tail wheel installation on their aging TF-51D fleet and issued a technical order to have the unit placed in a permanent down position.

The ideal configuration for a dual-control Mustang was found by Temco—extend the cockpit area and install a much larger canopy. The pilot of 44-84670 posed his aircraft against a buildup of clouds over Dallas. The zinc chromate area distinguishes the modified portion of the upper fuselage decking. Note the instrument hood for the second seat.

A Royal Air Force P-51K-10-NT awaits delivery under Lend-Lease as a Mustang Mk. IV.

As at Inglewood, Mustang operations at Dallas continued well into the night as a batch of Mustang Mk. IVs for the RAF had their engines tested. Aircraft in the foreground is P-51K-10-NT 44-12334. The flash photograph emphasizes the different tones of aluminum.

modification worked well, allowing pilots to lessen the stick forces required to maneuver the fighter, particularly in combat. The structural integrity of the ailerons was also improved through the employment of three hinge bearing attachments rather than two.

With the addition of two extra Browning M2 weapons, the P-51D could tote 1,840 rounds of ammunition, divided into 400 rounds for each inboard weapon, while the center and outboard .50s had 260 rounds apiece. Capable of firing 800 rpm, the M2 had a muzzle velocity of 2,810 fps, with a maximum range of 7,200 yards, but the effective combat range was about

The first P-51D-5-NT of the NA-111 contract has its compass swung at Dallas.

800 yards maximum. The early P-51B/Cs had lots of armament problems since the weapons were installed at a rather extreme side angle to allow feed chutes easy access from the ammunition trays, but this caused jams due to casings and links becoming entangled in the feed belts. Further snags were encountered with the weapons' oil and grease lubricant, which would often congeal at rarified operational ceilings despite being fitted with heaters (usually actuated near the combat area). These major problems were rectified by repositioning the weapons and issuing instructions to pilots to activate the heaters after the weapons had been charged.

The P-51D was to be the shining light of NAA's wartime fighter production with the Inglewood plant alone constructing 6,502 D-NA Mustangs. The Dallas factory would go on to contribute a further 1,600 D-NTs to the overall total, which included the photo-recon variants. The Dallas-built P-51K was similar to the D, but featured an Aeroproducts propeller, and 1,500 of these machines were completed. By any standard, the P-51D was a resounding production, as well as combat, success.

A WASP ferry pilot prepares to board her Mustang. As this book goes to press, an intensive search is being carried out in the Pacific for a WASP pilot who was lost in her Mustang shortly after takeoff from Mines Field.

With victory in sight, NAA began to plan for postwar life in America—a life that was predicted (incorrectly) to include a huge increase in private aircraft. Edgar Schmued designed the NA-145—an efficient four-seat aircraft that was originally named NAvion 51 as a play on NAA, the French word for bird, and the association with the P-51. Built incredibly strong, nearly 2,000 Navions (as they are popularly named) are still flying today.

CHAPTER FIVE

THE LIGHTWEIGHTS

In an attempt to obtain more performance from the Mustang, North American engineers came up with a completely new design built to British structural strength standards.

An axiom with the military is that if a combat aircraft remains in service long enough, then more performance is demanded from the basic design. Even though the NAA P-51 Mustang was the most aerodynamically efficient of all World War II fighter aircraft, enemy fighters in several different flight regimes could best it. For example, a comparable Mark of Spitfire could attain a set altitude in about one-third less time than a Mustang while a newer Luftwaffe Fw 190 had twice the roll rate of a Mustang. Much of the Mustang's slightly downward trend in performance was due to the fact that each variant had more and more combat equipment and extra fuel added which increased weight.

Accordingly, Edgar Schmued was given top priority travel instructions and dispatched to Britain on 9 February 1943 for a two-month trip to meet with British designers and study fighter combat philosophy and compare design and production techniques. The designer would later record, "The American air attaché in England was, in this case, Col. Tommy Hitchcock, a very famous polo player and

Parked among a diverse collection of aircraft including P-51Bs, a B-25, and Douglas SBD Dauntlesses, Bob Chilton starts the V-1650-3 fitted to XP-51F USAAF s/n 43-43332. Hand-crafted in the NAA experimental shops, the XP-51Fs were beautiful, finely finished aircraft with great attention to streamlining detail—as can be seen by the closely fitted stainless-steel exhaust shrouds.

As the Mustang design matured, so did the sophistication of the wind tunnels. Tunnel testing proved that lengthening of the canopy and scoop fairing would improve overall performance.

Ground personnel fit an external starter to the XP-51F's V-1650-3, which leads to the speculation that a starter was not fitted on the engine or the unit was not operational. With the long bubble canopy in the open position, Bob Chilton scans the instruments prior to start.

In the weight reduction program, every component of the Mustang was considered. An engineer points out a detail on a magnificent fuselage model to NAA assistant chief engineer H. A. Evans. For the Mustang enthusiast, this photo also has a couple of other points of interest—the Rolls-Royce Silver Wraith ashtray and the original P-51D painting on the wall done by famed artist Reynold Brown.

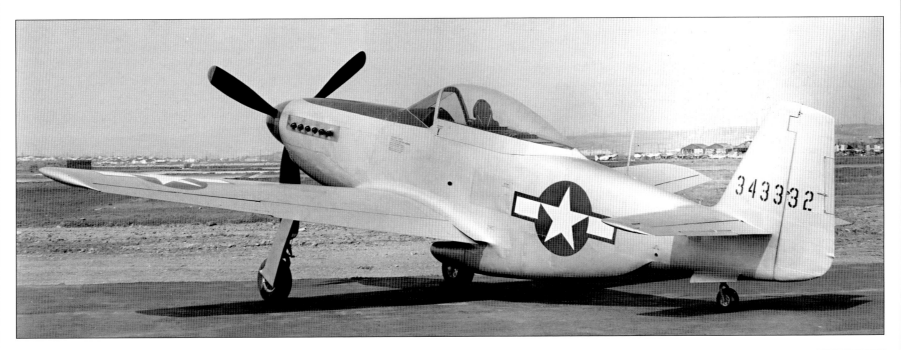

The lovely lines of the first XP-51F are well displayed in these three-quarter rear views that show the size of the bubble canopy to advantage. The large canopy actually helped streamlining—its length smoothing out airflow. As can be seen, the entire airframe (except for the cowlings and inspection panels) was filled, sanded, and then finished with a special silver lacquer to achieve a very smooth finish.

sportsman, who flew the P-51 with pleasure. He did help out on searching out problems that somebody had discovered and he verified them, if he could. He was really very instrumental in making my visit to England successful. He saw to it that I had all the papers, reservations, and the priority to go to New York to start on a flight to England on a Boeing 314 Clipper.

"It was a slow flying boat, but extremely comfortable. After waiting eight days in wintertime New York for the ice to clear, I finally got on the plane and flew to Lisbon. We were put up in a hotel overnight, and the next day we went off to Ireland.

"There was something very funny about the Irish. They really seemed to be under-the-table allies of the Germans and they did not like the idea that I, as a former German, was working to help the British in their war against Hitler. But it was always clear to me that once you change your nationality; your loyalty belongs to your new country. Their treatment was not particularly friendly. I was isolated as an individual and only at the last moment was I permitted to board the airplane that took me to London.

"I was most happy to get all the support from the British that I could have asked for. They were the most genial and nicest people I have ever met. They were building the first Vampire… and they insisted that I see this brand-new

Test pilot Bob Chilton in the cockpit of the XP-51F. Of note is Bob's modified football helmet—which served as one of the first hard hats utilized by test pilots. The large deeply cut windshield offered improved forward and downward visibility. As a point of interest, Bob was rather short of stature and had to sit on two phone books to enable the photographer getting his hero shot.

The instrument panel of the third, and final, XP-51F, USAAF s/n 43-43334. The layout of the panel was simplified over earlier Mustang variants. Note the V-shaped instrument panel shroud and how the rudder pedals have been drilled out to reduce weight—no step was too small in the aircraft's overall weight reduction program.

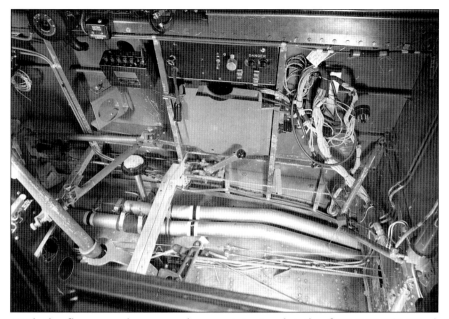

With the floor panels removed, some interior details of XP-51F USAAF s/n 43-43332 are revealed on both sides of the cockpit.

Floor panels in place (the lightweights utilized thin aluminum rather than the varnished wood floor panels on earlier Mustangs), this view illustrates the substantial control lock attached to the stick.

Detail of the XP-51F's tail wheel unit, which was reduced in size and weight compared to earlier Mustangs.

XP-51F/G DIMENSIONS

	Wing	Horizontal Tails		Vertical Tails	
	W	H	H1	V	V1
Root Profile	NACA 66, 2-18155 a = 0.6	652-012*	NACA Symm. 10.22% thick	652-101*	NACA Symm. 10% thick
Tip Profile	NACA 66, 2-18120 a = 0.6	652-010*	NACA Symm. 9.65% thick	652-019*	NACA Symm. 7.63% thick
Root Chord (in.)	105	49.64	49.9	69.75	74.94
Tip Chord (in.)	50	28.79	28.9	32	29.1
Taper Ratio	2.1:1	1.725:1	1.725:1	2.18:1	2.57:1
Sweepback of Leading Edge	3o39'33"	9o41'	9o45'	24o3'	26o46'
Geometric Twist	2.5o	0	0	0	0
Dihedral	5o	0	0	—	—
Mean Aerodynamic Chord (in.)	80.07	—	—	—	—
Area (sq ft)	235.6	41.96	41.04	20.4	20.58
Span (ft)	37	13.18	13.17	4.64	4.47
Aspect Ratio	5.811	4.14	4.24	1.16	1.17

* Straight lines from trailing edge to points of tangency with basic contour

Frontal Area of Fuselage = 12.27 sq ft

Frontal Area of Cockpit Enclosure = 2.19 sq ft

Radiator Duct:
Cross-sectional area at lip of inlet = 165 sq in
Cross-sectional area at inlet pitot tubes = 170 sq in

Cross-sectional area at front face of radiator core = 557 sq in

Radiator Exit Door: (dimensions used in hinge moment calculations)
Mean Chord = 2.833 ft
Area aft of hinge line = 4.669 sq ft

Full-Scale Propeller:
11.167 ft diameter; four-blades; planform and twist of Hamilton Standard 6487A-24 blade

airplane with the Whittle engine… I told them that 'I did not come here to pry into your secrets,' but they insisted I see it. Colonel Hitchcock and I made a trip to de Havilland and saw the Vampire in the mockup stage. That's as far as they had gotten.

"In the meanwhile, the British had developed a new version of the Merlin, the RM.14.SM. It was a Merlin engine which had a manifold pressure of 120 inches and developed 2,200 hp. This was the answer to our many prayers; more power without increasing weight. Every airplane designer likes to hear that and so did we.

"I went to Derby to visit the Rolls-Royce people and get all the dope on the new 14.SM engine. When I arrived at the factory, there was a large room reserved for the meeting. I sat in the middle and in half-circle formation sat all the experts of Rolls-Royce. I was shooting questions out and somebody, without directing, picked up his slipstick [slide rule], started working, and 15 to 20 minutes later gave me the answer.

"It was a marvelous demonstration of cooperation and ability to manage. I obtained all the information I needed to use their new 14.SM engine in the P-51 including the cooling and the installation requirements. I had all the information I could possibly have asked for."

Rolls-Royce's Bill Lappin would write, "It has been a most valuable thing to have Schmued visit us, and after meeting him a few times, one has no difficulty in realizing why the Mustang is a good aeroplane."

Schmued came back to North American invigorated with new information and ideas. Using his newly acquired acknowledge, he interfaced with USAAF officials. "Then came the idea from the field [the USAAF] that our airplanes were too heavy. American airplanes were heavier than the British and they [the USAAF] wanted to know why. That was not an easy thing to answer."

North American Aviation field personnel, upon Schmued's request, began weighing different Spitfire components and came up with a weight statement on the aircraft. "There were a number of reasons why the British airplanes were lighter than ours," wrote Schmued. "First, the high angle-of-attack load factor was 12 in America, but only 11 in England. Second, there was a side-load factor on the engine mount in America of 2g, which the British didn't have at all… then the landing gear load factors that we used were 6g, but were only 4g in England. We used all these lower factors to help whittle out a good deal of weight in a new design."

Back at Inglewood, Schmued wrote down his thoughts and observations in a report, one example of which was received by Gen. Henry "Hap" Arnold. Always looking for a cutting edge in combat design, Arnold called his old friend Dutch Kindelberger and suggested that the company should build a lightweight fighter. Accordingly, North American got busy on a proposal for the lightweight fighter and submitted data to the USAAF. On 20 July 1943, the government issued a contract for five aircraft under the company designation

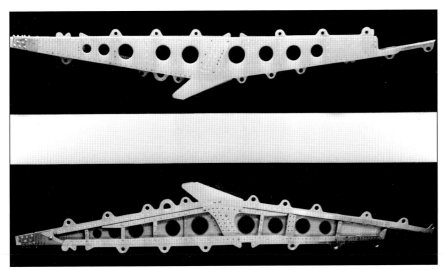

The motor mounts for the lightweights were designed not only to decrease weight, but also to increase structural strength.

Resting in its motor mount and with all accessories installed, a V-1650-3 is prepared for mounting on an XP-51F airframe. The lower portion of the motor mount has the airframe's exterior skin attached.

Detail of the XP-51F instrument panel hood also shows the aircraft's recognition light panel. The three lights (red, green, and amber), located under the wing, would be used to display the colors of the day and identify the Mustang to friendly forces.

These high-angle views show the overall slim configuration of the XP-51F to advantage. The very slick and smooth external finish to the overall airframe contributed to performance, but certainly could not have been maintained in the field. At this point in the test program, the spinner had been painted bright red.

Direct side view of 43-43332 highlights two of the lightweights' main recognition features—the elongated canopy and scoop fairing. Edgar Schmued greatly enjoyed his visit to Britain during spring 1943 and his stop at the Rolls-Royce facility confirmed his view point that airframe improvements had to go hand-in-hand with the increasing power coming from Merlin variants.

NA-105. Rolls-Royce and the British government would supply five new RM.14.SM engines and two Rotol five-blade propellers in return for two completed airframes.

Schmued would later write, "This was our go-ahead to build the P-51F. It was a marvelous exercise for us because we already had an airplane that was very, very light [the P-51 in comparison to the P-47 Thunderbolt and P-38 Lightning]. Now, by using some of the British load factors and design requirements and our design improvements, we actually whittled 600 pounds off the empty weight of the airplane… we took some great pains to save weight everywhere.

"For instance, the part of the engine cowling at the engine mount was actually a structural member of the engine mount, with a substantial weight saving. It also provided a better attachment of the engine cowling. The fuselage skins, aft of the firewall, used to be .065 aluminum alloy. At that time we had heard the Aluminum Company of America [Alcoa] had a stronger new alloy—75 ST—so we asked them to send us the material for our new airplane. They told us you can't get that material before next year.

"We then decided we were going to make our own 75 ST material by using 25 ST and stretch-forming and heat-treating it so we got the same values as the 75 ST material. But we bought ourselves a great deal of problems… when you rivet a .065-inch skin, you can cut-countersink for the head of a rivet, but you can't do that with the thin .042 skins we had to replace the .065 skin. There was no way of counter-sinking it.

"The only thing we had left was dimpling. We took these high-quality materials, 75 ST sheets, and started dimpling. We discovered to our dismay, that every time the punch came down, a little slug fell out. Instead of dimpling, we punched a hole in the sheet.

"Our research department was then asked to develop a method that we could use for punching these dimples into the sheet without cracking them or breaking them through. They came up with what they called a 'coin-dimpling' process. In this case, a punch came down against the surface and held the sheet of aluminum alloy tight against the surface underneath while the punch came down and formed the dimple."

Using creative thinking, the design team was able to greatly reduce weight in almost all areas. The first XP-51F flew from Mines Field on 14 February 1944 with Bob Chilton at the controls. The F was a beautiful aircraft and would be viewed, by today's definition, as being dedicated to one role: that of a high-altitude, high-performance fighter. When the USAAF contract for the F was issued during April 1943, there was no mention of ground attack, dive bombing, reconnaissance, or any other role that would detract from the aircraft's primary mission.

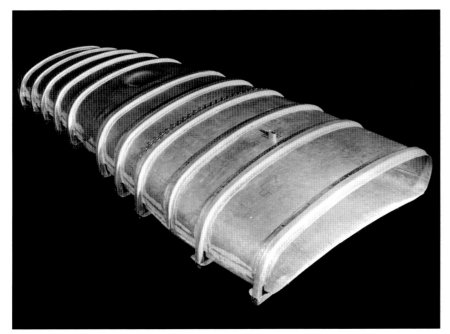 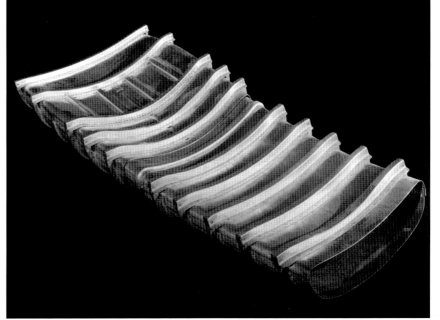

The XP-51F induction trunk was simplified to reduce weight and maintenance.

XP-51J PERFORMANCE

Gross Weight	7,400 lbs	Service Ceiling	43,700 ft (same for all ratings)
Fuel	105 gallons	Climb to 20,000 ft	3.3 minutes (war emergency rating, 150-grade fuel)
Wing Loading	31.4 lbs/sq ft		3.6 minutes (war emergency rating 130-grade fuel)
Max Speed (war emergency	424 mph @ sea level		5.0 minutes (military rating)
rating, 150-grade fuel)	495 mph @ 25,000 feet		
Max Speed (war emergency	409 mph @ sea level	Takeoff to Clear 50-ft Obstacle	1,098 ft
rating, 130-grade fuel)	491 mph @ 27,400 ft (critical altitude)	Landing to Clear 50-ft Obstacle*	1,595 ft
Max Speed (military rating)	369 mph @ sea level	Landing Speed*	83.4 mph
	470 mph @ 36,000 ft (critical altitude)		
Max Rate of Climb (sea level)	6,600 fpm (war emergency rating, 150-grade fuel)	* Based on gross weight = 7,085 lbs (basic gross weight less half fuel)	
	5,900 fpm (war emergency rating, 130-grade fuel)		
	4,230 fpm (military rating)		

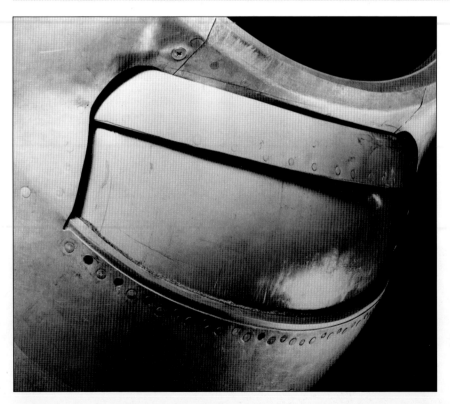

Rolls-Royce was keeping a close watch on the development of the lightweight Mustangs and Ernest Hives visited NAA and in a 28 September 1943 report he commented, "I saw the new lightened machine. My estimate is that it should be flying by the end of the year. It should be an outstanding machine. They have improved the pilot's view considerably from the original scheme. So far, they have orders for five of these machines—three for the USA and two for England. The anticipated production will start in September 1944. I strongly recommended that they should try and make 20 of these machines before their production is in hand.

"No one in the USA appeared to know that the requirement for fighters in this country [UK] was 25-percent high-altitude and 75 percent low-altitude."

Rolls-Royce chief engineer A. G. Elliott also visited NAA and made the following comments, "I had a good look at one of the XP-51F machines, which are the first lightened versions having the V-1650-3 engine, the reason for using the V-1650-3 engines being that the V-1650-9 is now going to have the high supercharger gear ratios. This machine incorporates the oil system and aftercooler

Although it was not installed on the lightweight airframes, NAA designed and built this ram air gate, which is illustrated in a closed position. Controlled by the pilot, it would let filtered air in through a panel on the side of the cowling (also not installed on the flying aircraft since the lightweights would not be going into the field). The mechanism was installed in the induction trunk and hot air from the engine opened the gate. In the open position, the filtered air went directly to the carburetor.

heat exchanger with its combined aftercooler radiator and oil cooler radiator. It also incorporates the North American style of rocker cover breathers, which differ considerably from the RM.14.SM arrangement. The oil heat exchanger certainly appears on the face of it to make a rather neat installation and so far is stated to be functioning very well. The one I inspected was of a somewhat temporary nature and the pipe work was not quite up to the usual North American standard. The aftercooler and oil cooler radiator is, of course, quite big... this radiator of course is mounted behind the main engine radiator in the same duct."

At this time, the P-51D was beginning to roll off the production line and the D's weight was used as a guide. Schmued wanted to keep the empty weight of the

With the background carefully removed by NAA photo lab technicians, the attractive lines of XP-51G USAAF s/n 43-43336 are displayed to advantage. Nearly complete, the aircraft was fitted with the Rolls-Royce RM.14.SM powerplant and four-blade Aeroproducts propeller. Note the open gun bays on the wing. This high-angle view also shows how the Mustang's distinctive cranked leading edge was eliminated courtesy of the smaller landing gear, wheels, and tires.

Although the compact and trim lines of the XP-51G went quite well with the Rotol propeller, flight testing was less than satisfactory and the unit was quickly replaced with the Aeroproducts propeller. It appears that the gun ports for the four .50-cal. Brownings had been faired over but the shell ejection chutes can be seen on the lower surface of the wing. Also note how the fairing for the scoop had been extended almost to the tail wheel—once again aiding in streamlining.

Pushed out to an open portion of ramp for photographic purposes, XP-51G USAAF s/n 43-43335 is seen prior to its first flight with the five-blade wooden composite Rotol propeller. The small dorsal fin was an interim attempt to improve stability.

XP-51F at 5,700 pounds and he did—the completed aircraft weighed in at 5,635 pounds. Streamlining was accentuated and a very long bubble canopy was added which helped smooth out the airflow (It must be remembered that the B was slightly faster than the D and this was because of the streamlining offered by the built-up rear fuselage). The radiator scoop was also lengthened for the same reason. Armament was reduced to four .50-cal. machine guns, a new landing gear was designed with smaller wheels and tires that eliminated the Mustang's cranked leading edge, and a three-blade Aeroproducts Unimatic hydraulic constant-speed propeller with hollow blades was added which also reduced weight.

Inspection panels were reduced in number but, at the same time, they were redistributed and made more efficient. The cowling for the V-1650-3 was also redesigned and the number of components greatly reduced, which allowed quicker and easier access to the powerplant and accessories.

The finish of the XP-51F was also a matter of considerable attention. The airframe was entirely flush riveted while the surface of the aircraft, with the exception of the cowling and inspection panels, was filled with special putty that had been developed by NAA. After drying, the putty was sanded down, reapplied where necessary, and then sanded down again before being primed and painted with a special silver lacquer. The company even went as far as to ensure that each and every rivet dimple had been smoothly filled.

Right from the start, Bob Chilton knew the XP-51F was a winner. "When we were doing the initial ground testing of the engine, we could not run the throttle up unless the aircraft was firmly chained down. On the early test flights I found that I had so much power on my hands that I had to advance the throttle by increments to prevent the plane from taking off prematurely. By the time that I had reached only 30 inches of manifold pressure, the F was off and flying!"

Flight testing of the XP-51F was sandwiched between the many other flight tests that were being conducted at NAA and Chilton recalled, "We were dealing with such a huge volume of new aircraft that time for testing new projects, unless they were of the highest priority, was strictly limited. On an overall total, the XP-51Fs probably accumulated no more than 100 flying hours.

Head-on view illustrates the wonderfully streamlined shape of the XP-51G.

"The USAAF did not like the idea that the XP-51F was built to British load specifications. They had gotten used to the incredibly rugged strength designed into almost all American fighters. They felt that the Japanese had gone way too far in sacrificing structural strength for additional performance. The USAAF was also none too pleased with the European and British practice of dropping some structural strength in favor of boosted performance. This was not to say that the XP-51F, or any of the lightweight Mustangs, was not a strong aircraft. They were not as strong as the basic D model, however."

Reducing weight and streamlining made the XP-51F into what Bob Chilton fondly remembered as my favorite Mustang. He recalled, "It was not uncommon to climb out of Mines Field at 7,500 feet per minute. The F handled like a finely tuned racecar and it was hard to find an angle-of-attack that would keep the aircraft slow enough to achieve its 250-mph climb-out speed. It was not uncommon on test flights to climb to 45,000 feet and that led to some interesting problems.

"Firstly, the F was, of course, not pressurized and, secondly, flying at altitudes of such extreme height was still a bit novel and the personal equipment for high-altitude flying had not kept pace with the aircraft. You would dress with as many layers of clothing as possible, to which was added a heavy flying jacket.

"I had been doing some experimental work with the University of Southern California in their new centrifuge, testing the effects of various aeronautical situations on the human body. For the high-altitude flights in the XP-51F, we obtained a Canadian experimental vest that wrapped completely around the upper torso of the body. Oxygen from the fuselage tanks passed through the vest, which made it very tight and uncomfortable with the pressure.

"However, the pressure was a great help at altitude. I had a British-built manually controlled regulator that hung on a strap around my neck and this device was calibrated so that I could dial the pressure required to keep the oxygen blood level at its correct percentage. In effect, I was having about 18 pounds of pressure shoved down my throat, which made speaking over the radio extremely difficult. The heavy pressure from the vest helped somewhat but I could only transmit one word at a time and that was only possible when I was exhaling, making it very difficult for the ground personnel to understand my messages.

"The heater, at 45,000 feet, was just putting out more frozen air but there were certain benefits. Passing through 30,000 feet, it seemed that the air was very clear. But when I broke 35,000 it seemed that I had passed into an entirely new strata of really clear air. I could look back and see an almost razor-sharp demarcation line and it made for a very awe-inspiring sight. One

The Rolls-Royce RM.14.SM awaiting installation in the XP-51G.

day, I was flying at 45,000 feet between Los Angeles and San Diego and the air was so clear that I could pick out a specific mountain peak almost 600 miles away in Arizona. The beauty of those high-altitude flights is something I will never forget."

NAA failed to get the benefit of 500-mph publicity from the XP-51F, not due to any lack of work on the part of Native American George Mountain Bear who, as with the NA-73X, spent day after day polishing the surface of the fighter. However, George's hard work could not get the aircraft past the magic 500-mph mark. With the first XP-51F (6,296-pound gross on the first flight), Chilton was able to achieve 491 mph at 21,500 feet (taking off with a loaded weight of 7,340 pounds). "We were in sort of a war with Republic and their P-47," recalled Chilton. "Republic was doing everything they could to get over the 500-mph mark and this included publishing some really inaccurate figures. I would start out with the F at 30,000 feet and begin a descent to 21,500 feet at maximum military power—67 inches. I would then level out and go to 90 inches with water/alcohol injection. We came close, but not close enough. To illustrate his integrity, a few individuals wanted Edgar to 'fudge' and state we hit 500. He would not."

Few unsatisfactory characteristics were uncovered while testing the F models. As with the P-51B, there was a lack of directional stability in level flight while at maximum power. Also, the F's flaps retracted in a very rapid three seconds and this caused equally rapid, and undesirable, trim changes.

The USAAF was apparently content to let the XP-51Fs slip into obscurity without issuing further contracts for development (the second XP-51F flew on 22 May 1944 with Chilton while the third aircraft got airborne two days earlier and was shipped to Britain on 30 June as Mustang V FR409). It is presumed that the two USAAF XP-51Fs ended their days on the scrap heap.

The next step in the development of the lightweight Mustangs was the XP-51G (NA-105A), which featured the Rolls-Royce RM.14.SM power-plants. This engine was an experimental Merlin with a critical altitude of 25,000 feet and capable of producing 1,675 hp on takeoff. The engine also used a fuel-control metering unit instead of a carburetor and this resulted in considerable testing and modification of the air intake scoop until the right combination was found.

A. G. Elliott reported back to Rolls-Royce on 8 June 1944 that, "The main reason for my visit to North American was to see the progress which has been

XP-51G 43-43335 was stripped of its wings and tail surfaces and mounted on this fixture once the limited test flying program was finished. The aircraft was fitted with a four-blade needle propeller—all test flights were done with the four-blade Aeroproducts prop except for the one contractual flight with the Dowty Rotol unit. It appears that NAA wanted to test the RM.14.SM to destruction and by the oil-soaked fuselage it appears they were successful. Fortunately, the fuselage was saved by John Morgan who now has the G under long-term restoration.

made with regard to the installation of the two RM.14.SM engines which you have sent here… I got the impression that they were not now so interested in flying the RM.14.SM engines as they would have been had these engines been made available to them some months earlier. The reason for this is that they are not contemplating making any production machines with your engines but that the corresponding P-51H machines with the V-1650-9 engines will, of course, be installationally somewhat different, and seeing that they expect to get some V-1650-9 engines before the end of the year for their prototype flying, the XP-51G machines will probably not be of as much use to them as they might have been. The first machine [XP-51G] will not be ready to fly for about three weeks, whereas the second one will not be ready until some time later. In any case, they do not propose to fly either machine until they have had some tests on one engine in order to find how the ratings of the engine compare with its British rating when using the available American-grade 150 fuel.

"I had an interesting talk with Mr. W. Templeton who is, of course, the Rotol representative who was sent out recently on this job. It appeared to me that it was rather lucky that he arrived on the scene when he did because he is the only person apparently who has had any connection with this job who knew how to adjust the Merlin 66 type of boost control with which these engines are fitted, and J. E. Ellor [R-R advisor at Packard] will know enough about North American to know what I mean when I say that anything which can be taken to pieces is liable to be pounced upon as soon as it enters the Inglewood factory.

"It is the intention to fly the first machine, first with an Aeroproducts propeller and then with one of the Rotol propellers, in order to obtain a direct comparison between the two, but Templeton has not as yet unpacked any of his Rotol propellers as he does not feel it desirable to have them laying around the shop to get damaged as they evidently will not be required for some little time yet.

"They tell me that they are expecting two more RM.14.SM engines in the very near future, one of which is to be sent direct to Inglewood and the other to Wright Field for altitude chamber tests, and it seemed to me that there was

Upper portion of the instrument panel of XP-51G USAAF s/n 43-43335 showing the instrument shroud and partial mount for the gun sight (which was probably never installed).

Second XP-51G 43-43336 (photographed at the factory on 26 February 1945) was finished in basic RAF markings and shipped to Britain. Once in Britain, the aircraft was camouflaged and tested at Boscombe Down where it reportedly achieved a top speed of 495 mph.

going to be a tendency for the North American flight tests to hang fire until they got this third engine, so that it could be used for ground tests.

"In order to make the two RM.14.SM engines suitable for installation in the XP-51G aircraft, quite a few external installation modifications had to be made and these were carried out by the Packard representative Mr. Freeman. When Mr. J. W. Wheeler came over he brought with him... a curve showing the performance of Mustang FX858 with RM.14.SM engine No. 90353 in it [this was one of the RAF Mustangs assigned to R-R for Merlin engine development work].

"I took this curve with me and Mr. Schmued was very surprised to see it as he stated that the performance shown therein was very poor, particularly with regard to maximum speeds which only come to about 445-mph true air speed at 17,600 feet in high gear with 25 pounds boost. He says he is hoping for at least 500 although of course he realized that this particular Mustang is not of the lightened variety."

The first XP-51G, USAAF s/n 43-43335, was flown for the first time by Ed Virgin on 10 August 1944. Bob Chilton was next and after a few flights with the Aeroproducts propeller, the five-blade Rotol unit was fitted. Bob remembered, "A British technician was sent out with the propeller but it was a full five months before we could get around to testing the unit. The Brit certainly enjoyed his lengthy vacation with trips to Hollywood and other tourist spots. Once we got a breather in our testing program, we had the Rotol unit fitted. The aircraft made just one flight with the propeller and, unfortunately, I was at the controls. The propeller made the XP-51G directionally unstable, especially over 250 mph when any touch of the rudder would cause the aircraft to start wandering in a most erratic manner." The Aeroproducts unit was re-installed after this flight and the aircraft was sent off to the USAAF after a total of 37 test flights. The USAAF accepted the aircraft on 26 September.

The second XP-51G, USAAF s/n 43-43336, was assigned to the RAF. The aircraft made its first flight on 14 November with Joe Barton at the controls. With North American, the aircraft made 54 test flights. Given the serial FR410, this aircraft was also briefly test flown—the vertical fin and rudder increased slightly in height—and fitted with a four-blade Aeroproducts propeller.

The final version of the experimental lightweight Mustangs was the XP-51J (NA-105B) and these aircraft were built for a USAAF contract issued on 30 June 1944. Two J models were built and they were very similar—from the firewall back—to the F

The two XP-51Js nearing completion in the NAA experimental shop. The simplified engine mount is immediately apparent, as is the large access panel in the side of the fuselage. A vertical tail of increased height had been fitted to this aircraft.

and G. The main reason for the construction of the J was to test the installation of the Allison V-1710-119 powerplant and the Allison-developed infinitely variable supercharger. With the standard two-stage supercharger unit that was fitted to the Merlin, there was a definite gap between the point when the first stage of the supercharger would become inefficient and the point when the second stage blower would cut in.

However, Bob Chilton felt that the Allison left something to be desired and "the cylinder head design of the Allison had never changed since day one. This caused improper fuel distribution between cylinders, causing popping and detonation when high power settings were applied. We put British plugs on the Allison and this helped but did not cure the problem. However, the supercharger appeared to work just fine and was an improvement on the two-stage system." Joe Barton had made the first XP-51J flight on 23 April 1945, but little flying was done with the two J models (the first aircraft had seven flights, the second just two) and the aircraft were turned over to the USAAF on 15 February 1946. Both XP-51Js were transferred to the Allison Division of General Motors for testing the V-1710-143 engine that would be used in the F-82E Twin Mustang.

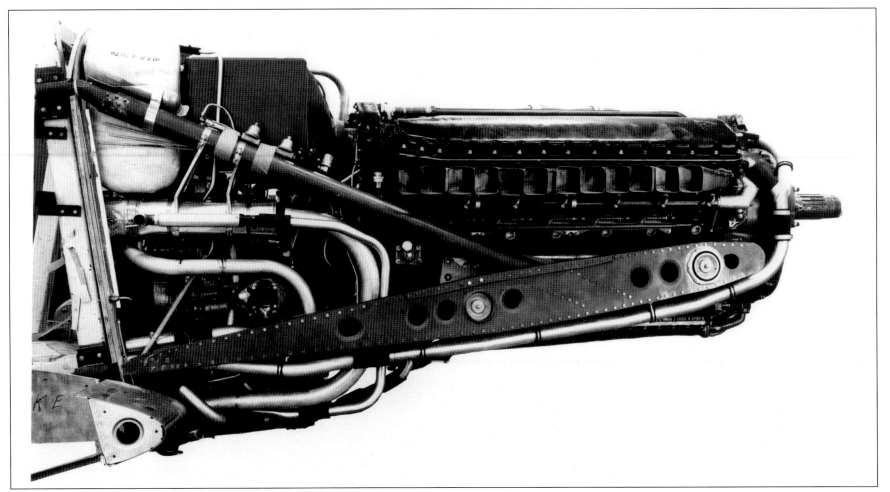

Allison V-1710-119 installed in the XP-51J's motor mount to test installation of equipment. The motor mount is attached to a mockup installation and not the actual aircraft.

A final look at the experimental lightweights leaves one with the impression that they were more an exercise in design management than a direct assault on a new generation of propeller-driven fighter. Schmued once said that *can't do* wasn't in his vocabulary and he certainly did prove that the lightweight Mustangs could be built and offer very high performance figures. USAAF planning had changed during the developmental time period and the lightweights never achieved the production line but the design goals were usually reached and, in many cases, exceeded. The lessons from the experimental lightweights would be applied to the ultimate Mustang—the P-51H. As a final note, when the Korean War took America by surprise, it was not the P-51H that was ordered to the front line. It was the old and reliable D model. Apparently it was felt that the structural strength and load carrying capability of the H was insufficient.

The Aeroproducts paddle blade propeller helped absorb the Allison's high horsepower ratings.

Rear view of an XP-51J in the experimental shop. Note how the fuselage has been carefully filled. After NAA testing, both J models were transferred to Allison for further development work on the -143 powerplant. Note the lightening holes drilled in the landing gear clamshell doors.

Beautifully handcrafted cowling covered the XP-51J's Allison V-1710-119 powerplant. The cowling was greatly simplified when compared to its P-51B counterpart. Carburetor air was ducted through the main radiator scoop, thus eliminating any forward opening on the cowling.

XP-51J SPECIFICATIONS

Wing

Total Area (including area covered by fuselage)	235.73 sq ft
Span	37.03 ft
Aspect Ratio	5.82
Mean Aerodynamic Chord	80.17 in
Approximate Surface Area Exposed to Airstream	441.74 sq ft

Airfoil Section

Root	66,2 - 18155 (a = .6)
Tip	66,2 - 1812 (a = .6)

Horizontal Tail Surfaces

Total Area	41.96 sq ft
Span	158.12 in
Aspect Ratio	4.14
Approximate Surface Area Exposed to Airstream	76.38 sq ft

Airfoil Section

Root	65,2 - 012
Tip	65,2 - 010

Vertical Tail Surfaces

Total Area	20.40 sq ft
Approximate Surface Area Exposed to Airstream	39.75 sq ft

Airfoil Section

Root	65,2 - 010
Tip	65,2 - 009

Fuselage

Maximum Cross Sectional Area	12.27 sq ft
Approximate Surface Area Exposed to Airstream	2.97 sq ft
Overall Length	32 ft 11.3 in

Cockpit Enclosure

Maximum Cross Sectional Area	2.79 sq ft
Surface Area - Added to Fuselage	17.78 sq ft

Radiator Scoop

Maximum Cross Sectional Area	3.19 sq ft
Surface Area - Added to Fuselage	28.1 sq ft

Miscellaneous

Height of MAC Above Ground	Static 57.43 in
	Oleo Extended: 63.74 in
Total Frontal Area (not including wing and empennage)	18.2 sq ft
Total Surface Area	900.94 sq ft

Powerplant

Manufacturer	Allison Division of GMC
Model	V-1710-119 (F32R)
Propeller Gear Ratio	
Engine	8:1:1
Auxiliary Variable Speed Drive Coupled	7.64:1
Impeller Diameters	
Engine	9.5 in
Auxiliary	2.8 in
Power Ratings: Static	
War Emergency (150 grade fuel)	2,100 bhp/3,200 rpm/sea level
War Emergency (130 grade fuel)	1,900 bhp/3,200 rpm/sea level
Military	1,425 bhp/3,200 rpm/sea level
Takeoff	1,500 bhp/3,200 rpm/sea level

Exhaust Stacks

Jet Area	4.0-sq-in cylinder

Propeller

Manufacturer	Aeroproducts Division of GMC
Type	Self Contained Hydromatic
Hub Model	A542
Blade Design	H-20-156-24M/

	H-25P-156-23M5
Number of Blades	4
Diameter	11 ft
Thickness - Chord Ratio	h/b at 75%
	Radius = .068

Weight Schedule (Basic Version)

7,400 lbs including 105-gallon fuel, 6-gallon oil, four .50-cal. machine guns, 1,000 rounds ammunition

Instrument panel of XP-51J USAAF s/n 44-76027. Try as he might, the author has been unable to unearth any aerial shots of the three lightweight experimental variants, which means that the aircraft may not have been photographed in the air or that such negatives and photographs were simply discarded after the program had come to an end.

Right console of the XP-51J illustrating the aircraft's simplified cockpit.

The XP-51Js compiled very little time while with NAA, and after being transferred to Allison it appears that one aircraft was kept flyable while the second served as a parts source.

The most stream-lined of the light-weights, the XP-51J also featured a taller vertical tail that helped cure stability problems at high speed.

Fully equipped Allison V-1710-119 with infinitely variable supercharger fitted to the XP-51J. A power takeoff shaft drove an auxiliary supercharger impeller and the unit required a separate lubrication system. The compressed air output was ducted to the normal engine supercharger. The V-1710-119 could produce 1,720 hp at 20,000 feet with water injection but water injection was not installed on the XP-51J due to problems calibrating the speed density unit.

CHAPTER SIX

LAST OF THE PONY SOLDIERS

With the P-51H, North American and the Army Air Forces hoped to update all the attributes of the Mustang's design into a new long-range fighter. Timing is everything.

To paraphrase T. S. Eliot, production of the Mustang ended not so much with a bang, but with more of a whimper. With the P-51D/K firmly established in the skies over the Axis powers, consideration was being given to extending the usefulness of the piston-engine fighter aircraft. However, aerodynamically, the piston-engine fighter had run into an aerodynamic wall—the airframe could only go so fast, the engine could be developed only so far. All over the combat world, the writing was clearly on the wall; the future would belong to turbo-jet-powered combat aircraft.

This fact did not stop companies such as Republic, Supermarine, Grumman, and NAA from going that last step in extending the life of their current production products. At NAA, a great deal had been learned from the experimental lightweights, but would it make sense to apply these advances to a production fighter?

Apparently so. However, numerous issues had to be addressed. First, the USAAF wanted an aircraft built to their strength specifications (over +7.33g) and not those of the British. Second, the great range of the Mustang had

Test pilot Bob Chilton breaks away from the camera plane in P-51H 44-64164. This aircraft was utilized by NAA for extensive testing of the type. This view gives good detail of the wing, illustrating the lack of the characteristic Mustang wing leading edge kink along with details of the underwing pylons and rocket stubs (all Hs were delivered with these installed). Also of note is the fact that the entire wing has been painted except for the flaps and ailerons. The lengthening of the radiator fairing is evident. Regarding P-51H performance, Chilton recalled, "Previous aircraft would begin to porpoise at Mach .74, but the H could do Mach .8. At that point, it would not porpoise, but there would be a lot more buffeting, shaking, and rattling."

As with all NAA mockups, special attention was paid to outfitting the NA-117's cockpit. Even though it looks like metal, the majority of the cockpit was wood. Placards were added in appropriate places (even if they were incorrect for the type of aircraft—the engine limitations' placard is for a V-1650-3).

Mockup of what would become the P-51H. When the photograph was taken, the project was proceeding as Model NA-117. NAA, as well as other aviation companies, employed skilled carpenters to build the exacting mockups.

proven to be one of its most valuable combat assets and this was due, in great measure, to the addition of the fuselage fuel tank as well as the ability to carry large underwing auxiliary fuel tanks. The configuration of the lightweight canopy and its associated hydraulic mechanism meant that a meaningful fuselage tank could not be fitted. Also, the underwing pylons were limited to 500 pounds and combat Mustangs were regularly toting 1,000-pound bombs under each wing to cause havoc among Axis ground forces. With the lightweights, gun bays were limited to four .50-cal. weapons, and the USAAF wanted more.

In the lightweights, NAA had created what basically would be defined as a point interceptor. The USAAF wanted to take some of the performance increases and combine them into a warplane that had all the attributes of the P-51D. Arthur Patch was assigned as project engineer and he and his crew got busy on a design that would increase performance of the overall Mustang concept. Accordingly, the project became NAA Model NA-117 (this model designation had been originally assigned on 10 August 1943) with an official start date of 20 April 1944 (this was soon changed to NA-126 and aircraft under the contract W33-038 AC-1752 were canceled and transferred to the new model designation, but retaining the same contract number and information). This was before the invasion of Europe and the USAAF was in need of more fighters with increased performance so, after a review of the assembled data, the design proceeded under the designation P-51H. The aircraft would be powered by the V-1650-9 and fitted with an Aeroproducts propeller some 11 feet 1 inch in diameter.

Initially, 1,000 of the new fighters were ordered but this increased to 2,400 examples as the invasion of Japan was contemplated. Although looking quite a bit like the earlier P-51D/K, less than 10 percent of the P-51H's components were interchangeable with the earlier aircraft.

One of the most noticeable changes was the wing, which eliminated the characteristic Mustang kink. Utilizing a NAA/NACA laminar high-speed airfoil, the new wing was much thinner in cross section and, following USAAF dictates, designed to tote six .50-cal. Browning M2 machine guns while the two underwing racks were stressed to carry 1,000 pounds each (the lightweights had provision to jettison the racks in flight, but this feature was deleted with the H). The Brownings were fitted with J-4 heaters and G-9 solenoids and the weapons were installed with a -2-degree deflection at a normal convergence of 800 yards. The cockpit was fitted with either a K-14A or K-14B gunsight that could be utilized in computing or fixed modes. The wing was also configured to carry rocket-launching stubs for six T-64 5-inch HVARs, but with the elimination of the bomb racks, this number could be increased to eight.

For the long-range air war, the interior of the wing was designed to hold two internal fuel tanks. The left tank could hold 110 gallons (of which 104

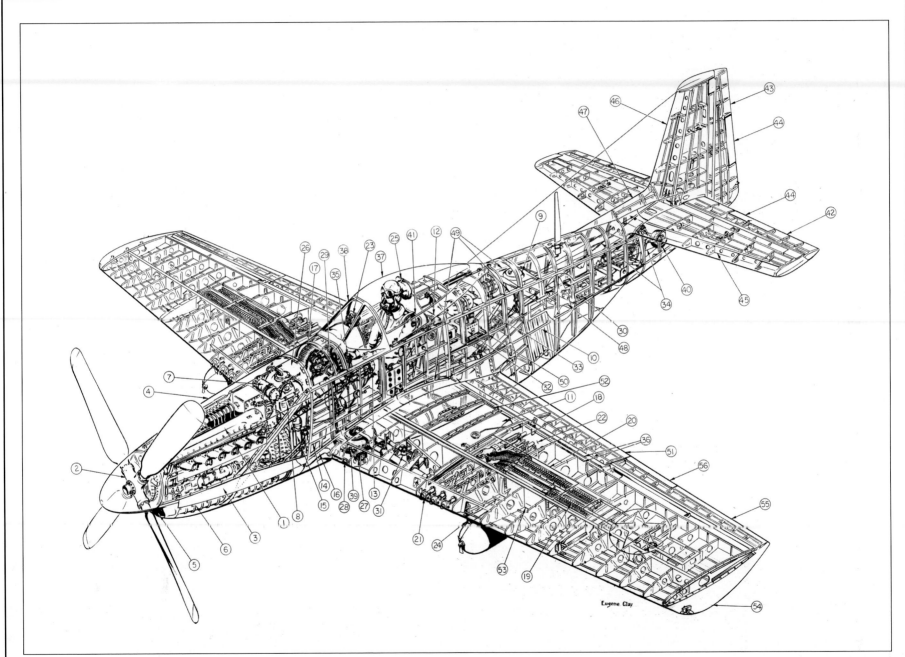

North American factory technical illustrations showing the P-51H in both cutaway and exploded views. Callout numbering refers to specific aircraft structure and components listed in NAA brochure.

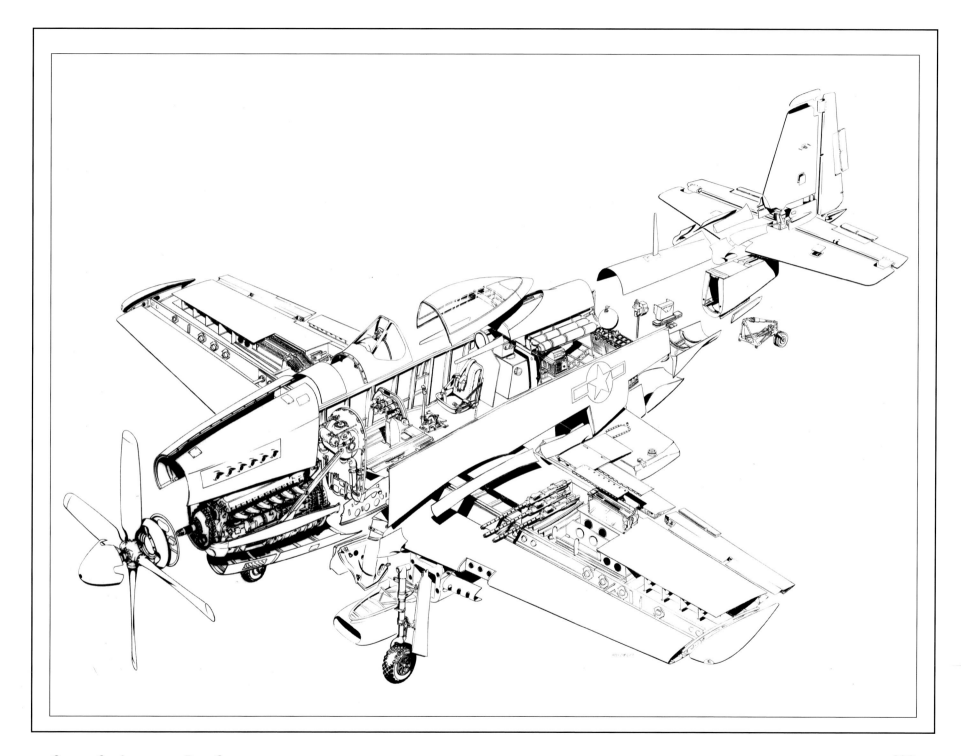

FLIGHT TESTING THE P-51H

Flight Test Division Memorandum Report No. TSFTE-2029: Flight Test of P-51H USAAF 44-64182

Introduction:

A. Flight tests have been conducted at Wright Field on P-51H 44-64182 at the request of the Production Section, Procurement Division. The tests were flown by Capt. John W. McGuyrt, Fighter Operations Section, Flight Test Division, for a total of approximately 48 hours. AN-F-33 fuel was used throughout the tests, making it possible to obtain up to 90 inches of mercury manifold pressure with water injection.

B. The original intent of the request was for complete performance data, but due to a series of interruptions the airplane did not arrive at Wright Field until the later part of December 1945. During this delay, the contractor obtained performance and range data on a similar P-51H and sent the information to Chief, Technical Data Laboratory, Engineering Division for preparing the figures presented in performance tables in the Technical Order on this airplane. For this reason, the scope of the tests was limited primarily to obtaining data for checking the contractor's figures.

Conclusion:

A. Control and handling characteristics of the P-51H are good under the conditions tested with the exception of a slight tendency to hunt directionally at indicated speeds above 400 mph. The elevator tab is inadequate for level flight trim when flying at 3,000 rpm and 90-inch manifold pressure.

B. The performance results in this report are satisfactory for use in checking the figures presented in the Technical Order.

Recommendations:

It is recommended that:

A. Additional nose down elevator trim be provided.

Condition of Aircraft Relative to Tests

A. The P-51H differs from earlier models in that the fuselage lines are somewhat cleaner, the wing has been redesigned for lower drag, the empennage section has also been redesigned, and the airplane is equipped with four-bladed Aeroproducts propeller.

B. All tests at the fighter configuration (bomb and rocket racks only) were flown at a takeoff weight of 9,544 pounds and approximately 25.4 percent MAC, wheels up, and 25.9 percent MAC, wheels down. This included ballast for 1,820 rounds of .50-cal. ammunition, six .50-cal. guns, and a full supply of fuel, oil, and water.

C. Items were added to the airplane at the gross weight to obtain the following configurations and corresponding takeoff weights. One additional flight was made for each condition to measure the drag of the external equipment.

Flight No.	Configuration	T/O Weight
16	Two 1,000-pound bombs	11,545 pounds
17	Six 5-inch HVAR/two 500 pound bombs	11,345
18	Ten 5-inch HVAR	10,880
19	Six 5-inch HVAR/two 110-gallon tanks	11,860
20	Two 500-pound bombs	10,525
21	Two 110-gallon tanks	11,040

For flight 18 it was necessary to replace each bomb rack with two rocket racks. For flights 19 and 21, the tanks were loaded with 79 gallons of water each to simulate fuel weight.

D. The airplane was equipped with a Packard-built Rolls-Royce Model V-1650-9 engine, equipped with water injection for use at war emergency powers exceeding 67-in. Hg. manifold pressure, a Bendix Stromberg PD-18D-3A carburetor, and an 11-foot 1-inch diameter four-bladed Aeroproducts propeller H-20-162-29M5, design no. 86892.

E. All flights were made with wheels up, flaps neutral, canopy closed, mixture run, and manual boost control. The airplane has a normal unpainted finish. All level flight power calibrations were run with the coolant shutter in the flush position. Climbs were run with the coolant shutter in automatic. All horsepower figures are based on power curves Nos. 2493 and 2494 dated 2 November 1945, furnished by the Power Plant Laboratory.

Flight Characteristics

A. Taxiing and Ground Handling: The airplane has good ground handling characteristics. The tail wheel is steerable 6 degrees either side of center, and is held securely in the steerable position when the control stick is in neutral or aft of neutral. When the control stick is held in the forward position, the tail wheel is full swiveling and brakes must be used for control and slow speeds. Forward visibility is not improved materially in this model when in the 3-point attitude, making S turns necessary for forward vision. Ground handling can be easily accomplished in crosswinds.

B. Takeoff and Climb: Takeoff characteristics are normal. The takeoff power setting is 3,000 rpm and 61-in. Hg. For short field operation and best obstacle clearance, 15 to 20 degrees of flaps should be used; rudder trim should be set 7 degrees right, elevator 1 degree nose heavy, and the aileron tab in the neutral position. The slowest takeoff speed attempted was approximately 103 mph, indicated. Sawtooth climbs indicated the best climb speed to be approximately 162-mph IAS for low blower and 154-mph IAS for high blower.

C. Stability: No extensive stability investigation was made. Aside from a slight tendency to hunt directionally above 400-mph IAS, the characteristics were good and no deviation from previously reported characteristics was noted.

D. Trim and Balance: Trim tabs are located on all control surfaces. Any variation in airspeed and power or external configuration, which require a change in trim in the normal operating range, may be easily corrected. However, at the high manifold pressures approaching 90-in. Hg. where water injection is necessary, the elevator trim is inadequate and it is necessary to exert excessive forward pressure on the control stick to maintain level flight.

E. Controllability: The airplane has good control characteristics throughout the speed range except for the insufficient nose down trim mentioned in the preceding paragraph.

F. Maneuverability: The airplane is very maneuverable within the range of speed tested. The radius of turn is comparatively small and the rate of roll is high. No buffeting is encountered in tight turns until the stalling speed is approached.

G. Stalling Characteristics: Stalling characteristics were very good in all configurations. The stalls were not violent, the approach was easily controlled, and recovery was easily accomplished in all cases. The airplane enters the stall gradually, giving the pilot a sensation of mushing instead of complete stall.

H. Spinning Characteristics: Not investigated.

I. Diving Characteristics: Not investigated.

J. High Altitude Trials: Under test conditions, the pilot determined 36,000 feet to be the maximum practical condition for cruising. At this altitude, three satisfactory level flight points using 3,000, 2,700, and 2,500 rpm were obtained. Above 36,000 feet, the maximum level flight indicated airspeed at normal rated RPM begins decreasing rapidly with altitude. No serious difficulty with freezing of trim tabs or other low temperature conditions was encountered.

K. Approach and Landing: The approach is normal, the landing flaps operated quickly, and there is very little tendency to float. Visibility is

Capt. John McGuyrt airborne in P-51H 44-64182 near Wright Field. As a point of interest, Capt. McGuyrt describes the aircraft as being unpainted, but, as can be clearly seen, the wing has been filled and painted per NAA specifications.

good with the gear down and is increased slightly when the flaps are lowered. Normal landing speed is approximately 102-mph IAS, normal speed for the glide is between 120 and 125 mph. The P-51H is easily controlled on the landing roll with the steerable tail wheel or brakes and has no ground looping tendencies. Final trim tab settings (power off) and landing is 2 degrees right rudder and 9 degrees nose-up elevator.

L. Noise and Vibration: Noise level is normal and not objectionable except when using over 74-in. Hg. MP. Most of the noise is caused by the short exhaust stacks just forward of the pilot. Vibration is slight above 420 IAS, below that it is negligible. There is little buffeting of the controls except with gear and flaps down. Vibration increases below 2,000 rpm.

M. Pilot's Report on Vision and Cockpit Layout: The visibility in taxiing, takeoff, and climb is normal for single-engine aircraft. In the air, in level flight, visibility for combat and cross-country is good. The visibility on approach for landing is satisfactory. There are no distortions in the side windshield canopy, or bulletproof glass. The P-51H is equipped with the standard AAF bucket type seat. Shoulder and elbow room is sufficient. Rudder pedals are in a comfortable position, however, the control stick is mounted slightly forward of the desired position.

Performance Data

A. Airspeed Indicator Calibration: The airspeed position correction was obtained by flying with P-51D 44-74570 pacer airplane. All indicated airspeeds quoted in this report are corrected for instrument error only.

B. Altimeter Correction: The altimeter calibration was calculated for the position error of the airspeed pick up.

C. Critical Altitude: The critical altitudes for normal rated power climb (46-in. Hg. MP and 2,700 rpm) are 17,400 feet for low blower and 30,700 feet for high blower. The critical altitudes for war emergency power climb (90-in. Hg. water injection and 3,000 rpm) are 16,000 feet for high blower and by extrapolation, approximately 2,200 feet for low blower.

D. Maximum Speeds, Coolant Shutters Flush, Wheels and Flaps Up. Data at war emergency rating with water injection at 3,000 rpm:

Altitude	True Airspeed	MP Hg.	Blower	Throttle Setting
SL	401 mph	90	Low	Part
6,800 feet*	431	90	Low	WO
13,400**	423	90	High	Part
21,200***	451	90	High	WO
25,000	448	78	High	WO

* Low Blower Critical Altitude for 90-in. Hg. MP
** Altitude for Blower Shift
*** High Blower Critical Altitude for 90-in. Hg. MP

Data at military power rating at 3,000 rpm, no water injection:

Altitude	True Airspeed	MP Hg.	Blower	Throttle Setting
SL	353 mph	67	Low	Part
10,000 feet	396	67	Low	Part
15,200*	418	67	Low	WO
20,800**	408	67	High	Part
29,000***	438	67	High	WO
36,000	413	47.5	High	WO

* Low Blower Critical Altitude for 67-in. Hg. MP
** Altitude for Blower Shift
*** High Blower Critical Altitude for 67-in. Hg. MP

Comparative speeds with various configurations at 14,5850 feet at 3,000 rpm and 1,600 chart brake horsepower:

Configuration	Gross Weight	True Speed
Clean	9,420 pounds	410 mph
Two 500-pound bombs	10,410	379
Two 110-gallon fuel tanks	10,900	375
Two 1,000-pound bombs	11,410	370
Ten rockets	10,740	367
Six rockets, two 500-pound bombs	11,230	361
Six rockets, two 110-gallon fuel tanks	11,724	354

E. Climb Tests, Coolant Shutters Automatic, Wheels and Flaps Up: Climb data for normal rated RPM (2,700) are summarized below. It will be noted that the altitude for blower shift as determined from the rate-of-climb curve is approximately 22,000 feet whereas from the brake horsepower curve this altitude is indicated as being 23,500 feet.

This discrepancy is attributed mainly to the inaccuracies of power charts for the determination of brake horsepower:

Altitude	True Airspeed	Climb	Time of Climb	MP Hg.	Blower	Throttle Setting
SL	164 mph	1,740	.0 fpm	46	Low	Part
10,000 feet	191	1,810	5.4-min	46	Low	Part
17,400*	215	1,860	9.6	46	Low	WO
21,700**	220	1,410	12.3	46	High	Part
30,700***	254	1,380	18.6	46	High	WO
36,000	282	720	23.2	39	High	WO

* Low Blower Critical Altitude for 46-in. Hg. MP
** Altitude for Blower Shift
*** High Blower Critical altitude for 46-in. Hg. MP

F. Fuel Consumption, Coolant Shutter Flush, Wheels and Flaps Up: Fuel consumption throughout the operating range of speeds and altitude of the aircraft in the clean configuration is Fuel Flow – lbs/hr versus Brake Horsepower:

Altitude	Air Miles Per Gal	True Speed	Blower	Gross Weight
4,600 feet	4.25	226 mph	Low	9,485
14,800	5.00	267	Low	9,425
24,900	4.80	287	High	9,340
29,800	5.22	332	High	9,300
34,600	5.10	338	High	9,250
36,000	4.97	338	High	9,235

G. Stalling Speeds: Precision measurements of stall for the determination of lift coefficients were not obtained. The following approximate stalling speeds were reported for a takeoff gross weight of 9,540 pounds without any bombs, rockets, or external fuel tanks installed:

Configuration	Indicated Stalling Speed	Approx. Power Setting
Cruise	106 mph	2,300 rpm, 36 inches
Climb, NRP	100 mph	2,700 rpm, 46 inches
Approach for Landing	97 mph	2,000 rpm, 23 inches
Landing	102 mph	Power off, Flaps and Gear Down

H. Takeoff and Landing Tests: Takeoff and landing data was originally obtained on P-51H 44-64182, but because of difficulty in reading the camera film due to haze in the background and faulty breaks in information was discarded and the tests rerun on P-51H 44-64703. The takeoff and landing distances and speeds were measured by the camera method. All distances and speeds are corrected to a gross weight of 9,500 pounds. The takeoffs were made at 3,000 rpm and 61-in. Hg. MP with the wing flaps neutral. The airplane was not equipped with a sensitive airspeed indicator and, therefore, the reported values of indicated airspeed must be regarded as approximations:

Indicated Airspeed at T/O	True Airspeed at T/O	Ground Roll	Over 50-foot Obstacle
120 mph	128 mph	1,730 feet	2,740 feet
95 mph	115 mph	1,400 feet	2,310 feet

Landing tests were made using full flaps. The pilot was unable to obtain indicated airspeeds at contact and the gliding speed at the 50-foot obstacle was recorded instead:

Indicated A/S Over 50-foot Obstacle	True A/S at Contact	Ground Roll	Distance Over 50-foot Obstacle
115 mph	99.5 mph	1,460 feet	3,390 feet

were useable) while the right tank contained 107 gallons (104 useable). The fuselage tank held 50 gallons (all useable) and NAA, with the importance of the long-range mission, designed each tank to be fitted with an electric booster pump that meant the Merlin would keep on running if the engine fuel pump failed or was damaged in combat—particularly reassuring for pilots having to fly long stretches over the Pacific. Going back to the lightweights, the fuselage tank and left wing tank could be removed so that the P-51H could assume the role of point defense if so required. Also, armament could be reduced for four .50-cal. machine guns for this mission. However, given the stage of the war, the USAAF was on the offensive and not defensive, but point defense could have come into play if the invasion of Japan had taken place and fighters would have to be scrambled from captured airfields to intercept incoming kamikaze attacks (the Japanese had retained over 8,000 aircraft to utilize on suicide missions against the American invaders).

With the NA-117, NAA engineers attempted to make the cockpit as comfortable as possible for the pilot, who would often be flying long-range missions. For example, the control stick and the seat had been placed closer together to help eliminate arm fatigue.

NA-117 instrument panel illustrating how the flight and engine instruments had been separated to make scanning easier for the pilot. At this point, the mockup still had hand-written notes regarding placement of equipment. To illustrate the cockpit's detail, blank USAAF and NAA data plates had been installed on the former in the lower right-hand corner.

As with earlier Mustangs, the fuselage was broken down into three sections comprising the main fuselage, engine mount, and empennage. The three components were bolted together. Of semi-monocoque aluminum alloy, the fuselage employed flush riveting. As with the D/K, two channel section transverse beams were utilized as lower and upper longerons while also acting as spar flanges on each side of the fuselage. Cockpit width, at maximum point, was 3 feet. Given the rigors of the long-range mission, some thought was given to improving the pilot's comfort and a new seat was designed to have 12 positions in order to alleviate fatigue on the long flights. Also, cockpit heating was improved with a Janitrol heater that was thermostatically controlled and

Some sources state that the P-51H was equipped with just four .50-cal. M2 Brownings—it wasn't and all aircraft were delivered with six such weapons. However, apparently taking a lesson from the earlier lightweights, the original wing for the NA-117 was created to hold just four Brownings, as can be seen in this photo of a wing section mockup.

Another view of the NA-117 armament mockup illustrates the use of wood, aluminum, and plexiglass. Often, to conserve war materials, the carpenters would work with whatever bits of scrap metal they could find.

utilized aviation fuel lit by a glow plug. However, Janitrol heaters had built up a reputation for catching fire in flight and many pilots would endure the rigors of extreme temperature rather than engaging the heater. Windscreen armor glass was 1.5 inches thick while a 5/16-inch-thick armor plate was installed behind the pilot's seat and the headrest had a sheet of 7/16-inch armor plate. Also, visibility over the nose from the cockpit had been improved from 0 to 5 degrees downward. Again with a nod to long-range operations, the instrument panel was designed to group flight instruments and engine instruments in separate sections on the panel, making them easier for the pilot to scan and thus reducing workload.

A comparison can be found between the landing gear of the lightweights and that of the P-51H. Redesign of the gear was the biggest weight saver on the P-51H with some 300 pounds being shed. However, with the redesign came trouble. Reduction came through the use of lightweight dural aluminum forgings and these did not have the strength of the magnesium forgings used on the earlier Mustangs. The main gear, as those on the lightweights, appeared visually spindly and for good reason—as testing continued it was discovered the gear would easily collapse with the introduction of lateral stress loads (such as in a ground loop). If the gear cycle was interrupted during raising or lowering, trouble would result, as the system would be thrown out of kilter. The fairing doors would go into incorrect cycling while one gear leg would go

The NA-117 designation was assigned 10 August 1943, but this was changed to NA-126 with contract AC-1752 that was signed on 20 April 1944. When the mockup's V-1650-9 installation was photographed on 31 March 1944, the project was being referred to by NAA as NA-117 so this designation was utilized right up to the time the contract was made official.

SERVICE TESTING THE *P-51H*

October 1946 - Air Proving Ground Command, Eglin Field, Florida, Final Report On Service Test of the P-51H Airplane

Combat Comparison: Completed between a P-51H-1-NA and a P-51D-25-NA, comparison consisted of turning circle, rate of aileron roll, level flight and dive accelerations, and full-power zoom from level flight and from a dive; these maneuvers were conducted at both 10,000 and 25,000 feet, and pilots repeated aileron roll and turning circle tests after exchanging airplanes. Throughout the comparison, the P-51D was limited to its war emergency rating of 67-in. Hg. manifold pressure and the P-51H used the tentative rating of 80-in. Hg. manifold pressure with water injection.

At both altitudes, no real difference in minimum turning radius could be noted between airplanes. Maneuver flaps were used on the P-51H, but no advantage was gained.

For corroboration, rate of roll comparison was done at both altitudes, with the airplane alternating in leading a shallow line-astern dive. Up to an indicated airspeed of 400 mph, the airplanes were about equal; then the P-51D had the higher rate of roll. P-51H-1s and later series airplanes have been modified to increase aileron effectiveness, but no opportunity to investigate the modified system was presented.

In level flight acceleration and dive acceleration, the P-51H was superior to the P-51D due to the greater power available and the resultant speed advantage. At both altitudes, the P-51H gained approximately 400 yards advantage after 3 minutes of a level flight acceleration run begun from cruising power. At both altitudes, the P-51H pulled slowly away from the P-51D in shallow, full power dives begun from cruising power level flight.

In zooms from full power level flight, and from a full power dive, the P-51H had gained an average altitude advantage of approximately 500 feet when indicated airspeeds had decreased to 130 mph. It was noted that the P-51H was extremely sensitive to ram effect on power, manifold pressure decreasing materially in a zoom or turn begun from full power level flight.

Range: The P-51D has a slightly longer radius of action than the P-51H due primarily to the larger internal fuel supply (269 gallons for P-51D, 255 gallons for P-51H), but this advantage is considerably reduced by the fact the P-51D is not sufficiently stable with a full fuselage tank to permit violent maneuvering.

Stability and Handling Characteristics: During the course of tests on the P-51H, undesirable elevator sensitivity and a tendency to porpoise during dives at high Mach number were encountered. Insufficient trim for high-power climb was also noted. These discrepancies were later corrected by manufacturer's modification. No stick-force reversal was reported during high acceleration turns with a full fuselage tank (this condition was most objectionable with the P-51D). The P-51H was much more stable than the P-51D with a full external load and was easily trimmed for various flight conditions. Stall characteristics, stability during final approach and landing, and visibility during landing and taxiing were better than the P-51D and, in general, the P-51H is easier to fly.

It was the opinion of pilots that the airplane is preferable to the P-51D as a gunnery platform, and as a dive-bomber. View over the nose for deflection shooting is better and the airplane is more stable during a dive-bombing run.

Cockpit Arrangement: The cockpit arrangement of the modified P-51H (-5) is satisfactory. Moving the seat forward and the stick to the rear has aided pilot comfort. Functioning of the heater during tests was satisfactory and the cockpit is better ventilated than the P-51D.

Maintenance: It is the opinion of the maintenance personnel who have worked on both types of aircraft; the P-51H is more easily maintained than the P-51D. The accessibility of the engine accessories and other equipment is very good, making it much easier to accomplish necessary maintenance on the P-51H than on the P-51D.

- Tail Wheel Down Lock: Throughout the entire time that the P-51H was flown at this station, periodic difficulties were encountered with tail wheel collapse during taxiing and landing, resulting in considerable damage.
- Wheel Brakes: During the test, it was found that the Goodyear three-spot brakes are more easily burned out by extensive use than are the multiple disc brakes of the P-51D although the braking effect obtained from this type of brake is considered superior to that of the multiple disc-type brake.

up as the other went down. If this happened, the pilot would have the choice of taking to his parachute or attempting a hazardous one-leg-down landing. The tail gear was also (as can be seen in test reports) subject to problems—mainly collapsing. Since the P-51H would be built in relatively small numbers compared to the D/K, little effort was expended to solve this problem and the fix was to simply lock the tail wheel in the down position. The tires for the main gear were 24 x 7.7-inch eight-ply units made for high pressure, meaning they were thinner and less forgiving than D/K tires, and this limited operation to smooth runways only.

With the success of the F-6D/K, the P-51H was designed to accommodate cameras between the intercooler exhaust shutter and the tail wheel installation. The P-51H could carry either K-17 or K-12 cameras while for work below 10,000 feet, a K-24 would be installed. However, fitting these cameras was

rare.

Test pilot Bob Chilton viewed the P-51H as a fully developed XP-51F with a longer fuselage and shortened canopy. Besides the accident described in the sidebar, Chilton saw the P-51H as an aircraft with few testing problems, although, during a 500-mph dive he did have the skin on one flap peel back and depart the airplane. Summing up, Bob stated, "The P-51H was probably no better or no worse than other Mustangs tested."

As the USAAF began their own flight-testing, pilots discovered that maneuvering the aircraft under high g loads could cause wing buckling. Also, the collapsing of the tail gear was noted early on. Further testing showed that the P-51H wing would buckle at around 9g and perhaps depart the fuselage at 9.5g. This testing, which started in June 1945, also eventually discovered another defect—the fuselage could buckle under high g. As the test pilot

As with the lightweights, the cowling of the P-51H was greatly simplified and the lower portion of the mount actually was also part of the exterior skin. On the mockup, the motor mount was made of wood and this necessitated the use of bracing to support the heavy weight of the Merlin.

Overhead view of a partially complete Merlin in the NA-117 mockup illustrates just how tight the cowls would wrap around the engine. In the field, the V-1650-9 was rated at 1,380 hp at sea level with 61-in. Hg. manifold pressure and 3,000 rpm.

report defined, "The fuselage longeron joins of station 187.2 cracked under excessive load." An attempt to correct this problem saw .015 aluminum side panels riveted over the area. Other USAAF recommendations led to modifying the gun bay latches so that the bay doors would not open in flight, stiffening the main gear doors, and some reinforcement to the wing trailing edge skins.

The P-51H received little in the way of publicity at NAA. The production

Ground servicing the V-1650-9 engine before Bob Chilton flew the first P-51H a few days later. The initial NA-117 contract called for 2,500 aircraft, but when the contract was switched to NA-126, production was cut to 2,400 aircraft and the cuts would continue as the H models rolled off the production line. At the NAA Dallas facility, plans were underway to build some 1,700 P-51Ls (NA-139), which were identical to the P-51H except for the installation of a V-1650-11. This contract was canceled before production could begin.

With the P-51H, the aircraft went from mockup directly into production without the use of prototypes. By this time, NAA had learned enough from the D/K series and the lightweights that there really was no need for a prototype since the P-51H did not feature any radical departures. The first H, USAAF s/n 44-64160, was photographed receiving final work al fresco near one of the classic Mines Field buildings.

With dozens of Mustang test flights taking place each day; the first flight of the P-51H went almost unnoticed except for those involved with the NA-126 project.

The first P-51H-1-NA pulled out from the ramp for photographs before the initial flight. The plane was not fitted with armament nor were the rocket stubs and underwing racks installed. The plane also had the initial small vertical tail.

For the test flights, 44-64160 was fitted with a yaw sensor probe under the left wing. Walt Disney designed the NAA Flight Test logo on the vertical fin. Under the logo, the antenna for the AN/APS-13 tail warning radar set is visible. This unit provided a visible and audible warning to the pilot on the presence or approach of aircraft from the rear. The warning system consisted of a signal light mounted on the right side of the instrument panel shroud and a warning bell on the right side of the cockpit, adjacent to the pilot's seat. The radio set was located on the right side of the cockpit, adjacent to the AN/ARC-3 radio. Controls for the set were on the forward end of the upper radio panel on the right side of the cockpit. The antenna system included the vertical stabilizer mounted six-pronged antenna with three prongs protruding horizontally from each side.

line was not well photographed (or, if it was, then these negatives were destroyed, along with virtually tons of other Mustang material, when Rockwell came into power) and the last P-51Hs on the line were accompanied by the new jet-powered P-86A Sabres which were gaining all the publicity. To give an idea of P-51H production, NAA had delivered 221 aircraft by 30 July 1945 and by V-J Day, 2 September 1945, the total had risen to 370. When the 555th and last P-51H was rolled out of the factory, there really was neither celebration nor special photographs taken of the event. The P-51H headed into service where it would not gain any particular distinction and its career would

Finding the correct vertical tail size for Mustangs was a subject of much experiment—from the P-51B/C through the H, various vertical tails were tried in an attempt to improve the aircraft's overall stability. This interesting photograph illustrates P-51D-5-NA 44-13253 (the first production example) with P-51H-1-NA 44-64162 (third example) followed by stock P-51D 44-64001 and another P-51H. The first D-5 had been retained by NAA for testing and is illustrated with a modified vertical tail featuring a fin cap, metalized rudder, and non-standard dorsal fin. Also, in the cockpit a camera mounting had been installed on the pilot's seat, facing to the rear. With the H, an order was issued to install the fin cap beginning with 44-64192 (the 13th example), but not all aircraft were so fitted on the production line so some modifications were carried out in the field.

FORCED LANDING

With a failed engine over a populated area, test pilot Bob Chilton was faced with a difficult decision:

"I was on a test flight in the first P-51H when an unusual vibration passed through the airframe, quickly followed by a violent shaking." North American test pilot Bob Chilton was recalling a February 1945 test flight in the first P-51H. What followed was an example of how cool thinking prevented a potentially disastrous situation.

As with any new variant of a military aircraft, factory and military test pilots would extensively test the first few examples, and the P-51H was no exception. Bob Chilton was NAA's chief Mustang test pilot and had flown literally thousands of aircraft as they came off the production line. Testing revealed that the H had pluses over the D, but it also had its negatives. Testing the prototype, Chilton found that the aircraft was a bit easier to fly than the D and had improved performance in several categories. However, he would sum up the P-51H by stating, "It was pretty much just another Mustang."

On 6 February 1945, Chilton was up in 44-64160 on a standard test flight. Over the past three days, the H had been flown some six times.

Famed Pearl Harbor fighter pilot George Welch, now an NAA test pilot, had also flown the aircraft. Bob was a bit over 2 miles away from the airfield, but he knew he would not make it, as the Aeroproducts propeller started to runaway. To people on the ground, the run away prop made an unholy shriek as the Mustang passed overhead.

Bob was near the Hollywood Race Track and, even in 1945, housing was encroaching the airport. Pulling the throttle all the way back, Bob put the prop control in full decrease and prepared for a crash-landing. He did not want to take to his chute since the H was over a populated area.

Pulling his straps as tight as possible and getting off a quick emergency call over the radio, Bob left the gear up, aimed for a freshly plowed field, and started milking the flaps down. The ground below was not exactly even and, with the runaway prop, Bob touched down hard. The Mustang skidded forward with great velocity and Bob saw a deep culvert ahead that could spell disaster. He pulled back on the stick and the Mustang managed to cross the culvert—losing bits and pieces in the process. The Aeroproducts prop tore off at this point and did a great deal of damage as it struck the forward fuselage upon departure.

Intact but very bent, the first P-51H is carefully lifted on to a flat-bed truck for transportation back to the factory only a few miles away. Thankfully, the area surrounding the airport was still largely undeveloped in 1945, ensuring that chief Mustang test pilot Bob Chilton had enough open area in which to set the stricken aircraft down safely. NAA photographers recorded the cockpit, as was done after any aircraft incident, and those photos verified that Chilton had pulled the throttle all the way back and had set the prop in full decrease. Note the North American flight test logo on the upper vertical fin.

The P-51H finally skidded to a stop and Bob hastily exited the cockpit. The craft came down near Crenshaw Boulevard so emergency vehicles were soon on hand. Fortunately, the test pilot was not injured and later, the airframe was lifted up, placed on a truck bed, and driven back to the factory. The plane was too badly damaged to consider rebuilding, and ended its days as an instructional airframe. Of all the Mustangs that he tested, Bob said, "That H was the only one I badly bent."

The departing Aeroproducts propeller ripped a large gash on the right side of the fuselage.

This photograph shows the Mustang's straight path and the departed propeller. Bits of the aircraft littered the area.

This deep culvert could have spelled doom for Chilton and the Mustang. Fortunately, the plane still had enough forward momentum to skip safely over the obstacle.

Detail of the sheared nose case of the P-51H's Merlin engine.

Accident investigator records the Mustang's path. Note the nearby housing development.

150 POUNDS SAVED
IN WINGS

80 POUNDS SAVED
IN FIXED EQUIPMENT

130 POUNDS SAVED
IN ENGINE SECTION

30 POUNDS SAVED
IN FUSELAGE

300 POUNDS SAVED
IN LANDING GEAR

464164

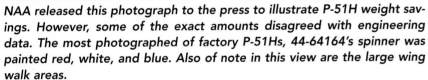

NAA released this photograph to the press to illustrate P-51H weight savings. However, some of the exact amounts disagreed with engineering data. The most photographed of factory P-51Hs, 44-64164's spinner was painted red, white, and blue. Also of note in this view are the large wing walk areas.

be overshadowed by the earlier and more widely used variants.

These two views are notable because the first shows 44-64164 with the original small vertical tail while 44-64161 has the revised vertical with the fin cap that amounted to 14.89 sq ft (including dorsal). When -161 received the updated tail it also had the twin radio masts and AN/ARA-8 Airborne Homing Adapter added. The single antenna under the left wing and close to the fuselage was for the AN/ARC-3 radio.

BUILDING THE P-51 MUSTANG

Left side of 44-64160 showing the compact throttle/propeller unit. Above and to the left is the fold-down pilot's armrest. The throttle incorporated a gate that allowed a maximum of 61-in. Hg. manifold pressure up to critical altitude of the engine. When the throttle was moved past the gate, breaking a light safety wire, a manifold pressure of as much as 67-in. Hg. dry and 80-in. Hg. with water injection was possible for War Emergency Power. The throttle was mechanically linked to the Simmonds automatic manifold pressure regulator used on the engine. A manual override linkage was added to the throttle linkage that permitted manual closing of the butterfly valve in the carburetor to prevent a runaway engine when starting. A twist grip on the throttle operated the K-14 gun sight range compensator. A push-to-talk button for radio transmission was located on the end of the twist grip. The throttle-locking lever was located on the face of the throttle quadrant to permit holding a desired setting.

Right side cockpit of 44-64160. The large crank was for operating the canopy. On the lightweights, the canopy was operated by a hydraulic mechanism and this prevented the installation of a fuselage fuel tank. The round piece of equipment with attached tubing is the oxygen regulator and the gauges directly above and to the left are oxygen instruments. Three large cylindrical oxygen tanks were mounted directly behind the pilot in the fuselage.

Detail of the right side gear well showing the gear leg and retracting linkage—a weak point for the P-51H if too much side load was added during takeoff or landing. The round panel is the removable access door to the landing gear. Held in place with eight NAS 205-7 screws, the door could be easily removed for quick inspection.

For NAA, the P-51H flight test program was rapid and extensive. However, the same could not be said for the USAAF who, at this point, was ready for jet fighters. This view of 44-64264 (before the tall fin update) shows the rather spindly gear and narrow high-pressure tires to advantage. The tires alone limited the P-51H to operation from smooth, paved strips—something their D/K brethren in the Pacific were certainly not doing. The length of the radiator fairing is quite apparent and one of the improvements brought forward from the lightweights.

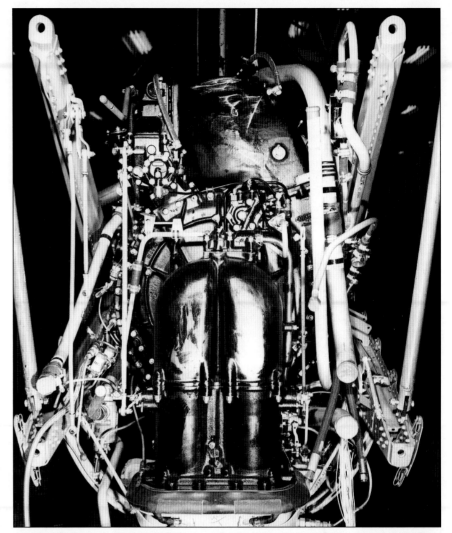

Unusual view of the V-1650-9's rear before being mated to the P-51H firewall. The powerplant had its problems with the Simmonds pressure regulator and the Bendix-Stromberg updraft injection carburetor, which was fully automatic. The Simmonds device maintained manifold pressure between 25- and 67-in. Hg. (dry). If the pilot or crew chief had not shut the engine down according to procedure, the next to start would find that the boost would instantly start where it had been left. If the pilot's reactions were not quick enough, the P-51H would stand on its nose and a new prop and possibly a new engine would be required.

Even though 20mm (and larger) cannon had become accepted armament in many foreign warplanes, the USAAF remained loyal to the Browning .50-cal. machine gun. In its defense, a well-aimed burst from the .50s would destroy just about any aircraft. As a P-51H wing moved along the line, the .50-cal. weapons were installed in the wing armament bays. The P-51H was equipped with either a K-14A or K-14B computing gun sight. Both sights were basically the same. However, on the K-14A, the sight gyro motor had a separate switch; on the K-14B, the battery-disconnect switch operated the sight gyro motor. The sight computed the correct lead angle at ranges varying from 200 to 800 yards. The sight was equipped with two optical systems, fixed and gyro. The fixed optical system projected on the reflector glass a cross surrounded by a 70-mil ring. The 70-mil ring could be blanked out by the reticule masking lever. Normally blanked out, the ring was used only in case of mechanical failure of the gyro or for ground strafing. The gyro optical system projected on the reflector glass a pattern of six diamonds surrounding a central dot. The size of the diamond pattern is varied by changing the setting of the span scale lever on the face of the sight and by rotating the throttle twist grip.

Partially complete tail cone awaits installation on a fuselage. At this point, the dorsal fin was attached as well as the horizontal stabilizer, which was wrapped in protective paper. The mountings for the tail gear assembly were in place, but the tail wheel unit had yet to be installed (note the tail wheel doors in the closed position at bottom of structure). It is interesting to note how the dorsal fin literally wrapped around the tail cone.

P-51H CHARACTERISTICS

Span   37 feet 5/16 inch
Length   33 feet 3.25 inches
Height   12 feet 7.75 inches
Height (tail wheel   13 feet 3 inches
    down, prop vertical)
Weight (dry)   7,000 pounds (no ammunition)
Weight (wet)   9,250 pounds (ammunition, fluids)

Wing
Airfoil Section   NAA/NACA high-speed/low-drag
Chord   8 feet 9 inches (at root)
Chord   4 feet 1 inch (wing station 214 near tip)
Incidence   +1 degree (at root)
Dihedral   5 degrees (at 25% line)
Sweepback   3 degrees 39 minutes 34 seconds (at leading edge)

Horizontal Stabilizer
Span   14 feet 10 5/32 inches
Max Chord   4 feet 3.5 inches
Incidence   .5 degrees
Dihedral   None

Fuselage
Width   3 feet (maximum)
Height   7 feet 6 3/16 inches (maximum)
Length   22 feet 2 inches (firewall to rudder attachment)
     28 feet 11 inches (with engine mount)

Areas
Wings   221.59 sq ft (less ailerons)
Ailerons   13.41 sq ft (total)
Flaps   31.74 sq ft (total)
Horizontal Stabilizer   35.50 sq ft
Elevators   12.85 sq ft (including trim tabs)
Elevator Trim Tabs   1.44 sq ft (total)
Vertical Stabilizer   14.89 sq ft (including dorsal fin)
Rudder   10.24 sq ft (including tabs)
Rudder Trim Tab   .74 sq ft (total)

Fuel Capacity
Right Wing Tank   104 gallons
Left Wing Tank   102 gallons
Fuselage Tank   50 gallons
Drop Tanks (2)   75 gallons each
     110 gallons each
Total Fuel   206 gallons (wing tanks)
     256 gallons (wing and fuselage)
     406/476 gallons (wing, fuselage, drops)

Oil
Tank   16.0 gallons
Expansion Space   2.25 gallons
Total System Capacity   18.25 gallons

Cooling System
Tank Capacity   2.0 gallons (coolant header tank)
Expansion Space   2.0 gallons
Total System Capacity   14.4 gallons

Aftercooling System
Tank Capacity   1.0 gallons
Expansion Space   .25 gallons
Total System Capacity   6.2 gallons

Contracts/Serials

Variant	Contract/Approval	Serials
P-51H-1-NA	AC 1752/30/6/44	44-64160 through 44-64179
P-51H-5-NA	AC 1752/30/6/44	44-64180 through 44-64459
P-51H-10-NA	AC 1752/30/6/44	44-64460 through 44-64714

(c/n 126-37586 through 126-38140)

Funding for the contracts was classified J, which meant funding had been allocated in 1944.

P-51H-2-NA 44-64166 fitted with the massive 165-gallon underwing drop tank. If deployed to the Pacific, the H would have needed the fuel for B-29 escort missions to Japan. The -2 in the designation is unusual and probably indicates a factory modification or upgrade.

Assigned to the 47th Pursuit Squadron, 15th Pursuit Group, at Wheeler Field, Hawaii, George Welch managed to get airborne during the 7 December 1941 Japanese sneak attack and shot down two enemy aircraft while damaging two more. Welch left the service in July 1944 and, with the recommendation of Gen. Hap Arnold, went to work as a test pilot at NAA. Welch, seen here with a P-51H, was purported to have broken the sound barrier in a P-86 on the morning of 14 October 1947, just minutes before Air Force Capt. Chuck Yeager accomplished the feat in the Bell X-1 rocket plane. Welch was killed on 12 October 1954 when the F-100A Super Sabre he was flight-testing disintegrated in midair at high speed.

Complete V-1650-9 fitted in a production P-51H. This view illustrates how the lower motor mount incorporated exterior skin.

Interesting comparison of how P-51H instrument panels changed on the production line. The first photograph shows an early production panel (44-64166) while the second photograph illustrates a later production panel (44-64211) that has cleaned up and simplified the earlier variant.

The new seat installed in an H cockpit. A connecting attachment for a g-suit was located on the left side of the seat. The large package on the seat contained all the documents for this particular aircraft.

With long-range missions in mind, NAA designed a new metal tube seat that was adjustable in 12 positions—a big step from the wooden seats of the earlier Mustangs.

A P-51H fuselage in maneuvered on the overhead conveyor to be joined with the wing in the foreground.

The means to an end—a U.S. Army Air Forces ferry pilot takes official delivery of a factory fresh P-51D-5-NA Mustang at North American's plant in Inglewood, California, as a North American ground crewman hands up the aircraft logs and paperwork.

MUSTANG VARIANTS AND SPECIFICATIONS

NAA MUSTANG VARIANTS

NA-73X: This was literally a hand-built prototype with civil registration NX19998 (c/n 73-30997) for the British requirement. Unarmed with polished natural metal finish, this aircraft was powered by an Allison V-1710-30 rated at 1150-hp. The airplane was heavily damaged on an early test flight, but was rebuilt, and the test flight program continued. Final fate of this aircraft is unknown.

XP-51-NA: The USAAF acquired two early production Mk. Is (c/n 73-3101 and 73-3107) to test for possible purchase potential. These airplanes had carried RAF serials AG348 and AG354, but were assigned USAAC serials 41-038 and 41-039. Initially flown in natural metal finish, both aircraft went through several different paint schemes. They were powered by the Allison V-1710-39.

P-51-NA: Similar to British Mk. I Mustang, 150 P-51s were built with four 20mm cannon in wing and with American style instruments, radios, and controls replacing similar British items. Construction numbers 91-11981 through 91-12130 airframes were given RAF serials FD418 through FD597. Fifty-seven aircraft were converted to P-51-1-NA standards (later F-6A-NA) and carried two K-24 cameras (airframes 41-37320 through 41-37339; 41-37352 through 41-37366; 41-137368 through 41-37371 ; 41-37412 through 41-37429). One aircraft (41-7426/FD524) was transferred to the U.S. Navy as BuNo 57987. Most aircraft were delivered in either RAF-style camouflage or U.S. Olive Drab/Neutral Gray.

A-36A-NA: This variant was a P-51A airframe optimized for ground attack. Aircraft retained machine gun armament, but had dive brakes mounted above and below each wing panel. Also had underwing racks for carrying 500-lb bombs. P-51As were delivered in Olive Drab and Neutral Gray with individual serial numbers stenciled in yellow on the rear fuselage.

XP-51B-NA: These were two P-51-NAs (41-37352, 41-37421) rebuilt with 1380-hp Rolls-Royce Merlin V-1650-3 engines. Many detail modifications were made to areas such as the radiator, engine cowling, and ailerons. These aircraft were originally designated as XP-78-NA before switching to XP-51B. Olive Drab/Neutral Gray camouflage.

P-51B-NA: Total of 1988 B-models constructed, of which 71 B-10-NA were converted to F-6C-NAs. Early versions were powered with V-1650-3/1380-hp. Four Browning M2 .50-cal machine guns were mounted in wing (two-per-panel). Later versions had the V-1650-7. Five hundred and fifty Bs became B-7s with the addition of a fuselage fuel tank. Underwing racks held drop tanks and bombs. Fuselage tank was retrofitted to earlier aircraft. Delivered in Olive Drab/Neutral Gray until AAF change eliminated camouflage.

P-51C-NT: These aircraft were basically identical to the P-51B except for fact of being built at NAA Dallas (Grand Prarie), Texas, plant. A total of 1750 P-51Cs were completed including 20 converted to F-6C-NT. The P-51C-1 was powered with a V-1650-3, but the remaining 1400 aircraft carried the -7 engine.

XP-51D-NA: Conversion of two P-51B-10s (42-106539, 42-106540) with cut-down rear fuselage and bubble canopy. Numerous detail modifications. Olive Drab/Neutral Gray.

P-51D-NA: Production bubble canopy Mustang. Four P-51D-1-NAs completed with original built-up canopy (this is speculation from examining photographs — total may have been only two). A total of 6502 D models were built at Inglewood. Dorsal fin was added after production commenced, while other aircraft were retrofitted with field kits.

P-51D-NT: Some 1454 P-51D-NT aircraft were built at Dallas. Dallas also delivered 135 F-6D-20-NT/-25-NT tactical reconnaissance airframes. All were delivered in natural metal finish.

TP-51D: Stock P-51Ds modified for full dual controls with extensive reworking carried out in cockpit area for provision of a second seat and full instrument panel and controls. NAA TP-51D conversions originally carried out under original canopy, but an enlarged and bulged bubble was latter added to facilitate a bit more space in the rear seat. Post-war Temco TF-51D conversion was undertaken with a much larger cockpit space created through cutting back fuselage deck. Also, a much larger bubble canopy was added on a new frame.

P-51E: This was the original designation for Dallas-built D models, but was dropped in favor of D-NT (T for Texas).

P-51K-NT: Similar to P-51D-NT, but built with Aeroproducts propeller instead of Hamilton Standard unit. A total of 1500 Ks were built, including 163 as F-6K-NTs; 594 transferred to RAF as Mustang IV. With the K-10-NT, underwing rocket stubs were added.

P-51M-NT: Dallas-built version of the P-51D-30-NT with V-1650-9A. One was completed (although there was no photographic evidence), but remaining order for 1628 was cancelled with the end of the war.

XP-51F/G/J: These three models were an experimental series of lightweight Mustangs built to British standards in order to further improvements in Mustang performance. None were ever put into production, but lessons learned were incorporated in the next variant.

P-51H: The P-51H, considered by many to be the ultimate Mustang, incorporated the production standard of the lightened Mustang concept, but was built to higher American tolerances. Arriving too late to see operational service during WWII, the type also did not serve in the Korean War and was the last of the single-engine P-51s to be built.

ROYAL AIR FORCE MUSTANG VARIANTS

Mk. I: Some 620 Mustang Mk. Is were built, with ten being transferred to the Soviet Union (over American protest), and two delivered to the USAAF. The Mk. I was powered by the Allison V-1710-39 rated at 1150-hp.

Mk. IA: This aircraft was the same airframe as the Mk. I, but contained four 20mm cannons in wing. Part of this order was kept by the USAAF.

Mk. II: Fifty aircraft similar to P-51A.

Mk. III: Some 852 aircraft with transfers to RAAF and USAAF. Similar to P-51B/C.

Mk. IV/IVA: Similar to P-51D/K.

Mk. X: The Mk. Xs were essentially Mk. Is converted to test Rolls-Royce Merlin 61 and 65 powerplants. They were fitted with four-blade props, different radiators, and differing nose configurations. Photo shows a P-51B to illustrate a four-blade propeller and unusual nose configuration as it would have appeared on the Mk. X Mustang.

NAA MUSTANG MODEL DESIGNATIONS

NAA	DESIGNATION	MILITARY SERIALS
NA-73X	NA-73X	None (civil NX19998)
NA-73	Mustang I	AG345 to AG664
RD-1058	XP-51	41-038/-039
NA-83	Mustang I	AL958 to AL999 AM100 to AM257, AP164 to AP263
NA-91	P-51	41-37320 to -37469, FD418 to FD587
NA-97	A-36A	42-83663 to -84162
NA-99	P-51A	43-6003 to -6312
NA-101	XP-51B	41-37352 to -37421
NA-102	P-51B-1	43-12093 to -12492
NA-103	P-51C-1, -5, and -10	42-102979 to -103378 42-103379 to -103978, 43-24902 to -25251
NA-104	P-51B-5, -10, and -15	43-6713 to -7202, 42-106429 to -106538, 43-6313 to -6712, 42-106541 to -106978, 43-24752 to -24901
NA-105	XP-51F/G/J	43-43332 to -43-43336 44-76027 to 44-76028
NA-106	P-51D-1	42-106539/-106540
NA-107	P-51D-1	42-103379 to -103978 Cancelled, moved to NA-103 43-24902 to -25251 Cancelled, to NA-103
NA-109	P-51D-5, -10, and -15	44-13253 to -15752
NA-110	P-51D-1	None, disassembled to Australia
NA-111	P-51C-10, P-51D-5, P-51K, P-51D-20	44-10753 to -11152 44-11153 to -11352 44-11353 to -12852 44-12853 to -13252
NA-112	P-51D	Cancelled, transferred to NA-109
NA-117	P-51H	Cancelled, transferred to NA-126
NA-122	P-51D	44-63160 to -64159, 44-72027 to -72126, 44-72127 to -73626, 44-73627 to -75026
NA-124	P-51D	44-84390 to -84989, 45-11343 to -75025
	P-51M	45-75026
NA-126	P-51H	44-64160 to 44-64714
NA-127	P-51D	Cancelled
NA-138	P-51D	Cancelled, end of war
NA-139	P-51H	Cancelled

MUSTANG SERIAL NUMBERS

XP-51-NA	41-038/-039
P-51-NA	41-37320 to -37469
P-51A-1-NA	43-6003 to -6102
P-51A-5-NA	43-6103 to -6157
P-51A-10-NA	43-6158 to -6312
XP-51B-NA	41-37352/-37421
P-51B-1-NA	43-12093 to -12492
P-51B-5-NA	43-6313 to -6352, 43-6353 to -6752, 43-6753 to -7112
P-51B-10-NA	43-7113 to -7202, 42-106429 to -106538, 42-106541 to -106738
P-51B-15-NA	42-106739 to -106908, 42-106909 to -106978, 43-24752 to -24901
P-51C-1-NT	42-102979 to -103328
P-51C-5-NT	42-103329 to -103378, 42-103379 to -103778
P-51C-10-NT	42-103779 to -103978, 43-24902 to -25251, 44-10753 to -10782
P-51C-11-NT	44-10783 to -10817
P-51C-10-NT	44-10818 to -10852
P-51C-11-NT	44-10853 to -10858
P-51C-10-NT	44-10859 to -11036
P-51C-11-NT	44-11037 to -11122
P-51C-10-NT	44-11123 to -11152
XP-51D-NA	42-106539/-106540
P-51D-5-NA	44-13253 to -14052
P-51D-10-NA	44-14053 to -14852
P-51D-15-NA	44-14853 to -15252, 44-15253 to -15752
P-51D-20-NA	44-63160 to -64159, 44-72027 to -72126, 44-72127 to -72626
P-51D-25-NA	44-772627 to -73626, 44-73627 to -74226
P-51D-30-NA	44-74227 to -75026
P-51D-5-NT	44-11153 to -11352
P-51D-20-NT	44-12853 to -13252
P-51D-25-NT	44-84390 to -84989, 45-11343 to -11542
TP-51D-NA	44-84610/-84611
TP-51D-NT	45-11443/-11450
P-51K-5-NT	44-11553 to -11952
P-51K-10-NT	44-11953 to -12752, 44-12753 to -12852
P-51L-NT	44-91104 to -92003 (cancelled)
P-51M-NT	45-11743
P-51H	44-64160 to -64714

ROYAL AIR FORCE MUSTANG SERIALS

Mk. I	AG345 to AG664, AL958 to AL999, AM100 to AM257, AP164 to AP263
Mk. IA	FD418 to FD567
Mk. II	FR890 to FR939
Mk. III	FB110 to FB399, FR411, FX848 to FX999, FZ100 to FZ197, HB821 to HB961, HK944 to HK947, HK955 to HK956, KH421 to KH640, SR406 to SR440
Mk. IV	KH641 to KH670
Mk. IVA	KH671 to KH870, KM100 to KM492, TK586, TK589, KM744
	KM799 (cancelled)

THE MUSTANG CONTRACTS

CHARGE NO./DATE	DESIGNATION	CONTRACT	FACTORY C/Ns	QTY.
NA-73X 24/4/40	NA-73X	—	73-3097	1
NA-73/29/5/40	Mustang I	A-250	73-3098 to -3416, 73-4767 to -4768, 73-7812	320
RS-1058	XP-51	AC-15471	73-3101, 73-3107	2
NA-83 24/9/40	Mustang I	A-1493	83-4769 to 83-5068	300
NA-91 7/7/41	P-51	DAW535/AC140	91-11981 to -12130	150
NA-97 16/4/42	A-36A	W535/AC27396	97-15881 to -16380	500
NA-99 23/6/42	P-51A	W535/AC30479	99-22106 to -22415	310
NA-101 25/7/42	XP-51B	AC-32073	91-12013 and -12082	2
NA-102 26/842	P-51B	AC-33923	102-24541 to -24940	400
NA-103 8/10/42	P-51C-1/-10/-15	AC-3940	103-22416 to -22815 103-25933 to -26882	1350
NA-104 20/10/42	P-51B-5/-10/-15	AC-30479	104-22816 to -23305 104-24431 to -24540 104-24941 to -25340 104-25343 to -25930	1588
NA-105 2/1/43	XP-51F	AC-37857	105-26883 to -26885	3
	XP-51G		105-25931/-25932	2
	XP-51J		105-47446/-47447	2
NA-106 27/12/43	P-51D	AC-30479	106-25341/-25342	2
NA-107 12/4/43	P-51D	Ac-33940	Cancelled, to NA-103	
NA-109 13/4/43	P-51D-5/-10/-15	AC-40064	109-26886 to -28885 109-35536 to -36035	2500
NA-110 23/4/43	P-51D-1	AC-389	110-34386 to -34485	100
NA-111 3/5/43	P-51C-10	AC-40063	111-28886 TO -29285	400
	P-51D-5		111-29286 TO -29485	200
	P-51K		111-29486 TO -30885 111-36036 TO -36135	1500
	P-51D-20		111-36136 TO -36535	400
NA-112 7/5/43	P-51D	AC-40064	cancelled, to NA-109	
NA-117 10/8/43	P-51H	AC-1752	cancelled, to NA-126	
NA-122 11/3/44	P-51D	AC-2378	122-30886 to -31885 122-31886 to -31985 122-38586 to -40085 122-40167 to -41566	4000
NA-124 14/4/44	P-51D	AC-2400	124-44246 to -44845 124-48096 to -48496	1001
NA-126 26/4/44	P-51H	AC-1752	126-37586 to -38140	555
NA-127 22/8/44	P-51D	AC-3449	cancelled, to NA-126	
NA-138 26/1/45	P-51D	AC-8387	cancelled	

BRIEF SUMMARIES OF MUSTANG SPECIFICATIONS

NOTE: More detailed specifications are in the main text

XP-51

Span	37.04 ft
Length	32.25 ft
Height	12.2 ft
Wing Area	233.19 sq ft
Empty Weight	6280 lbs
Loaded Weight	8400 lbs
Max Speed	382 mph
Cruise Speed	300 mph
Ceiling	30,800 ft
Climb	2500 fpm (initial)
Combat Range	750 mi (no drop tanks)
Powerplant	Allison V-1710-39/1150 hp

P-51

Overall Dimensions	As XP-51
Empty Weight	6550 lbs
Loaded Weight	8800 lbs
Max Speed	387 mph
Cruise Speed	307 mph
Ceiling	31,300 ft
Climb	2200 fpm (initial)
Combat Range	750 mi (no drop tanks)

P-51A

Overall Dimensions	As XP-51
Empty Weight	6430 lbs
Loaded Weight	9000 lbs
Max Speed	390 mph
Cruise Speed	305 mph
Ceiling	31,400 ft
Climb	2300 fpm (initial)
Combat Range	750 mi (no drop tanks)
Powerplant	Allison V-1710-81/1200 hp

P-51B

Overall Dimensions	As XP-51
Height	13.67 ft
Empty Weight	6980 lb
Loaded Weight	11,800 lb
Max Speed	439 mph
Cruise Speed	362 mph
Ceiling	41,500 ft
Climb	30,000 ft/12.1 min
Combat Range	755 mi (no drop tanks)
Powerplant	Packard V-1650-3/1380 hp

P-51D

Overall Dimensions	As XP-51
Height	13.67 ft
Empty Weight	7100 lbs
Loaded Weight	11,600 lbs
Max Speed	437 mph
Cruise Speed	362 mph
Ceiling	41,900 ft
Climb	20,000 ft/7.3 min
Combat Range	1155 mi (no drop tanks)
Powerplant	Packard V-1650-7/1490 hp

P-51H

Span	37.04 ft
Length	33.33 ft
Height	13.67 ft
Wing Area	233.19 sq ft
Empty Weight	7040 lbs
Loaded Weight	9500 lbs
Max Speed	487 mph
Cruise Speed	381 mph
Ceiling	41,600 ft
Climb	20,000 ft/6.8 min
Combat Range	755 mi (no drop tanks)
Powerplant	Packard V-1650-9/1380 hp

BIBLIOGRAPHY

In the course of assembling research material for this book, numerous North American, USAAF, and RAF manuals were consulted along with field and technical orders. Aviation periodicals, both past and present, often supplied gems of information that were difficult to find elsewhere. Interviews and meetings with people involved in developing and building the P-51—most notably Edgar Schmued—took place over the last several decades. The staffs of the National Museum of the USAAF and the San Diego Aerospace Museum were also able to supply copies of obscure documents, drawings and illustrations, interviews and recordings pertaining to the history of the Mustang.

Aldrich, Nelson W., Jr., Tommy Hitchcock. *An American Hero*. Fleet Street Corp. 1984

Avery, Norm. *North American Aircraft 1934-1998 Volume 1*. Narkiewicz/Thompson, 1998.

Birch, David. *Rolls-Royce and the Mustang*. Rolls-Royce Heritage Trust, 1987.

Butler, Phil with Hagedorn, Dan. *Air Arsenal North America*. Midland Publishing, 2004.

Carter, Dustin W. & Matthews, Birch J. *Mustang: The Racing Thoroughbred*. Schiffer Publishing, 1992.

Davis, Larry. *P-51 Mustang In Action*. Squadron/Signal Publications, 1981.

Davis, Larry. *P-51 Mustang in Color*. Squadron/Signal Publications, 1982.

Davis, Larry. *P-51 Mustang*. Squadron/Signal Publications. 1995.

Ethell, Jeffrey. *Mustang: A Documentary History*. Janes, 1981.

Freeman, Roger A. *Camouflage & Markings USAAF 1937-1945*. Ducimus Books, 1974.

Freeman, Roger A. *The Mighty Eighth in Color*. Specialty Press, 1992.

Hardy, M.J. *The North American Mustang*. Arco Publishing, 1979.

Hawker, R.W. *Rolls-Royce From the Wings 1925-1971*. Oxford Illustrated Press, 1976.

Hooker, Sir Stanley. *Not Much of an Engineer*. Airlife Publishing, 1984.

Johnsen, Frederick A. *North American P-51 Mustang*. Specialty Press, 1996.

Kinzey, Bert. *P-51 Mustang*. Squadron/Signal Publications, 1997.

Lloyd, Ian. *Rolls-Royce: The Merlin At War*. Macmillan, 1978.

Ludwig, Paul A. *Development of the P-51 Mustang Long-Range Escort Fighter*. Classic Publications, 2003.

Matthews, Birch. *Wet Wings & Drop Tanks*. Schiffer Publishing, 1993.

O'Leary, Michael. *North American Aviation P-51 Mustang*. Osprey Publishing, 1998.

Rohmer, Richard Maj. Gen. *Patton's Gap - Mustangs Over Normandy*. Stoddart, 1981.

Scutts, Jerry. *Mustang Aces of the Ninth & Fifteenth Air Forces & the RAF*. Osprey Publishing, 1995.

Scutts, Jerry. *Mustang Aces of the Eighth Air Force*. Osprey Publishing, 1996.

Wagner, Ray. *American Combat Planes*. Doubleday & Company, 1982

Wagner, Ray. *Mustang Designer*. Orion Books, 1990

White, Graham. *Allied Piston Engines of World War II*. Society of Automotive Engineers Inc., 1995.

Whitney, Daniel D. *Vee's For Victory!* Schiffer Publishing, 1998.

INDEX

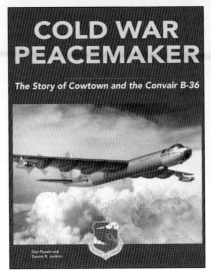
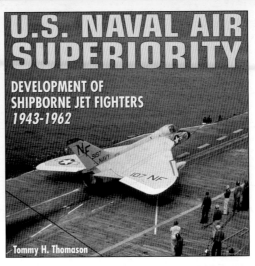
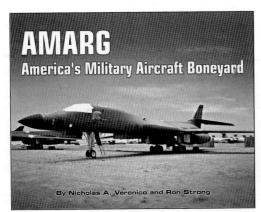